d States, in order to form a more perfect Union, establish Justi

the general Welfare, and secure the Blessings of Liberty to ourselves

ted States of America.

Article. II.

Section. 1. The executive Power shall be vested in a President of the United States of America. He shall hold his Office during the Term of four Years, and together with the Vice President, chosen for the same Term, be elected as follows

Each State shall appoint, in such Manner as the Legislature thereof may direct, a Number of Electors, equal to the whole Number of Senators and Representatives to which the State may be entitled in the Congress: but no Senator or Representative, or Person holding an Office of Trust or Profit under the United States, shall be appointed an Elector.

The Electors shall meet in their respective States, and vote by Ballot for two Persons, of whom one at least shall not be an Inhabitant of the same State with themselves. And they shall make a List of all the Persons voted for, and of the Number of Votes for each; which List they shall sign and certify, and transmit sealed to the Seat of the Government of the United States, directed to the President of the Senate. The President of the Senate shall in the Presence of the Senate and House of Representatives, open all the Certificates, and the Votes shall then be counted. The Person having the greatest Number of Votes shall be the President, if such Number be a Majority of the whole Number of Electors appointed, and if there be more than one who have such Majority, and have an equal Number of Votes, then the House of Representatives shall immediately chuse by Ballot one of them for President; and if no Person have a Majority, then from the five highest on the List the said House shall in like Manner chuse the President. But in chusing the President, the Votes shall be taken by States, the Representation from each State having one Vote; A quorum for this Purpose shall consist of a Member or Members from two thirds of the States, and a Majority of all the States shall be necessary to a Choice. In every Case, after the Choice of the President, the Person having the greatest Number of Votes of the Electors shall be the Vice President. But if there should remain two or more who have equal Votes, the Senate shall chuse from them by Ballot the Vice President.

The Congress may determine the Time of chusing the Electors, and the Day on which they shall give their Votes; which Day shall be the same throughout the United States.

No Person except a natural born Citizen, or a Citizen of the United States, at the time of the Adoption of this Constitution, shall be eligible to the Office of President; neither shall any Person be eligible to that Office who shall not have attained to the Age of thirty five Years, and been fourteen Years a Resident within the United States.

In Case of the Removal of the President from Office, or of his Death, Resignation, or Inability to discharge the Powers and Duties of the said Office, the Same shall devolve on the Vice President, and the Congress may by Law provide for the Case of Removal, Death, Resignation or Inability, both of the President and Vice President, declaring what Officer shall then act as President, and such Officer shall act accordingly, until the Disability be removed, or a President shall be elected.

The President shall, at stated Times, receive for his Services, a Compensation, which shall neither be encreased nor diminished during the Period for which he shall have been elected, and he shall not receive within that Period any other Emolument from the United States, or any of them.

Before he enter on the Execution of his Office, he shall take the following Oath or Affirmation:— "I do solemnly swear (or affirm) that I will faithfully execute the Office of President of the United States, and will to the best of my Ability, preserve, protect and defend the Constitution of the United States."

Section. 2. The President shall be Commander in Chief of the Army and Navy of the United States, and of the Militia of the several States, when called into the actual Service of the United States; he may require the Opinion, in writing, of the principal Officer in each of the executive Departments, upon any Subject relating to the Duties of their respective Offices, and he shall have Power to grant Reprieves and Pardons for Offences against the United States, except in Cases of Impeachment.

He shall have Power, by and with the Advice and Consent of the Senate, to make Treaties, provided two thirds of the Senators present concur; and he shall nominate, and by and with the Advice and Consent of the Senate, shall appoint Ambassadors, other public Ministers and Consuls, Judges of the supreme Court, and all other Officers of the United States, whose Appointments are not herein otherwise provided for, and which shall be established by Law: but the Congress may by Law vest the Appointment of such inferior Officers, as they think proper, in the President alone, in the Courts of Law, or in the Heads of Departments.

The President shall have Power to fill up all Vacancies that may happen during the Recess of the Senate, by granting Commissions which shall expire at the End of their next Session.

Section. 3. He shall from time to time give to the Congress Information of the State of the Union, and recommend to their Consideration such Measures as he shall judge necessary and expedient; he may, on extraordinary Occasions, convene both Houses, or either of them, and in Case of Disagreement between them, with Respect to the Time of Adjournment, he may adjourn them to such Time as he shall think proper; he shall receive Ambassadors and other public Ministers; he shall take Care that the Laws be faithfully executed, and shall Commission all the Officers of the United States.

Section. 4. The President, Vice President and all civil Officers of the United States, shall be removed from Office on Impeachment for, and Conviction of, Treason, Bribery, or other high Crimes and Misdemeanors.

Article III.

Section. 1. The judicial Power of the United States, shall be vested in one supreme Court, and in such inferior Courts as the Congress may from time to time ordain and establish. The Judges, both of the supreme and inferior Courts, shall hold their Offices during good Behaviour, and shall, at stated Times, receive for their Services, a Compensation, which shall not be diminished during their Continuance in Office.

Section. 2. The judicial Power shall extend to all Cases, in Law and Equity, arising under this Constitution, the Laws of the United States, and Treaties made, or which shall be made, under their Authority;— to all Cases affecting Ambassadors, other public Ministers and Consuls;— to all Cases of admiralty and maritime Jurisdiction;— to Controversies to which the United States shall be a Party;— to Controversies between two or more States;— between a State and Citizens of another State,— between Citizens of different States,— between Citizens of the same State claiming Lands under Grants of different States, and between a State, or the Citizens thereof, and foreign States, Citizens or Subjects.

In all Cases affecting Ambassadors, other public Ministers and Consuls, and those in which a State shall be Party, the supreme Court shall

AMERICAN
CONSERVATISM

AN ILLUSTRATED

HISTORY

Left to right.

John Dickinson

William Franklin

James Madison

Henry Clay

Daniel Webster

Abraham Lincoln

Left to right.
Grover Cleveland

William McKinley

Theodore Roosevelt

William Taft

Warren Harding

Calvin Coolidge

AMERICAN CONSERVATISM

AN ILLUSTRATED HISTORY

Robert J. Nagle

Library of Congress Cataloging-in-Publication Data

Nagle, Robert J.
    American conservatism—An illustrated history

    1. Conservatism—United States—History.   2. Conservatism—
United States—History—Pictorial works.
3. United States—Politics and government. 4. United
States—Politics and government—Pictorial works.
I. Title.
E183.N34   1988   320.5'2'0973   87-15208
ISBN 0-8022-2535-7

Design by Charles Davey
Manufactured in the United States of America.

This book is dedicated in loving gratitude to my Father and Mother

Contents

Preface

I was six years old when Barry Goldwater ran for President in 1964, too young to vote for him (not that it would have helped) but not too young to forecast the size of his debacle. One of my older sisters, then a high school student and far more conservative than she is now, took me across the street from our house to the public school that was serving as the local polling place, put an "AU H_2O placard around my neck, and gave me strict instructions to march back and forth shouting "Why doesn't everybody vote for Goldwater?" When my father came home from work a little while later and went to vote, he found his youngest son marching back and forth shouting "why doesn't *anybody* vote for Goldwater?" In terms of precociousness that may not rank with Mozart, but it was one of the earliest examples of accurate exit polling in America.

In his introduction to the *The Rise of the Right*, William A. Rusher writes that his work is not the definitive history of conservatism in America. Let me rush to make the same disclaimer here. That book remains to be written. My hope is that this book will serve as an enticing introduction to those who wish to know more about conservatism, and a useful overview of its history for the already-initiated.

No author ever writes a book by himself, and no acknowledgments section is ever adequate to give credit to all of the people whose help and encouragement are essential to a writer. But, short of putting dozens of names on the cover, it is the only method available.

First, I wish to express my gratitude to Edward A. Capano, associate publisher of *National Review* magazine, who got me involved in this project in the first place. My treatment of *NR* in the book is limited to its editors and contributing writers, but let me say here that it is a better magazine and a better-read magazine than it would be if Ed were not there. His understanding of the publishing business, and of conservatism, is complete; his understanding of baseball is another matter.

John P. Fowler showed enormous patience by listening to me when I called at all hours to kick around ideas, read passages, or complain about writer's block. (His lovely wife Sharon showed even more.) Virtually all of his suggestions were incorporated in the book. I hope that I can be as much help to Jack on his next book as he has been to me on this one.

Frank Costello said "Let me know if I can help," and meant it; I thank him for that. David Jaco was unfailingly supportive and unfailingly late for lunch.

The staff at the Philosophical Library, expecially publishers Rose Runes and Ginger Najar, have been enthusiastic and helpful from the start. A special word of thanks to their associate, George Nammack, for his wake-up calls and contraband ashtray.

The encouragement of many people has been far more valuable to me than they could possible realize. Among these people are Dennis Linehan, Douglas McKay, Donald Healy, Michael and Ann Duignan, Michael Cirrilli, Kieran McTague, Kenneth Cooper, Patrick Healy, Eugene Seip, Nelson Alicea, Michael Staunton, my six brothers and sisters, and a host of others too numerous to mention by name. They know who they are, and I'm grateful to them all.

The formation of any political philosophy is basically an attempt to to transform personal moral and social values into a platform acceptable to a great mass of people. My own personal values—moral, social and political—were instilled in me by the example of my parents, who are, bar none, the two finest people I have ever been privileged to know.

Though a conservative myself, I have tried to be as objective as possible in analyzing conservatism both as a philosophy and as a political force in our nation, as well as in viewing historical conservative characters as human beings. I may not always have been as successful in this endeavor as I would have liked. Any less-than-objective slant that may have crept in, as well as any factual errors that may have slipped by, are entirely my fault.

Robert J. Nagle
New York City
July 27, 1988

AMERICAN
CONSERVATISM

AMERICAN
CONSERVATISM

Paul Revere's depiction of
the Boston Massacre.

Entered according to Act of Congress

THE DESTRUCTION

OF TEA AT BOSTON HARBOR.

A View of the Attack against Fort Washington and Rebel Redoubts near New York on the 16 of November 1776 by the British and Hessian Brigades. Drawn on the spot by Tho.ˢ Davies Esq.ʳ R.ᴬ of Artillery.

A view of the attack against
Fort Washington on
November 16th, 1776.

Opposite, left. John Adams.

Right. Alexander Hamilton.

*General Washington on a
White Charger.*

Below. George Washington,
his wife Martha, and his
stepchildren.

Following pages. Washington
crosses the Delaware to
attack the British at Trenton,
Christmas, 1776.

Jefferson's abhorrence of centralized government marked him as a liberal in his own day. This would put him squarely in the conservative camp today.

The American Civil War, 1861-1865, transcended politics, and was fought for moral principles.

1 The Mists of History 1765–1787

England—the very name conjures up images of green fields and graceful towers, imposing castles and stately halls, of kings and queens, pomp and pageantry, of glory gained and empire lost. And of mist, ever-present, wrapping the land as if in a shroud, becoming a part of the character of that place. But from this mist, this England, would emerge the men and ideas who set the American experiment on the course it has followed to the present day. The roots of the American political system, and thus the roots of American conservatism, are firmly planted on the misty shores of England.

Conservatism, as an impulse, is as old as history, but philosophic conservatism as we know it was shaped in large measure by a fiery genius who would be an understanding friend of the American Revolution and the most implacable foe of the French one. Edmund Burke, born and educated in Ireland, came to London as a young law student and would go on to be acclaimed as Parliament's most brilliant orator. He took a deep and abiding interest in the welfare of England's colonial subjects: in Ireland, in India, and in the thirteen colonies of America.

After his election to Parliament in 1766, Burke cut his political teeth in active opposition to the Stamp Act. Passed the year before, the Stamp Act provided for a tax on every public document printed in the American colonies. No contracts could be signed, no bills introduced in colonial legislatures, no legal briefs filed, no sermons or newspapers published without payment made to a British tax collector. It was a fatal error. By uniting businessmen, lawyers, legislators, ministers and journalists—the shapers of public opinion in colonial America—against the Crown, Parliament had set the wheels of revolution in motion. Boycotts were organized, petitions were signed and sent to the King, mobs broke out into violent demonstrations. Burke led the movement for repeal in the House of Commons. In his own mind, he was not advocating revolutionary ideas or defending revolution—quite the opposite. He believed that tradition must be upheld—and that rights and liberties traditionally granted to the colonists (albeit mostly by benign neglect) could not arbitrarily be abrogated by the mother country.

Burke and the pro-American party in the Commons carried the day when their efforts, combined with pressure from London merchants who were losing profits, forced Lord Rockingham, then Prime Minister, to agree to repeal. But Parliament passed a companion act asserting its right to tax the colonies. Burke realized that the government had missed the point, and opposed this act as well. (When told that members of his own pro-repeal coalition were fighting among themselves over whether or not to support the companion bill as a compromise, Burke remarked, "Birds of prey are not gregarious.")

Parliament, Burke believed, theoretically did have a right to tax the Americans, but to do so would be an exercise in tyranny. Tax after tax was imposed, always under a different guise, always met with virulent opposition by the Americans, who would admit no British right to direct taxation. The situation grew explosive, and Burke tried one last time to

THOMAS PAINE.

Thomas Paine. A radical, his famous writings in favor of the French Revolution were rebutted by such conservative philosophers as the Englishman Edmund Burke, and the American John Adams.

avert a war. In what is perhaps his most famous speech to the House of Commons, "Conciliation with America," which he delivered on the eve of the Revolution, Burke admonished King and Parliament with these words: "The question with me is not whether you have a right to make your people miserable, but whether it is not in your interest to make them happy." He recognized that the rights of free men superseded the rights of legitimate government acting tyrannically, and he felt that England was leaving the colonies no choice but to go their own way. Viewed by many as an outrageous liberal and defender of traitorous revolutionaries, Burke saw himself as a defender of traditional liberties—a conservative.

And that was the way he viewed the American Revolution—as a conservative, legal

Edmund Burke, whose conservative philosophy enabled him to support the American Revolution while vociferously opposing the revolt in France. His ideas would continue to influence American conservatives in the late 20th century.

revolution. Unlike their future French counterparts, the American revolutionaries were not utopians out to wrench a new social order from the twisted wreckage of one they had destroyed. The Americans were defending—by force of arms—rights and liberties they had long enjoyed. The aftermath of this revolution would not see the breakdown into chaos and civil bloodshed that has marked so many subsequent revolutions. The same cannot be said for the revolution in France—the one Burke so bitterly denounced.

Edmund Burke would come to be viewed as a conservative even in his own country because of the stance he took in opposition to the French Revolution. He opposed it for the very same reasons he had supported the Americans in their revolt—he felt that traditional and legal rights were being trampled on by the state. This time, "the state" was little more than a bloodthirsty mob who employed the revolutionary rhetoric they had borrowed from the Americans but left out their ideals. Burke's successful balancing act

King George III, who, despite long periods of mental illness, sat on England's throne for sixty years. He lost the American colonies.

George Grenville, the Prime Minister who created the Stamp Act and garrisoned the colonies with British troops.

of support for and opposition to the two greatest political upheavals of the eighteenth century, which were viewed by many in both countries as "sister revolutions," would help to shape the philosophical mold of conservatives down to our day. Modern conservatives generally support revolutions whose participants claim to be restoring rights lost to the state, as in Nicaragua, and oppose those whose participants advocate a new social order (often Marxist) as in El Salvador.

America's founding fathers would not have looked upon Edmund Burke as being particularly influential, even among those whom we would now consider the forerunners of modern conservatism. To them, he was a contemporary, sympathetic English politician whose thinking agreed with, rather than shaped, their own. His influence on conservative political philosophy would be felt more forcefully by later generations.

The events leading up to America's revolution divided the conservatives of the time. Many would agree with Burke and view the coming break as an inevitable struggle, pitting the rights of free citizens against the rights of a tyrant. Others, however, though they might be sympathetic to the grievances of their fellow colonists, and might well join the strident opposition to the encroachments on liberty being made by the British, still could not sanction revolution as a legitimate political tool to gain redress. These were the American Tories, and though despised by some on their side of the Atlantic, their reputation has been rehabilitated over the centuries, so that we now look on many of them as men who held to their principles despite the loss of their property, their liberty, and, in many cases, their lives.

Perhaps the most prominent among them was William Franklin, the illegitimate son of the patriot Benjamin Franklin. Always close to his father, he travelled to Europe with him on many of the elder Franklin's diplomatic missions, and was considered to have a bright political future himself. Commissioned a captain in the Pennsylvania militia before his twenty-first birthday, he fought in Canada during the French and Indian War, and then returned to Pennsylvania where his father, then that colony's Postmaster General, appointed him comptroller of the Philadelphia Post Office. He followed his father to London the following year, studied law, and was admitted to the bar in 1758. George III made him Royal Governor of New Jersey in 1763, and it was as the holder of this office that Franklin was first confronted with the question of where his loyalty lay.

He did not flinch. As Royal Governor he enforced the short-lived Stamp Act, which his father abhorred, and the myriad other taxes that came out of Parliament. Always considering himself an Englishman first and an American second, Franklin sided with the British when the war finally came. Imprisoned for two years (1776-1778) by order of the New Jersey legislature, Franklin was stripped of his property and titles. He returned to England in 1782, secure in the knowledge that he had done what he considered to be a patriot's duty. There he stayed for the rest of his life, dying quietly in 1813. His name is rarely mentioned in American history books.

One man whose name is found in those books is John Dickinson of Pennsylvania. A wealthy landowner, Dickinson was eloquent in his impassioned plea to the British government to reach accord with the colonies. Called "the Penman of the Revolution" for his famous "Letters from a Pennsylvania Farmer to the Inhabitants of the British Colonies," and selected as a delegate to the Second Continental Congress in Philadelphia, Dickinson nevertheless opposed the resolution to break with England and refused to sign the Declaration of Independence.

When war became a reality, though, Dickinson felt that he had no other course but to support his fellow Americans, however reluctantly. As the Revolution progressed, Dickinson became more enthusiastic about independence. He continued to serve in the Congress, and wrote the first draft of what would become the Articles of Confederation. In it, he hammered away in support of states' rights, which was his passion. He would go

29

Boston cannonaded.

on to serve at the Constitutional Convention in 1787, and die in 1808 much honored by his fellow countrymen, in contrast to William Franklin.

The life of John Dickinson may be considered a microcosm of the time and place in which he lived. Fiercely proud of his English heritage, he was bewildered by the British government's attempt to place on Americans restrictions of the liberties enjoyed by all citizens. He felt, right up to the outbreak of the war, that a political solution not only could but must be found. But when independence was declared and war came, he embraced the idea of a new American country with the same patriotic fervor he had previously reserved for England. When the revolution ended, he devoted the rest of his life to helping the young United States survive as a free and independent nation.

The resolution for independence which Dickinson initially felt was too radical for a conservative such as himself to support was, ironically, pushed through the Continental Congress by a man equally conservative, one who had also long believed that reason could be employed to prevail upon the British to restore the rights and privileges formerly enjoyed by the colonists. John Adams, born in Braintree, Massachusetts, the son of a farmer and cobbler, had graduated from Harvard College and was admitted to the bar in 1758. A man who never forgot his relatively humble beginnings, Adams worked hard to improve his lot and, after a few years, had a thriving law practice in Boston. Conservative by nature and philosophy, Adams' reaction to the Stamp Act and other colonial grievances was to file legal briefs in opposition to government policy, several of which were adopted as resolutions by neighboring New England communities.

While his activist cousin Samuel Adams organized mob violence against British garrison troops, John Adams continued to believe that the rupture between colonies and mother country was a temporary disturbance that, caused by King and Parliament, would be righted by King and Parliament when the colonists presented their case. His respect for

William Franklin, the son of
Benjamin Franklin, was the
last Royal Governor of New
Jersey. Among the most
prominent of American
Tories, he was imprisoned
during the Revolution and
exiled to England after its
conclusion.

the law was never more dramatically demonstrated than in 1770, when he undertook the legal defense of the British soldiers charged with murder after the Boston massacre. Despite howling mobs at his door, Adams persevered, and won. Five of six defendants were found not guilty, with the sixth convicted of the lesser charge of manslaughter.

Over the next few years however, British intractability on the subject of the colonies was becoming more and more apparent. Adams began to fear, like Burke, that the government was making revolution inevitable. With the imposition of the Tea Tax, Adams moved firmly into the independence camp, and he celebrated the Boston Tea Party, which his cousin had led.

Selected as one of Massachusetts' delegates to the Second Continental Congress, Adams arrived in Philadelphia resolved that the colonies must unite and act. He was determined to win a resolution for independence.

To that end, he wheedled, cajoled, threatened, begged and pleaded with his fellow delegates so much that not a few of them actually came to hate him. But for over a year he could not move them to action. Finally, with the fighting in New England intensifying, they agreed to allow a committee of five to draw up a declaration of independence for their consideration. Adams was chosen for the committee, as were Roger Sherman of Connecticut and Robert Livingston of New York. But Adams' greatest allies in the struggle were the men who were chosen to fill the two remaining places on the committee.

Thomas Jefferson was as different from John Adams as the North was from the South. The product of the union of two of Virginia's most distinguished families, Jefferson was

32

The Stamp Act set off a chain
of events which culminated
in the American Revolution
and the founding of the
United States.

Samuel Adams. Before the
American Revolution he was
far more radical than his
cousin John, even leading the
Boston Tea Party, but he
became increasingly more
conservative as post-war
Governor of Massachusetts.

SAMUEL ADAMS Efq.

tall and lean, a graceful aristocrat who wore an air of superiority as naturally as a waistcoat. Whereas Adams, the short, overweight son of lower-middle-class parents would be ridiculed by his enemies for "putting on airs," Jefferson's regal bearing was an integral part of his nature. Eight years younger than Adams, he was acknowledged to be the most gifted writer in Congress. Adams himself said that he deferred to Jefferson in the writing of the Declaration because "I had a great opinion of the elegance of his pen, and none at all of my own." (Adams also knew that a declaration written by him was bound to be voted down by his fellow delegates.) Truly a renaissance man, Jefferson was as much at home in the fields of architecture, agriculture, machinery, music, and science, as he was in politics.

Having graduated from the College of William and Mary in 1762 at the age of nineteen, young Jefferson busied himself with running his inherited plantation before opening a law practice in 1767. Elected to Virginia's House of Burgesses two years later, he allied himself with the faction led by Patrick Henry in opposition to British encroachment on colonial sovereignty. He declared for independence after Virginia's Royalist Governor dissolved the colonial legislature in response to the radical Virginia Resolves in 1769. He, like Adams, arrived in Philadelphia determined to come away with nothing less than a new country.

The final member of the committee was Benjamin Franklin of Pennyslvania. His legendary wit and lighthearted writings have caused his humorous nature to be more fully presented in modern portrayals of the man, at the expense of his intellectual achievement. It is an inaccurate portrait. Of all the accumulated brilliance that crowded the stage during colonial America's passion play, only Jefferson could rival Franklin in sheer breadth of knowledge and mental accomplishment.

The fifteenth child and tenth son of a Massachusetts candlemaker and newspaper publisher, Benjamin Franklin was born in Boston in 1706 to his father's second wife. Apprenticed as a young man to his brother James, who had taken over their father's printing business, Benjamin soon demonstrated a flair for writing. After a falling-out with his brother, he made his way to Philadelphia, where he gained influential friends who persuaded him to travel to London. There he spent two years in the printing trade with two of the top firms in England, making the acquaintance of most of the important literary personalities of the day. Upon returning to Philadelphia in 1726, he resumed his work in the printing trade, and, three years later, was able to purchase the *Pennsylvania Gazette*. Turning the *Gazette* from a dull and failing paper into a widely-read success, he prospered financially.

In 1731, Franklin founded the first public library in America, and the following year published *Poor Richard's Almanac*, whose literary fame has survived to the present. Four years later, Franklin was appointed clerk of the Pennsylvania General Assembly, becoming deputy Postmaster of Philadelphia the following year. It was around this time that he organized Philadelphia's first fire company, and developed methods for improving street paving and lighting.

Aside from his literary, political, and civic achievements, Franklin's most productive years as a scientist were just beginning. He invented the Franklin stove, which made heat consumption more efficient, devised a way to reduce the excessive smoking of chimneys, and began his legendary experiments with electricity which greatly aided man's ability to harness the phenomenon as a source of energy.

He received honorary degrees from the University of Saint Andrew's in Scotland and Oxford University in England, became a Fellow of the Royal Society of London for Improving Natural Knowledge, and was awarded the Copley Medal for distinguished contributions to experimental science.

Franklin's positions as deputy Postmaster General of the Colonies, which he assumed in 1753, and Pennsylvania's delegate to the Albany Convention, called in 1754 to devise methods to deal with the oncoming French and Indian War, gave him a perspective on the interconnected workings of the colonies afforded few others. Accordingly, he drew up what came to be known as the Albany Plan, providing for a loose union of the colonies which would retain local sovereignty. But the plan was too radical for its time, and was rejected. Franklin believed to the end of his days that had the Albany Plan been adopted, the colonies could have presented a united front against England in the 1760s and averted the Revolutionary War ten years later.

It was during the French and Indian War that Franklin began his diplomatic career, serving as Pennsylvania's representative at Court. Over the course of the next twenty years, Franklin virtually lived in England, presenting the case for his colony and indeed all the colonies on a wide variety of subjects. Interrogated by the House of Commons about the effects in the colonies of the Stamp Act, his testimony swayed many members to vote for repeal. But as the years wore on, Franklin, like so many of his contemporaries, came to see war as inevitable and, in 1776, with great sorrow in his heart, he sailed for America and revolution. He had not been home for eleven years.

Though certainly all five members of the committee made important contributions, the Declaration of Independence was largely shaped by Adams, Jefferson, and Franklin; of these, Jefferson is rightly credited with being the author.

The document itself is a wondrous product of that historical moment. For if basically conservative men were to set themselves on a radical course of revolution, they would need a declaration of conservative principles to justify their radicalism. And so they produced one.

There is nothing subversive, nor even, by the standards of the day, anything terribly liberal in the Declaration of Independence. It begins by affirming what all of them could agree on: free men were endowed by God with certain rights that, considering their origin, were inalienable, and that among these were life, liberty, and the pursuit of happiness. This was not to say that a king—who ruled by God's will—could not deprive individual men of their freedom or their life, if justice so required. To believe that would make one an anarchist, and none of these men was that. But if a king were to deprive *all* men of their rights, if he were to strike at the rights themselves, then he was a tyrant. And free men who believed, as these men did, that government is in place to keep order and to guarantee their rights, had a duty to throw off a tyrant and restore government to its proper function.

To demonstrate their point, they listed their grievances against the King, told of their unsuccessful attempts to petition for redress, and declared that the King's willingness to abrogate their rights given by God made him a "Tyrant...unfit to be the ruler of a free people."

As Thomas Jefferson was the author of the Declaration of Independence, so John Adams was its political floor manager. Adams' greatest fear was that Massachusetts, where fighting had already broken out, would be left to face the British Army alone and would be annihilated—perhaps broken up and the pieces distributed to surrounding colonies. To save Massachusetts, he had to get all the colonies to unite and adopt the Declaration. A united country must face the British—even twelve out of thirteen would still give the British one safe haven for preparing an assault force and ensure the others' defeat. Thirteen separate declarations of independence would be equally fatal—no one colony was strong enough even to hold off the British Army, much less defeat it. The only hope was for thirteen colonies to make one nation—*E pluribus, unum.*

But if there was one colony of which all the others were suspicious, it was that same Massachusetts. Just as Adams knew that the Declaration was doomed to defeat if he wrote it, so he knew that the idea of unity was equally doomed if its basis was the defense of Massachusetts. Many of the delegates were of the opinion that the problems of the Bay

Benjamin Franklin. Though
some modern revisionist historians paint him as a radical,
Franklin accepted revolution
only as a last resort.

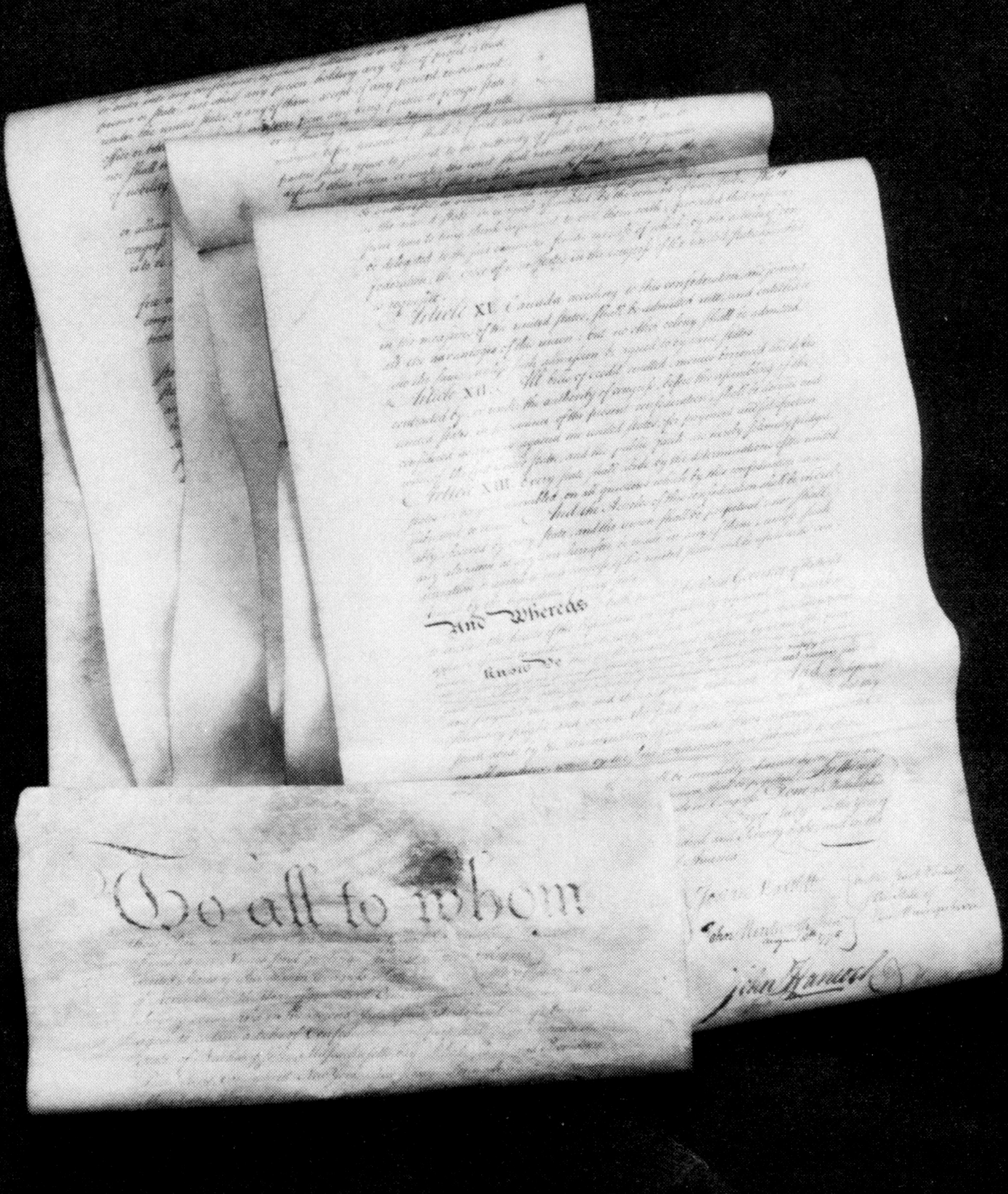

Article XI

Article XII

Article XIII

And Whereas

Know Ye

To all to whom

Opposite. The Declaration of
Independence.

Left. George Mason. He
helped to write the Constitution, then refused to sign it
because it did not contain a
Bill of Rights.

Colony were of its own making, and believed that they could strike a deal with England
if they were willing to let the British Army deal unhindered with Massachusetts. Adams
was well aware of this sentiment, and realized quickly that he had to put the fight on a
colonies-wide basis. No other colonies were going to send men to join the Massachusetts
militia to face the British. It was for this reason that Adams had, a year earlier, proposed
the idea of creating a Continental Army.

And it was Adams who argued that his colony was merely the place where the war was
beginning, that it would surely spread to all the others. The command of the army could
not, he knew, go to a New Englander. There was only one man it *could* go to—and Adams
proposed his name to the Continental Congress. His choice was many things—cool-
headed, seasoned, a bona fide war hero, a gentleman, and, most important of all, a
Virginian—George Washington.

Born on his father's estate in Westmoreland County in 1732, Washington had inherited his half-brother Lawrence's plantation, called Mount Vernon. Though he had little

formal education, he had been tutored, and was widely read in geography, military history, agriculture and science. He showed aptitude as a surveyor and, at the age of seventeen, wrangled an appointment as official surveyor of Culpeper County. He spent the next two years traipsing around the backwoods of Virginia, surveying what was then the American frontier.

In 1753 he received his first military commission, as a major, and served as adjutant commander of one of the military districts into which Virginia was divided. With war looming, he was chosen to deliver an ultimatum to the French forces to stop their build-up in the Ohio River Valley (they politely refused). Promoted to lieutenant colonel, he led an expedition back to the Ohio River to protect workmen building forts there for the British. Attack by a superior French force obliged him to surrender, though he and his company were allowed to leave the area. It was a bitter experience, never to be forgotten.

He resigned his commission. But the following year he came back, serving as a volunteer adjutant to General Edward Braddock, commander of the regular British forces in Virginia. During an ambush near Fort Duquesne, Braddock was mortally wounded and his troops thrown back in disarray. Washington assumed command, and, though he narrowly escaped death himself, was able to rally the troops and effect an orderly withdrawal.

His success at Fort Duquesne resulted in his appointment to command the Virginia militia with the rank of colonel. The official declaration of war between England and France in May, 1756, moved the bulk of the fighting northward, and Washington was able to keep Virginia's frontier safe from further invasion.

Throughout the war, Washington tried without success to get a commission in the regular British Army. It is one of those fascinating "What ifs?" that riddle history. What if Washington was in command of British troops when the American Revolution came? What would his sense of honor and loyalty have directed him to do? We will never know, because the British repeatedly turned down his request, and in 1758 he returned to his plantation as a civilian.

Having been elected to the House of Burgesses while still in command of the militia, Washington took his seat immediately upon his return and, like his younger friend Thomas Jefferson, allied himself with the anti-tax Henry faction. Washington, like most of Virginia's political leaders, grew increasingly more strident in opposition to British policy as the years progressed, and it was he who presided over the session that adopted the Virginia Resolves, a resolution of outright defiance.

Washington was elected as a Virginia delegate to both the first and second Continental Congresses and it was through them that Adams came to know and admire him. Having Washington in command of the forces in Massachusetts was a great step forward in the process of getting the other delegates to think of themselves as Americans, rather than as Britons or natives of their own colonies. The second Continental Congress unanimously adopted the resolution to appoint Col. Washington to lead the Continental Army. Washington took command of his troops at Cambridge on July 3, 1775.

For the next year, his poignant letters from the front did more than any other single factor to unite the Congress in its resolve to fight the British. Thus, when Adams presented the finished Declaration of Independence to Congress on July 2, 1776, it too, after two days of haggling, was unanimously adopted. Independence had been declared, but it was far from achieved. That would take a war.

The American Revolution, like the Declaration which marked its official beginning, was an historical curiosity. The most radical step that can be taken in politics was being taken by men who were lifelong conservatives and believed that they were upholding their conservative principles. This was not a revolution of the proletariat—as at Runnymede in 1215, this was a revolt of the aristocracy. It is no accident that we celebrate our Independ-

Sketch of General George
Washington at his command
headquarters, Valley Forge,
Pennsylvania, during the winter of 1777-78.

ence Day on July 4. We do not celebrate the day, six long years later, when independence
was achieved on the battlefield at Yorktown, or the day in 1784 when independence was
finally recognized by the British in Paris. We celebrate the day when independence was
declared in a legal bill promulgated by a legitimate authority—a very conservative-minded
way of doing things. We celebrate the legality of the action as much as the action
itself—what came afterward neither confirmed nor denied that legality, but merely
enforced it.

And that was the key for the conservatives of the era—not whether what they were
doing was morally right or wrong, for all felt that they were morally right, but whether
they were legally right or wrong. Some, as noted above, felt that the end could not justify
the means, and opposed the Revolution. Most others were able to accept the legality that
the Declaration lent to their actions and viewed the war as a military defense against a
nation that had already—legally—been declared a foreign country.

And so the war was fought, and won. The colonies had united to defend their common
rights, to repel their mutual enemy. But when it was over, there was no guarantee that they
would remain united, or that this new nation would survive. It almost didn't.

For the moment, the close of the war brought a return to normal life. Commerce was
resumed, farms were re-invigorated, men went back to work. But the way in which men
worked, and thought about work, was undergoing a change as revolutionary as the one
which had just affected their political fortunes. Adam Smith, a Scottish economist and
university professor, had published his *Inquiry into the Nature and Causes of the Wealth
of Nations* in 1776. But as most Americans were preoccupied with politics around that
time, Smith's arguments, which were being hotly debated in Europe, did not gain much
momentum in the United States until after the war. Briefly, Smith contended that the
sources of all income are rent, wages, and profits, with profits being of paramount
importance. Commerce flourishes, and greater profits are generated, when it operates
under conditions of *laissez faire*, or governmental non-interference. The more that
government involves itself with the economic life of the nation, the more injurious the
result to the people.

While much of this, naturally, did not sit well with the crowned heads of Europe, it was
accepted with alacrity by the commercial movers and shakers of the new United States.
Smith's "capitalist" system of economics seemed tailor-made for a democratic people

Cover of an 18th century
pamphlet supporting Shays'
Rebellion. Note that here,
Shays has been promoted to
General.

whose major interest in government was to place as many limitations on its power as
possible.

The central government of the United States had been formed as far back as 1776,
shortly after the Declaration of Independence. John Dickinson, who had refused to sign
the Declaration (and, though other delegates continued to sign for years afterward, never
did) agreed to head the congressional committee charged with formulating the proposal
for the new form of government. What he wrote would come to be called the Articles
of Confederation, though if it had been written in the second half of the twentieth
century, it might simply have been labelled "Catch-22."

The Articles gave the federal government—which was a continuation of the Continental Congress—veto power over concerted actions of the states, and the states veto power
over virtually any action of the Congress. The intent was to prevent the federal government from gathering too much power unto itself—they were not about to replace one
tyranny with another—while at the same time, preventing any of the states from taking any
action that would affect *all* of the states, some of which might not agree to it. Thus, the
Congress could not make alliances, declare war, or make treaties without the approval of a
majority of the states; no state could do any of these things unilaterally—it needed the consent
of the Congress, which meant the consent of a majority of the other states.

The effect of the Articles of Confederation was to prevent the United States from
formulating a coherent foreign policy, make a shambles of interstate commerce, and
almost kill off the new country when internal rebellion threatened its survival. The federal
government was powerless to deal with any of these problems, as it was constitutionally
limited in its authority, and too penniless to enforce the prerogatives it *was* entrusted
with—it could levy taxes on the states, but could not collect without the consent of each
state, a permission few states granted.

In the autumn of 1786 a crisis developed which would have implications far out
of proportion to the actual threat it posed. This was Shays' Rebellion, named for its leader,

Capt. Daniel Shays of Massachusetts. Armed men, mostly poor farmers who could not pay their debts due to economic depression, were demanding protective legislation, reduction of onerous taxes, and the abolition of the court of common pleas, which handled foreclosures. The mob broke up several sitting courts throughout the state; only when they marched to Springfield to seize the federal arsenal were they met by an opposing force, a private militia under the command of Gen. William Shepard, which was paid for by the Massachusetts legislature. Shays' men went home, and a second American Revolution was narrowly averted.

But the rebellion had thrown America's political leaders into a fit of panic, for they realized that the next rebellion might not be so easily put down. Economic depression was causing unrest throughout all the states. Only 800 men had taken active part in Shays' rebellion, but he was rumored to have 15,000 supporters in New England alone. An armed insurrection of that magnitude could not be dealt with—the federal government had no money with which to pay an army, if it could find one to fight.

Two things were clear: the economic depression must ease, and a central government powerful enough to deal with crises both economic and political must be set in place. The Articles of Confederation would have to go.

To accomplish this, a constitution governing the relationship among the states and between the states and the federal government would have to be written. The federal government—which must still be limited in its powers—would have to be strengthened. The fundamental concept of American government would have to be changed. And so a

Engraving depicts Daniel Shays leading his rag-tag army, which included young boys.

Following pages. Contemporary map showing Great Britain's North American colonies at the time of the Revolution.

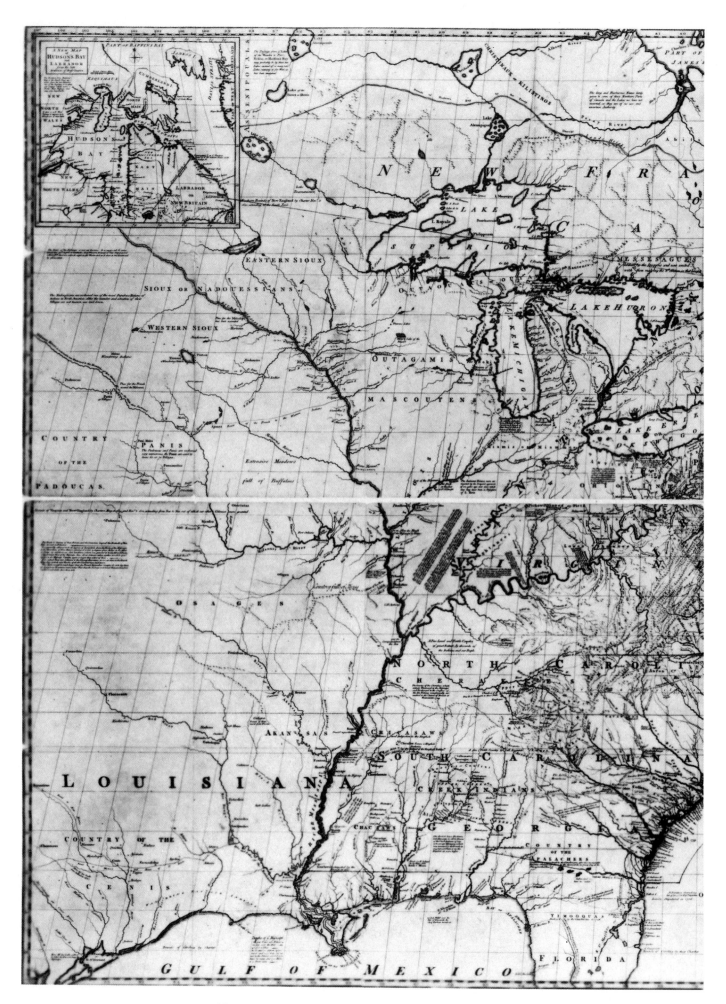

44

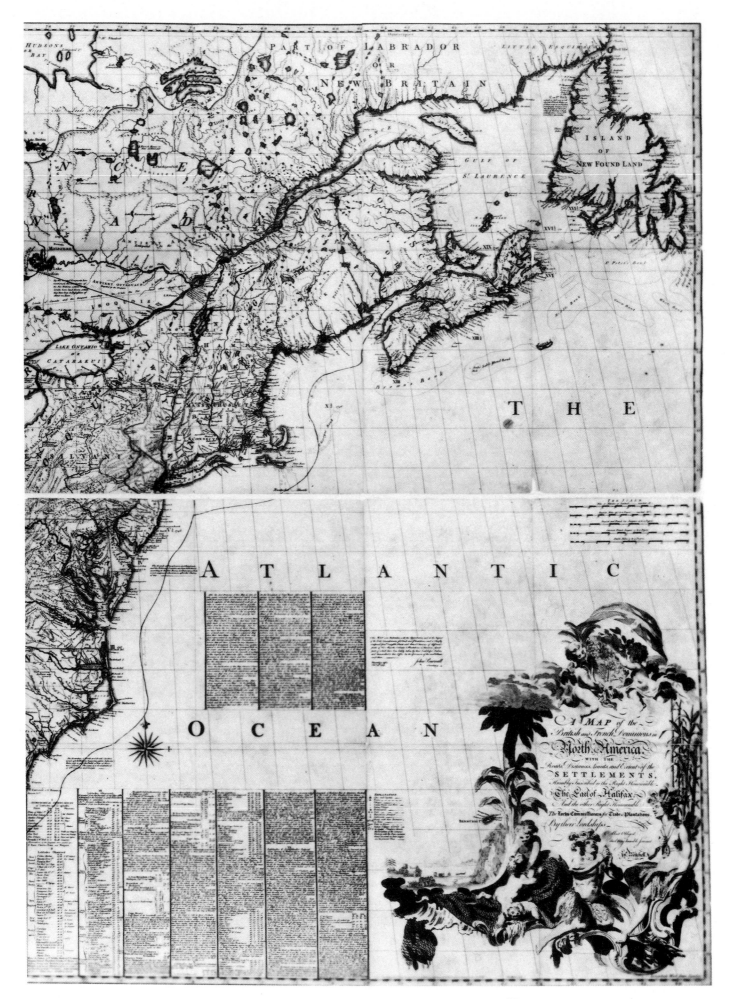

convention was called to write this new constitution. The place chosen as the site for the convention was, naturally, Philadelphia, then serving as the nation's capital. The date set for its opening was May 14, 1787.

As we might say today, most of the "usual suspects" were rounded up and sent as representatives to Philadelphia. Washington would preside; Franklin, Dickinson, Livingston, Sherman, and many other veterans of the Continental Congresses were present (Adams and Jefferson were out of the country on diplomatic missions). But many new faces appeared on the scene. The most important of these, as far as the Convention is concerned, were James Madison of Virginia and Alexander Hamilton of New York.

Madison, like Jefferson, was the son of a Virginia plantation owner who moved in the highest social circles. His early passion was agriculture, and Jefferson would one day call him "the greatest farmer in the world." He went north at the age of eighteen to attend the College of New Jersey at Princeton, and graduated two years later. When he returned home, his new passion was politics.

With independence declared, Madison served as a delegate to the convention called to form a new state government. His was a major voice in the writing of Virginia's constitution. He won election to the state legislature, where he formed a lasting friendship with Jefferson, newly returned from the Continental Congress and famous as the man who had written the Declaration of Independence. Madison lost his bid for reelection (because, it is said, he refused to honor the age-old tradition of plying the electorate with free rum) but was appointed to the council of state by Governor Patrick Henry. He was reappointed by Governor Jefferson.

As a member of Congress from 1780 to 1783, he got a first hand look at how dismally the country was organized under the Articles of Confederation. Despite his admiration, bordering on worship, for Jefferson, who wanted a weak federal government, Madison more often than not found himself in agreement with another young congressman, Alexander Hamilton, who was a forceful advocate of strong central government.

Hamilton was as different from Madison as Adams was from Jefferson, even more so, yet they too found themselves allied in a common cause. The illegitimate son of a Scottish trader, Alexander Hamilton was born on the West Indian island of Nevis in 1755, and was apprenticed to a counting house on St. Croix at the age of fourteen.

Within two years he was in charge of the business. With the aid of money raised by friends, he arrived in New Jersey in 1772, spending two years in a grammar school before entering King's College (now Columbia University) in New York. While a student there, he wrote pamphlets encouraging independence and refuting Loyalist calls for reconciliation. While originally attributed to John Jay or Robert Livingston, the pamphlets were soon to be revealed as the work of Hamilton, who won fame because of them.

Hamilton joined the Continental Army at the outbreak of the Revolution, rising to captain of artillery before being appointed aide-de-camp to General Washington in March, 1777. Though he had great influence with the General, Hamilton yearned for military glory in his own right. He took advantage of a rebuke from Washington to resign his post in 1781. Taking command of a regiment, he distinguished himself at the Battle of Yorktown.

At war's end he returned to New York to study law, and was elected to Congress in 1782. His single term there was fortuitous, for it was there that he met Madison and formed the alliance that would change the course of American history.

Madison and Hamilton would, on balance, do more than any others to determine the shape of the new national government. While Madison is justifiably called the "Father of the Constitution," Hamilton's contribution, and his influence on Madison, should not be underestimated. It would be futile to try to discuss here all that went on at the Constitutional Convention (which did not open on the appointed date—a quorum could

"An Attempt to Land a Bishop in America." Followers of the philosophy of Briton John Locke on occasion demonstrated violent anti-clericalism to insure the separation of Church and State.

General George Washington bids a final farewell to his old friend, Marie Joseph Paul Yves Roch Gilbert du Motier, Marquis de Lafayette, at Mount Vernon in 1794. Intimates of Lafayette called him "Gil."

not be reached for nearly two weeks). When it was over, Madison and Hamilton had won the day, calming the fears of those who did not want a strong central government with their system of checks and balances designed to prevent a recurrence of tyranny.

What emerged from the Convention was the American government as we recognize it today. Three branches—executive, legislative, and judicial—with power to defend the nation, conduct foreign policy, regulate commerce between the states, and crucially, to collect the taxes necessary to ensure its own survival.

If this was the beginning of modern American government, then it was also the beginning of our modern political system. Political parties, identifiable in England since mid-century, would form around the nucleus of particular issues. "Conservative" and "liberal" would take on new, previously unthought-of connotations. Campaigns would be waged, deals would be made, mud would be slung. All of this was right around the corner, but the time was not yet ripe.

First the people, weary from Revolution, bickering, disunity, disharmony, and near-rebellion, needed to take a deep breath before plunging headlong into the future. They needed something to rally around, something—or someone—to unify them as a people and consolidate them as a nation, even if only for a brief period. As in the past, when unity was the object and a rallying point was needed, there was one man pre-eminently suited to fill the bill. The man from Mount Vernon would be called upon again.

2 America Comes of Age
1787–1812

Debate raged throughout the United States over the wisdom of ratifying the new Constitution. Men who had fought so hard and suffered so much privation to win their independence during the late war were fearful of replacing one tyranny with another. Hamilton realized the crucial tests of ratification would come in his native New York and in Virginia, and set out to influence public opinion in those states in favor of the Constitution.

His chosen method was a series of letters, originally signed "A Citizen of New York," and later with the pen name Publius, that were published by influential newspapers in his home state, then published in pamphlet form and rushed to Williamsburg, to be used there virtually as a textbook on how to argue in favor of ratification. Though he wrote most of the eighty-five letters himself, several of the most powerful and persuasive ones were written by his Virginia ally James Madison, and several more were contributed by John Jay.

Jay, the scion of an aristocratic New York family, was born in New York City in 1745, and, like Hamilton, was a graduate of Columbia. Admitted to the bar in 1768, he was elected to both the First and Second Continental Congresses. After drafting the first constitution for New York, he was appointed that state's first chief justice in 1777. He was elected president of the Continental Congress the following year. In 1782, he went to Paris as a part of the negotiating committee that drew up the terms of peace between the United States and Great Britain.

In 1784, Congress appointed Jay secretary of foreign affairs, the forerunner of the office of Secretary of State. It was while he served in this capacity that Jay became convinced of the ineffectiveness of the Articles of Confederation and of the need for a strong centralized government. It was this conviction that led him to assist Hamilton and Madison in the writing of what would become known as *The Federalist Papers*.

To say merely that *The Federalist* was instrumental in convincing thoughtful men to support ratification of the Constitution is to grossly underestimate the importance and brilliance of the work. Throughout our country's history, *The Federalist* has been looked to and cited by legal scholars as the definitive interpretation of the Constitution by the men who wrote it. In our own day, when searching for the "intent of the Framers" has gained wide currency among conservatives as a brake on "judicial activism," *The Federalist* is enjoying a renewed popularity among students and jurists that rivals the acclaim it received when it was published.

The Constitution was ratified, by the requisite nine states, by June 1788, and thus became the supreme law of the United States. The first Congress organized under the new government met in New York, then the nation's capital, the following year, as did the first electoral college. As expected, that body unanimously selected General Washington to be

Right. John Dickinson. Though originally a pro-conciliation Tory who refused to sign the Declaration of Independence, Dickinson later formulated the conservative tenet of state's rights as the major author of the Articles of Confederation.

Below. The house in Philadelphia where Thomas Jefferson wrote the Declaration of Independence.

50

FEDERAL HALL

The Seat of CONGRESS

Printed & Sold by A. Doolittle New Haven 1790

Peter Lacour delin.

A. Doolittle Sculp.

Left. Federal Hall in New York, where the first United States Congress met and where George Washington was inaugurated for his first term as President in 1789.

the first President of the United States. John Adams was named on thirty-four of the sixty-nine ballots (each elector was required to name two choices), and thus became the first Vice President.

Naturally, every presidential act performed by Washington set a precedent. He gave the first inaugural address (and held the first inaugural ball), spontaneously added "So help me God" to the oath of office (and though it is not in the Constitution, no President has since omitted it), refused his presidential salary (a precedent that did not take hold), and delivered the first State of the Union address (a precedent that did take hold)—though it was not called that at the time. But the most important precedent set by Washington was to divide the executive branch of the government into departments, relying heavily on the advice of men he appointed to head those departments. It would not be formally called so until his second term, but these department heads constituted the first Cabinet.

Following pages. Left. Gouverneur Morris of New York, whose lack of success as President Washington's trade ambassador in England would lead indirectly to the disastrous Jay Treaty.

Right. George Clinton, seven-term Governor of New York, attempted to rebut *The Federalist Papers*, but, ever the pragmatic politician, later championed federalism.

51

President Thomas Jefferson.
Though considered the
father of American liberalism, Jefferson's accomplishments include much for conservatives to admire.

It was an illustrious Cabinet. Thomas Jefferson was appointed Secretary of State,
Alexander Hamilton Secretary of the Treasury, Henry Knox Secretary of War, and
Edmund Randolph Attorney General. His selections show Washington's keen understanding of the political situation in the country as it then existed. He knew Hamilton and
Jefferson to hold widely divergent views on the functions of the central government, and
knew also that they would be his most forceful and eloquent advisors. Knox, a cool and
studied soldier whom Washington trusted intimately, leaned toward Hamilton's political
views. Randolph was Jefferson's cousin. (In fact, in Cabinet meetings, Randolph usually
took notes and rarely expressed his opinion, which one might reasonably assume would
have been similar to his cousin's; Jefferson loathed him for it.)

As provided for in the Constitution, Washington also appointed the first Chief Justice
of the Supreme Court. For this position he chose John Jay, who had been chief justice
of the New York State Supreme Court.

It may fairly be said that the greatest achievements of Washington's first term were accomplished by Hamilton as Secretary of the Treasury. Hamilton felt it incumbent upon the central government to assume the war debts of the several states to France and Holland, and of the states to their own citizens, if the new government was to establish credibility abroad and at home. He was completely successful in repaying all the outstanding debts, aided by more effective tax laws than were available under the Articles of Confederation. In these efforts he was supported both by the President and by Jefferson. The Secretary of State, as part of a political trade-off, even supported Hamilton's original plan for a National Bank. But it was over the bank that they eventually had a bitter split, leaving Jefferson feeling badly used and determined to leave the Cabinet.

It may also be fairly said that the greatest controversy during Washington's first term was caused by Jefferson as Secretary of State. His support of the revolution in France, to the point where he hoped the United States would aid the French radicals in their war with England (despite the horror stories of mass bloodshed which were daily emerging from Europe), caused Washington grave concern and put him at odds with his own chief diplomat. Washington was determined to steer a course of neutrality, knowing how treacherous European politics was, and knowing that the young country could ill afford another war with England. Hamilton had convinced him that the best hope for American prosperity lay in a resumption of pre-Revolutionary levels of trade with England, and to that end, the President sent Gouverneur Morris of New York to London in an effort to negotiate a trade treaty. The British, still petulant over the Revolution and further offended by the growth of American support for the radicals in France, were having nothing to do with their former colonies as far as commercial trading went. Morris was spectacularly unsuccessful.

The duel between Alexander Hamilton (*right*) and Aaron Burr in Weehawken, New Jersey, July 11, 1804 that ended their rivalry and left Hamilton dead.

Throughout 1793, Jefferson petitioned Washington to allow him to resign his post and return to Virginia. He felt stymied by Hamilton's influence over Washington. It was Hamilton, he felt, who urged Washington to hold to the policy of neutrality when Jefferson desperately wanted the United States to intervene in Europe on the side of the French, and it was Hamilton who had convinced the President to petition Congress to charter the first National Bank, which Jefferson now held to be an evil thing that undercut the sovereignty of the states and was blatantly unconstitutional. He was further embarrassed by the Citizen Genet Affair, in which the representative of the radical government in France consistently flouted diplomatic protocol in his efforts to rally the American people to the cause of France. Jefferson originally welcomed Genet as a brother, and when Washington felt it necessary to ask for the Frenchman's recall in July 1793, it reflected very badly indeed on his Secretary of State. Still, Washington repeatedly asked Jefferson to stay on, until Jefferson could be persuaded no more and resigned in December 1793. Washington chose Randolph to succeed his cousin, much to Jefferson's disgust.

Washington was unanimously reelected in 1793, and hoped to devote his second term to putting the country on a stable financial and political footing for his successor. He hoped for tranquility. It was not to be.

America came alive politically during Washington's second term. The split between Jefferson and Hamilton led to the fomenting of genuine, recognizable political parties, and Washington feared they would divide the country irrevocably. The Federalists, led by Hamilton, supported neutrality in foreign affairs and commercial advantages at home, and looked to the national government to protect their interests. The Republicans, led by Jefferson, wanted the United States to actively support France in her tribulations in Europe, and favored an agrarian economy at home. They looked to the increased sovereignty of the states at the expense of the power of the central government as the surest means to protect their interests.

The President leaned toward the Federalists. Though one may speculate that his natural inclinations were closer to those of his fellow Virginian, Washington understood better than Jefferson what it meant to be the *first* President, and he felt it necessary to use his powers accordingly. Many have claimed that after Jefferson left the Cabinet there was no effective voice to counter the persuasive arguments of Hamilton (which is true, and a situation that Washington was fully aware of, hence his numerous entreaties to Jefferson to stay on), but the New Yorker had no Svengali-like influence over the President. The President was a Federalist because of the situation he found himself in, Hamilton or no.

Perhaps the one objective dearest to the hearts of all Federalists, and most especially the President, was a trade agreement with England. A *laissez faire* economy depended upon open markets. England, where most of the pre-war colonial trading was carried on, had done an effective job of bottling up American commerce. Not only would the British themselves not trade with the United States, but they prevented the young nation from trading with France, with whom England was at war. In an effort to break this commercial stranglehold, Washington had, as noted, sent Gouverneur Morris to London to negotiate, but his work had been fruitless. By 1795, the Federalists were clamoring for a new negotiator, while the Republicans were clamoring for war. Casting around for someone who could reason with the British, Washington almost bowed to Federalist pressure to send Hamilton himself (an idea which horrified the Republicans, who were afraid that he might be so successful that he would be assured of succeeding Washington), but in the end settled on Chief Justice Jay. Jay was sent to England to assert America's sovereign right to trade with whom she pleased, while at the same time assuring the British that she would be pleased to trade with England in a most-favored-nation arrangement. But Jay was outmaneuvered by his British negotiating counterparts, and he virtually gave away the store.

The treaty which Jay brought back with him would, on the surface, seem favorable to the Americans on several points. First, the British would open their West Indian colonies to American trading ships. Second, all other international agreements signed by the Americans (such as with France) would not be abrogated by any provision of this new treaty. Third, the British agreed to evacuate their western posts along the disputed Canadian border. But the concessions he had made to get these agreements were disastrous. He had allowed the British to set a limit on the size of ships that could trade in the West Indies—seventy tons, the size of virtually the smallest ships in the American commercial fleet. He had agreed to allow British men-of-war to search American ships bound for Europe and remove anything that could aid the French in their war effort—and for the beleaguered French, this could amount to almost anything. As to the Canadian proviso, the evacuation would not take place for nearly a year, and even then the British would be allowed free trade with the Indians in the American and Canadian West—the surest way to keep their influence strong among the tribes.

Washington knew the treaty was a disaster, but it was he who had wanted it, and to reject it now would mean almost certain war with England. To accept it would mean war with the Republicans. Ever the astute strategist, Washington opted for war on the home front.

The outcry from the Republicans was deafening, and the Federalists were hard put to defend either the treaty or Jay. Most men on both sides of the aisle saw him as a dupe who had been outwitted by the British; others saw him as an instrument in a plot to abandon the French in order to maintain American neutrality. Not a few accused him of treason.

But Washington had decided to accept the treaty, and he called upon his Federalist allies to get it through the Senate. The fight there was led by Fisher Ames of Massachusetts.

Born into an aristocratic New England family in 1758, Ames was brought up with a distaste for egalitarians, feeling that government should be left to those most suited to safeguard the public welfare—people like himself. He possessed a silver tongue, and his gift for oratory had brought him to the Senate at an early age. He was still only thirty-seven when the Federalist Party turned to him to lead the fight for ratification of this most unpopular treaty. And he was up to the task, for it is Ames who is credited with convincing his fellow Senators that while this treaty might not be very good, it was the best they could hope to get, and to reject it would mean a war that they were ill-prepared to fight. The treaty was passed, grudgingly.

Washington's prestige suffered badly during the fight over the Jay treaty. He was no longer aloof from politics, and politicians in both parties now felt free to attack him openly. One who did, and whose career was ruined, was the Secretary of State, Edmund Randolph. Randolph was shocked when, after a month of indecision, the President had decided to bring the full weight of his office to bear in support of the treaty, an agreement the Secretary vehemently opposed. Randolph made no secret of the fact that he was disgusted with the treaty, and with the President for supporting it. Enemies of Randolph within the government produced documents, supposedly captured by the British from a French warship and then passed on to high-placed Americans, which implicated Randolph as being in the pay of the French government. Confronted by the President, Randolph denied that he had spoken against the treaty for any reason but what he considered the best interests of the United States, and denied further that he had ever been in the pay of the French government. Washington was inclined to believe him (he loved him as a son), but Randolph then exploded in anger, saying he could not serve a President who would even bring such questions to him. Washington went to his grave believing that Randolph had at least flirted with treason, if he had not actually committed it.

Washington was glad to see his second term drawing to a close, and would set another

John Adams. Leader of the political fight for independence and second President of the United States, he was one of the most important conservative philosophers among the Founders.

precedent by refusing to run for a third term, to which he could easily have been reelected. On September 19, 1796, he released to the newspapers his Farewell Address, in which he warned the nation to be wary of foreign entanglements and denounced political partisanship as an invitation to national division and foreign intrigue. But by this time political parties were a fact of life, and they would determine the character of government from that time forward.

John Adams was viewed by many as the natural successor to George Washington, having served him as Vice President for the last eight years. He was backed by the Federalists, while the Republicans rallied around Thomas Jefferson, who had been living in retirement in Virginia. The election remained in doubt even after the electors were chosen because Hamilton, the acknowledged head of the Federalist party, had deemed Adams too independent and preferred the more tractable Thomas Pinckney, Federalist candidate for Vice President, to succeed Washington. Hamilton was able to maneuver enough Federalist electors out of the Adams camp and over to Pinckney so that it almost cost the Federalists the election. When the votes were counted, though, Adams had seventy-one electors in his column to Jefferson's sixty-eight, with Pinckney running third: Adams was President, Jefferson, Vice President.

The main thrust of Adams' Presidency, which undoubtedly cost him his chance for reelection, was his insistence on holding to Washington's course of neutrality in European affairs. When he took office, the Republicans were still demanding concrete executive action favoring France in her war with England, even if it meant military intervention against England. By the time his term of office was done, many in the nation would be clamoring for war with France.

Adams had achieved great personal and political success in the years after the American Revolution. Returning home to Massachusetts, he had written that state's constitution in 1779, then traveled to Paris the following year as part of the American delegation seeking peace terms with Great Britain. He remained in Europe for the next several years with his son, John Quincy, serving as Minister to England from 1785 to 1788. During this period, he had published his masterful three-volume *Defense of the Constitutions of the Government of the United States of America*, then returned home to be elected Vice President (an office which he referred to as "the most insignificant office that ever the invention of man contrived or his imagination conceived"). During the years he served under President Washington, he published his *Discourses on Davila*, a bulwark of conservative philosophy in which he denounced the revolution in France as being wholly incompatible with the American Revolution. Though the work deeply offended his old friend Thomas Jefferson, it ranks with Burke's *Reflections on the Revolution in France* as a conservative rebuttal to works such as Thomas Paine's *The Rights of Man* and *The Age of Reason*. But nothing in his previous career, not even the outright hatred he felt from some of his fellow delegates at the Second Continental Congress, had prepared him for the vitriol he would endure as President of the United States.

Adams made a serious political error immediately upon his succession to the office. He decided, out of respect for Washington, to keep the old General's cabinet officers in power in his Administration. But Washington had believed in bipartisan government, and so the loyalty of these men lay not to their new President, but to the heads of their respective parties. Hamilton in New York and Jefferson, right under Adams' nose, were better informed of what was going on in the government than President Adams was himself. Adams realized his mistake soon after he made it, but could not bring himself to dismiss many of these men for fear of alienating Washington.

Adams was barely in office when the crisis that would seal his political fate arose. France had been acting imperiously in her relations with the United States since the ratification of the Jay Treaty, refusing to recognize American diplomats and threatening even to hang

American seamen found serving on captured British war ships. Adams, though, tried to smooth relations, and dispatched new commissioners to France in 1798. He soon received word from his envoys that three agents of the French government, referred to in dispatches only as X,Y, and Z, had demanded bribes before any Americans would be allowed to present their diplomatic credentials to the French Foreign Minister, the redoubtable Monsieur Talleyrand. Adams' immediate inclination was to ask the Congress for a declaration of war against France in the face of this insult to the national honor, but then he reconsidered, and asked Congress only to relax the policy of neutrality enough to allow American merchant ships to arm themselves. He did not tell them about the inflammatory dispatches. His request for merchant arms was violently denounced as a threat to France by the pro-French Republicans. Adams then released the dispatches, making public what has ever since been known as the XYZ Affair, and all hell broke loose.

The Federalists demanded war, and with no apology forthcoming from the French government, Adams felt he had no choice but to oblige them. War preparations moved swiftly. Congress immediately created a Department of the Navy, then passed the Alien and Sedition Act, which empowered the federal government to imprison aliens or citizens who were suspected of working against the government. Adams then called General Washington back to duty as commander of the Army, a post which Washington accepted on the condition that Hamilton be appointed second-in-command.

Opposite. Alexander Hamilton, commander-in-chief of the American Army after the death of George Washington in 1799. It was in this role that the Democratic-Republicans feared him most, certain that any military victory would propel him to the White House.

The Republicans were horrified. Though deeply embarrassed by the actions of the French government, they had been pro-French and anti-isolationist too long to back down now. They knew they could not attack Adams directly for preparing for war, because war fever had swept the nation. Instead, they trained their sights on the Alien and Sedition Act, which had not been enforced against aliens (who seemed to have been cowed enough by it to keep their opinions to themselves), but had been used to put twenty-five pro-Republican, anti-Adams newspaper editors in jail. Working in concert, Jefferson and James Madison wrote the Kentucky Resolves, declaring that no one was subject to "unlimited submission" to the government. Jefferson in particular would have been struck dead had he known that the Kentucky Resolves would be used as a justification for secession from the Union to protect the institution of slavery some sixty years later.

In the end, it was Adams who undercut the Federalists and the war party and handed the Republicans a political victory by offering to send new envoys to France on the understanding that they would receive more courteous treatment. Some Federalist Senators threatened to vote a declaration of war without a request from the President; Adams promptly threatened to resign and leave the government in the hands of Jefferson. The Federalists had no choice but to back down, but they would not forget. War was averted, but Adams was ruined in his own party.

On the morning of December 13, 1799, it snowed more than three inches in Virginia, and the temperature hit a high of thirty degrees. General Washington, at home on his beloved plantation, Mount Vernon, noticed that he had a mild sore throat but, as was his custom, would not take anything for it. By midnight the following day he was dead, and the nation plunged into mourning. Perhaps no one in the country had greater reason to mourn the passing of America's first President than the second. Though Adams was now free to dismiss the holdovers from Washington's Administration (which he did), he knew that his political fate had already been sealed. If Washington had lived, his support would have been enough to ensure Adams' reelection, if he had been willing to publicly express such support. But now Washington was dead, and politically, so was John Adams. Hamilton, leader of the Federalists and now Washington's successor as commander of the Army, felt cheated of the glory he could have won in a war with France and again supported Pinckney for President in 1800. The Federalist Party was divided over Adams' handling of the XYZ Affair, and though he could count on some support as an incumbent

President, it was not enough to overcome the split in his own ranks. Each member of the Republican ticket, Thomas Jefferson and Aaron Burr, received seventy-three electoral votes in the election of 1800. Adams received sixty-five.

The flaws in the electoral system as it then operated were glaringly obvious with the election of 1800. The Republican Party had clearly backed Jefferson for President, and Burr for Vice President. It was because of the solid unity of the party that the election ended in a tie, and was thrown to the House of Representatives, as provided for in the Constitution.

Aaron Burr had been born in New Jersey in 1756, the son of the president of the College of New Jersey (now called Princeton University). He joined the Continental Army in 1775, rising to the rank of lieutenant colonel before retiring from active service due to illness. He went to New York, where he was admitted to the bar in 1782. Burr became a power in Republican (or Democratic-Republican, as the party was called in that state) politics, often clashing with Alexander Hamilton, leader of the Federalists both in New York and the country at large. Appointed Attorney General of New York State in 1789, Burr went on two years later to win election to the U.S. Senate, where he served one full term. He was among the most loyal of party regulars, one who took delight in thwarting Federalist plans as much to goad his rival Hamilton as to win a victory for the Republicans. The choice of Burr to run with Jefferson in 1800 was an early example of "ticket-balancing." The House of Representatives recognized the will of the electorate, and despite heavy political maneuvering on Burr's part, elected Jefferson President and the New Yorker, Vice President.

Opposite. Aaron Burr, who in his career managed to arouse the hatred of both Thomas Jefferson and Alexander Hamilton. He killed Hamilton in a duel in 1804.

As the new President, Jefferson moved quickly to reverse what he viewed as abuses of power by the previous Administration. He freed all persons who had been imprisoned by the Alien and Sedition Act, ordered major cuts in government expenditures, especially those pertaining to the military, and pushed Congress to lower taxes whenever and wherever possible.

The high-water mark of Jefferson's first term came with the purchase of the Louisiana Territory from France in 1803. When Spain ceded the vast territory to France in 1802, Jefferson, by now disabused of his admiration for the French Revolution, realized, "We must marry ourselves to the British fleet and nation," as the only power that could keep France in check. In no way wanting to undertake such a policy, he wrote to the American ambassador in Paris, Robert Livingston, instructing him to urge Napoleon to sell New Orleans to the United States. He sent James Monroe to Paris to assist in the negotiations.

To the amazement of the Americans, they found that Napoleon was willing to part with his entire North American territory for the sum of $15 million, which worked out to roughly three cents an acre. From this purchase all or part of thirteen future states would be carved out. Jefferson at first feared that a constitutional amendment would be needed to make the transaction legal, but recognized that the amount of time needed to get one passed was more than ample for Bonaparte to change his mind. Accordingly, he urged Congress to appropriate the necessary monies as quickly as possible, writing privately, "the less said about any constitutional difficulty, the better."

This unexpected expansion of the country was widely credited to Jefferson's political acumen, and was a major factor in his overwhelming reelection in 1804. Jefferson garnered 162 electoral votes to only 14 for his opponent, Federalist Charles Pinckney. Federalist, or conservative, political prospects were at their lowest ebb since the founding of the country. Jefferson's smashing victory in the 1804 race was disheartening enough, but even that paled in comparison with the blow the Federalists had received in July of that year.

Alexander Hamilton had come to view Vice President Aaron Burr as a much greater

John Randolph, another cousin whom Thomas Jefferson detested. He was one of Jefferson's severest critics during the President's second term; he later opposed the War of 1812, James Madison, the Missouri Compromise, and Henry Clay, with whom he fought a bloodless duel. Randolph died insane in 1833.

a Presidential election. Within twenty years, the party would peter out of existence entirely.

The duel also brought an end to the political career of Aaron Burr, though not to his time in the limelight. During Jefferson's second term, the nation would be rocked by the news that Burr had intended to set up a separate republic in the Southwest, either by fomenting a war between the United States and Mexico, or by invading Mexico himself with a private army and then forcing some of the territories of the Louisianna Purchase to join with whatever Mexican land he could seize. Jefferson got wind of the scheme and had Burr arrested, but after a six-month trial before the Supreme Court's Chief Justice John Marshall, he was acquitted for lack of concrete evidence. Burr went into exile in England. After suffering severe financial reversals, he returned to the U.S. to practice law, dying quietly in New York at the age of eighty in 1836.

Jefferson's second term was far rockier than his first. He considered the Burr acquittal a direct slap at him by Chief Justice Marshall. The impressment of American seamen by the British merchant navy brought the two nations close to war again in 1807. Jefferson wished devoutly to avoid such a war, and thus persuaded the Congress to pass the Embargo Act, which completely cut off American shipping to foreign ports. This act ravaged the New England economy, which was based on shipping, but the political strength of the conservative New England merchants had waned considerably, and the act stayed in effect until the end of Jefferson's term. It would not be the last time that a liberal President would use the embargo of American exports as a tool of his foreign policy, and thus earn the enmity of an entire region of the nation.

Opposite. French map of the Louisiana Territory sold by Napoleon to the United States in 1803.

Thomas Jefferson refused to even consider pleas from within his own party that he run for a third term, preferring instead to follow the example of General Washington and return to private life after two. He successfully supported his Secretary of State, James Madison, for the Presidency in the election of 1808, then retired for the last time to his plantation at Monticello. During his last years, he founded the University of Virginia, replenished the Library of Congress with his own collection of books after the original one had been burned by the British, and renewed his friendship with his predecessor, John Adams. Incredibly, the two died on the same day, July 4, 1826, fifty years to the day after the signing of the Declaration of Independence. Adams' last words were: "Still Jefferson lives." He was wrong.

James Madison came to the White House well suited to be President of the United States, for he had virtually been Jefferson's partner, at least in the conduct of foreign affairs, for the past eight years. But he also ascended at a time of great upheaval in foreign affairs, due principally to the two still-warring powers, France and Britain.

Shortly before leaving office, Jefferson had obtained the repeal of the Embargo Act, replacing it with the Non-Intercourse Act, which prohibited U.S. trade only with France and Britain. But the two European superpowers continued unabated their trampling of American rights at sea, and their intrigues against the young nation on its own continent. Britain in particular was blamed for fomenting Indian uprisings on America's western frontier, the most serious of which was put down by General William Henry Harrison at the Battle of Tippecanoe.

Madison was also faced with pressure from a group in Congress whom he referred to as the "war hawks." Led by Henry Clay of Kentucky and John C. Calhoun of South Carolina, this group advocated the military annexation of Canada from Britain and Florida from Britain's ally, Spain.

A threatened British blockade left Madison with no choice but to ask Congress for a declaration of war against Great Britain, which Congress approved on June 18, 1812. The United States was embarking on its second war with its former mother country, and was almost completely unprepared.

3 Manifest Destiny 1812–1856

Opposite. James Madison, author of many of *The Federalist Papers*, and father of the Constitution. Despite differing viewpoints, he greatly admired Jefferson and carried on his friend's work when he succeeded him as President of the United States.

The military forces of the United States in 1812, thanks largely to Jefferson's earlier cutbacks, consisted of an Army of about 10,000 troops and a Navy with only about twenty seaworthy fighting vessels. They were no match for the full might of Britain's military machine. But fortunately, the U.S. did not have to face Britain's full might, as most of her fighting forces were tied up in the war with Napoleon. Still, the forces they did send wreaked havoc on the United States.

The American military expeditions against Florida and Canada were almost complete failures, and when their campaign against Napoleon ended temporarily, the British sent a force strong enough to compel the President and the Congress to abandon Washington, D.C., which the British promptly burned—White House, Capitol, and all.

The American Navy, small as it was, acquitted itself well against a far superior British force, employing with good success the tactic of hit-and-run. And the American Army did defeat the British in the largest land battle of the war, at New Orleans on January 15, 1815, under the command of General Andrew Jackson. What neither Jackson nor his British counterpart knew was that by the time they fought the Battle of New Orleans, the war had been over for three weeks.

The British and the Americans had signed the Treaty of Ghent back on December 24, 1814, though the news did not reach the western commanders until much later. Despite heavy American losses in the field, the terms of the treaty declared neither side the winner or loser, simply stipulating that both sides return any captured territory they occupied at the end of the war. The British were tired of war after nearly fifteen years of continuous fighting in Europe, and did not wish to prolong their American adventure any more than they had to. The Americans, taking stock of their inferior forces and resources, were glad to have it done with, and requested no reparations for the burning of their lovely capital city. Most importantly, the defeat of the French in Europe meant that normal commercial shipping could resume unmolested on both sides, and thus removed the reason for the war.

Politically, the war had serious political repercussions in the United States. The New Englanders, still feeling slighted over the Embargo and Non-Intercourse Acts, had opposed the war from the beginning, and during the war, secession was a popular topic among New England legislators. Although tempers would cool with the end of the fighting and the resumption of normal commerce, it was obvious that the country was dividing along regional lines, rather than along any political lines that can easily be identified as "conservative" and "liberal."

President Madison is a case in point. He had been easily reelected in 1812 while the war was in full gear, defeating not a Federalist, but a disaffected member of his own Republican Party, De Witt Clinton of New York, who was nominated by the Federalists as a fusion candidate. He then finished off his defeat of the Federalist Party by, in effect, co-opting it.

De Witt Clinton of New
York. As a fusion candidate
for President in 1812, he
unsuccessfully opposed Madison's reelection.

His second term saw Madison implement many of the Federalists' most basic economic platforms, including the chartering of a new United States Bank and a call for a protective tariff.

Here was a President implementing the conservative party's platform after winning two terms as the nominee of the liberal party, yet finding his strongest opposition in the most conservative region of the country. It is interesting to note that the "conservative" ideas he advocated then would be anathema to conservatives today, and that his "liberal" stand in favor of a strict interpretation of the Constitution is a staple of the modern conservative diet. It is also interesting to note that the region from which he hailed, then considered the hotbed of liberalism, is now considered to be one of the most conservative in the country, while the conservative region that opposed him is now considered one of the most liberal. For reasons such as these, it is hard to peg our Founding Fathers as either "liberal" or "conservative," in the modern understanding of these terms.

But if "liberalism" and "conservatism" are something of a muddle in the early part of the nineteenth century, then "regionalism" is the soul of clarity, and it is this factor that would dominate American political thought and action for the next sixty years at least, culminating in the vicious and bloody War Between the States of 1861-1865. But the roots of that struggle lay much further back, and they shall be examined in due course.

One of Madison's last acts as President was to veto the "Bonus Bill," a measure proposed by Senator John Calhoun that would have provided federal funding for a national system of roads and canals. Madison announced that he had given the Constitution a thorough going-over, and could find no provision for such federal funding. Therefore, the project would have to be left up to the states. Madison wanted to make sure that everyone knew where he stood on strict construction of the Constitution, the document he had done so much to write.

The original Capitol building after being burned by the British during the sack of Washington, D.C., in 1814.

Upon leaving office Madison, like Jefferson, retired to his Virginia plantation, and like Jefferson, would serve as the rector of the University of Virginia. Upon his death in 1836, his wife turned over to the government his heretofore secret notes on the Constitutional Convention of 1787. Like *The Federalist Papers*, Madison's *Notes* are today enjoying renewed popularity among people who want to know more about the formation of our Constitution.

The roll call of America's Founding Fathers is studded with names of men so outstanding that it is difficult to believe that such a group could have come together in one nation at one time without such a gathering having been ordained by Divine Providence. Debates over which of these men was in fact the most outstanding of all would bring out proponents of at least a dozen factions. And one name that would be prominent even among such an illustrious list would be that of our country's fifth President, James Monroe of Virginia.

It is, in fact, easy to lose Monroe in the shuffle of great men of his era, or to confuse his accomplishments with those of his fellow Virginians, Jefferson and Madison. But the fact is that Monroe may well have equalled both of them in political accomplishment during his long years of public service.

He was born into a Virginia planting family in 1758, and attended the College of William and Mary, where he was a classmate and friend of John Marshall, the future

71

Chief Justice. When the Revolution came, he left William and Mary to accept a commission as a lieutenant in General Washington's Continental Army. He fought gallantly in many battles, and for his demonstrated heroism at the Battle of Trenton was promoted to captain by Washington himself. Before the war was over, he was a lieutenant colonel, carrying out special assignments for the governor of Virginia, Thomas Jefferson.

After the war, Monroe returned to Virginia, studied law, and was elected to the state legislature in 1782. The following year he was elected to Congress. Despite his youth, Monroe almost immediately began to make his voice heard in Philadelphia. Knowing that he might well alienate some powerful forces in his native region, Monroe nevertheless assisted Rufus King, an outstanding Federalist legislator from Maine, in the writing of the Northwest Ordinance, which subsequently made slavery illegal in the Northwest Territory ceded by Great Britain at the end of the Revolution. And despite his admiration for Jefferson, Monroe, like Madison, felt that the Articles of Confederation needed strengthening. But unlike Madison, he did not want a new constitution; instead he introduced a proposal that would have given Congress regulatory power over interstate commerce. His proposal was defeated.

Monroe opposed ratification of the Constitution when it was put forth in 1787, but softened his views and grudgingly supported the document after receiving assurances from Madison that a bill of rights would be added later. In 1788, he opposed Madison for a seat in the House of Representatives, but was defeated by his friend. Two years later, though, he was appointed to the Senate to fill a vacancy left by the death of Sen. William Grayson. It was while in the Senate that Monroe truly began to become a leader of Jefferson's Republican Party, causing such political annoyance to the Federalist leader Alexander Hamilton that those two almost fought a duel.

Always a Francophile, Monroe was appointed Ambassador to France by President Washington in 1794. It was during this period that Monroe caused himself some discredit by supporting the French Revolution to the point where Washington felt it necessary to recall him. After his recall, in a fit of pique, Monroe published *A View of the Conduct of the Executive*, in which he excoriated Washington and the Jay Treaty for the deterioration of relations with France.

Out of political favor, he returned to his farm, Ash Lawn, for three years, but in 1799 was elected governor of Virginia by the state legislature, a post in which he served with distinction. Monroe regained national stature in 1803, when he was sent by President Jefferson to Paris to assist Robert Livingston in the negotiations for the purchase of New Orleans. Largely because of the esteem in which he was held by the French people and government, Monroe was able to convince the French to sell the entire Louisiana Territory to the Americans. Even if James Monroe's political career had ended there, he would have earned a lasting place in American history.

But his career did not end there. For the next four years, he was the U.S. Minister to Great Britain, where he helped Jefferson to avoid, or at least postpone, war over freedom of the seas. Unable to convince the British to sign a treaty guaranteeing American shipping rights, and equally unable to convince the Spanish government in Madrid to cede Florida to the United States, Monroe returned to the U.S. in 1807, feeling somewhat defeated and extremely wary of the European powers. He resumed his life at Ash Lawn, until he was reelected governor of Virginia in 1811.

His second term as governor was short-lived, as he resigned later that same year when President Madison offered him the post of Secretary of State. Immediately Monroe was plunged into the war fever that gripped Washington, and he helped the President draft the proposal of war against Great Britain that Madison delivered to Congress. When the war was on, Monroe was in large part responsible for its prosecution, as Madison saw fit to appoint him Secretary of War in addition to his duties as Secretary of State, the only man

DEATH OF THE EMBARGO, WITH ALL ITS " RESTRICTIVE ENERGIES."

A wit first celebrated this great event in the FEDERAL REPUBLICAN, in the manner to be seen below ; but he has had the politeness to revise and correct the article for the Evening Post, with additions : in this improved state it is now presented to our readers, aided by an appropriate engraving devised by the author and admirably executed by one of our fellow-citizens. Here it comes—

" TO THE GRAVE GO SHAM PROTECTORS OF " FREE TRADE AND SAILORS'
RIGHTS"—AND ALL THE PEOPLE SAY AMEN !"

TERRAPIN'S ADDRESS.

Reflect, my friend, as you pass by ;
As *you* are, *now*, so, once, was *I* ;
As *I* am *now*, so *you* may be :—
Laid on your back to die like me !
I was, indeed, true Sailor born ;
To quit my friend, in death, I scorn.
Once Jemmy *seem'd* to be my friend,
But, basely, brought me to my end !
Of head bereft, and light, and breath,
I hold *Fidelity*, in death :—
For " *Sailor's Rights*" I still will tug ;
And, Madison to death I'll hug,
For his perfidious zeal display'd,
For " *Sailor's Rights and for Free Trade.*"
This small atonement I will have—
I'll lug down Jemmy to the grave.
Then Trade and Commerce shall be free
And Sailors have their liberty—
Of head bereft, and light, and breath,
The *Terrapin*, still true in death,
Will punish Jemmy's perfidy :
Leave *Trade*, and *brother Sailors Free !*

PASSENGERS REPLY.

Yes Terrapin, bereft of breath,
We see thee faithful still, in death :
Stick to't—" *Free Trade and Sailor's Right* :
Hug Jemmy—press him—hold him—bite—
Ne'er mind thy head—thou'lt live without it,
Spunk will preserve thy life—don't doubt it—
Down to the grave t'atone for sin,
Jemmy must go, with Terrapin.
Bear *him* but off, and we shall see
Commerce rester'd and Sailors Free !
Hug, Terrapin, with all thy might,
Now for " *Free Trade and Sailor's Right* :"
Stick to him, Terrapin, to thee the nation
Now eager looks :—then die for her salvation.
FLOREAT RESPUBLICA.

Banks of Goose Creek,
City of Washington,
15th April 1814.

in our nation's history to have the distinction of holding two cabinet positions at one time. When the war ended, he resumed his full-time activities as Secretary of State for the remainder of Madison's term.

And when that term was drawing to a close, Monroe was the natural choice to lead the Republican Party in the 1816 elections. His opponent was a well-known Federalist statesman and, in fact, an old friend, Rufus King.

Like Monroe, King had great breadth of experience in politics both domestic and foreign. After his success with the Northwest Ordinance, King was a prominent fixture at the Constitutional Convention, where he was a staunch ally of Alexander Hamilton. Moving to New York, he was elected to the U.S. Senate, where he was a vociferous partisan leader of the Federalists. He served as U.S. Minister to Great Britain under President John Adams, and was twice the Federalist Party's candidate for Vice President, both times unsuccessful. By 1816, again a U.S. Senator, he was the Federalist Party's last hope for capturing the White House. But it was not to be. The Federalist Party was making its final stand, and King could muster only 34 electoral votes to Monroe's 183.

The period of American history that followed was marked by such growth and stability that it has been known ever since as the "Era of Good Feeling." Monroe continued Madison's tradition of adopting the best policies and appointing the best men, be they Federalist or Republican, without regard to partisan politics. His cabinet, generally rated as the strongest in American history, included John Quincy Adams, son of the former Federalist President, as Secretary of State, and John C. Calhoun as Secretary of War. While domestic tranquility was the order of the day at home, Monroe enjoyed smashing success in the field of foreign policy.

The Rush-Baggot Agreement between the U.S. and Great Britain resulted in the elimination of all fortifications on both sides of the U.S.-Canadian border and set the stage for the unprecedented friendliness of those two neighboring states that continues to this day. Remembering his earlier failure to procure Florida for the U.S. from Spain, Monroe set to the task anew as President, and concluded the negotiations successfully in 1819. Spain's influence as a colonial power was waning on all fronts, and this presented Monroe with his greatest challenge—and his greatest triumph.

The election of 1820 saw what amounted to a temporary end to the two-party system in the United States. So successful in his administration, and so personally popular throughout the country after a whirlwind tour of all its regions, was James Monroe that in 1820 he ran unopposed for the presidency and received 230 of the 231 available electoral votes. One elector cast his vote for Secretary of State Adams to preserve for George Washington alone the honor of unanimous election.

But Monroe saw storm clouds gathering on the horizon that could well put an end to this period of tranquility. Since 1810 at least, the Spanish Empire throughout Latin America had been growing smaller and smaller, as many of the subjugated nations saw the power of the mother country weakening steadily and opted for independence. Most Americans, the President included, were delighted by this turn of events, as many of these newly independent countries sought to base their system of government on our own. But Madison recognized that these countries were themselves weak politically and militarily, and thus could be easy prey for exploitation and possible takeover by a strong imperial power such as Great Britain. With the assistance of John Quincy Adams and on the advice of the elderly Thomas Jefferson, Monroe formulated what has come to be known as the Monroe Doctrine, which he delivered to Congress as part of his Executive Address in 1823. In it, he declared that any attempt by any foreign power to establish a sphere of influence anywhere in the American Hemisphere would be viewed as an act of aggression against the United States and would be answered in kind. Like the Declaration of Independence, the Monroe Doctrine has become part of the organic law of the

AND IT LOOKED EASY, TOO.

United States, and is at the heart of modern conservative philosophy in regard to foreign relations.

Strangely, after leaving office, Monroe became the forgotten man of American politics, unable even to collect expense money that he claimed was owed him by the government. Forced to sell his Virginia plantation, he retired to New York, where he lived in poverty and obscurity until his death in 1831.

It would seem that by 1824 the nation had grown restless after ten years of stability and tranquility, and chose not to elect another conservative president. Accordingly, the electorate turned to the populist candidate Andrew Jackson of Tennessee, awarding him forty-three percent of the popular vote and ninety-nine electoral votes. His nearest rival was Secretary of State John Quincy Adams, who polled some thirty percent of the popular vote and received eighty-four electoral votes. But because there were two other candidates in the field—William H. Crawford, Secretary of the Treasury from Georgia, and Henry Clay, congressman from Kentucky—no candidate was able to garner an outright majority, and by the rules of the day, the election was thrown for the second time to the House of Representatives. Clay, with the fewest electoral votes, was dropped from consideration; but those same thirty-seven electoral votes which he controlled were enough to swing the election to the candidate of his choice. After some hard bargaining, he chose Adams, and while the country cried "Foul!" Adams was duly certified the winner by the House. When he went to the White House, Clay went along as Secretary of State.

Though no candidate ran with a party label in 1824, Adams was clearly heir to the old Federalist traditions, while his rival Jackson was forming a new party that combined his populist followers with the remnants of Jefferson's Republican-Democratic Party. His new party faithful simply called themselves Democrats, and it is to this party that the modern Democratic Party can truly trace its origins.

76

SCENE IN WASHINGTON

"I will now go home and look over Hoyle and calculate the odds in favor of my friend P-s Faro Bank, in which he proposes to give me d-n good interest."
(Soliloquy of Sir Harry Bluff.)

"Now go home G-d D-n you where you belong." Spoken by H. Clay in the Hall of the House of Representatives after the vote on the contested "Mississippi Election".

HOYLE'S GAMES
"Brag," "Sheep-
"Poker," "ker's Loo,"
"Bluff," "Old-
"Faro," "Stedge,"

In which the **PRESIDENTIAL CANDIDATE** of all the **DECENCY** or **RESPECTABLE WEBB** "**WHIG**" **PARTY**
enters the Hall of Representatives from his favorite amusement "**BRAG** and **POKER**".

Entered according
To Act of Congress in the Year 1838 by W. Chambers in the Clerks Office of the District Court of the Southern District of New York.

Opposite. John Quincy Adams, the son of John Adams and a leading conservative in his own right, nevertheless served opposition Presidents with distinction before his own uninspired term in the White House.

Left. Contemporary cartoon savaging House Speaker Henry Clay.

John Quincy Adams presided over the most unsuccessful Administration up to that time, and there is irony in that, for there is no doubt that he was highly qualified to be President. Under his father's Administration, he had served as diplomat throughout Europe, afterwards becoming a U.S. Senator from Massachusetts. Despite his Federalist background, he had served two Republican Administrations with distinction, leading the American negotiating team that drew up the favorable Treaty of Ghent, serving afterwards as Minister to England, and finally enjoying great success as Secretary of State for both of President Monroe's terms of office. But the manner in which he became president cut off any chance he had to be popular with the people, and an unpopular President gets no support from Congress, as Adams learned. His four years in office were uneventful, and the electorate seemed only to be marking time until they could elect Jackson outright.

This the electorate did by a wide margin in 1828, and so embittered was Adams that he refused to attend his successor's inauguration. Andrew Jackson came to the White House with a reputation as something of a wild man, still carrying several bullets from the countless duels he had fought, many of them over women—including his wife, Rachel, whose own reputation was somewhat suspect because of activities she engaged in during her youth. But Rachel had died between the time Jackson was elected and inaugurated, and so broken up was he about it that many of his friends feared he would not live out his term.

He also came to the Presidency with a more positive reputation of military heroism because of his part in the Indian Wars and as the hero of the Battle of New Orleans. Despite a widespread perception of him as a backwoods frontiersman, Jackson was in fact a highly successful lawyer who had served with distinction as a member of the Congress and Senate from Tennessee.

But his hot temper and thin skin did not serve him well during his first two years in office, when he found himself not on speaking terms with most of his cabinet over the affair of the wife of Secretary of War John Eaton, who would not be received into the homes of the other Cabinet minister's wives because of *her* dubious reputation. He also developed a passionate hatred for his Vice President, John C. Calhoun, when he learned that years earlier Calhoun had wanted President Monroe to arrest Jackson for seizing Spanish forts in Florida while fighting Seminole Indians, an incident that had almost precipitated war between the U.S. and Spain. (It was to Jackson's chagrin that he learned his staunchest defender in the Cabinet during this incident was Secretary of State John Quincy Adams).

But eventually the affair of Mrs. Eaton was put to rest, and Jackson, by now somewhat recovered from the shock of his wife's death, turned his considerable talents toward governing the country. Jackson had a series of political triumphs in the years to follow, winning his fight with Congress over the rechartering of the National Bank (which Jackson abhorred), and forcing Calhoun, who had resigned as Vice President to become a Senator from South Carolina, to back down over the issue of nullification. The principle of nullification held that a state legislature could nullify a federal law, and South Carolina threatened to secede if the federal government did not recognize its right to nullify federal tariff laws. Jackson threatened to hang Calhoun if South Carolina seceded, and Calhoun, knowing that the President wasn't bluffing, promptly decided that discretion was the better part of valor. The Union was preserved, and Jackson had reaffirmed the sovereignty of the Constitution.

Jackson easily won reelection over Henry Clay in 1832, and devoted his second term to sound finance. In 1835, his Administration became the first in the nation's history to fully pay off the national debt. The country entered a new period of growth and prosperity unmatched since the Monroe years.

Andrew Jackson is regarded as the founder of the modern Democratic party, and the godfather of populism and modern liberalism. While his insistence on solidifying the power of the central government at the expense of the states can hardly be considered conservative, few conservatives today would espouse the principle of nullification outright, and there is no doubt that Jackson's commitment to sound money and repayment of the national debt even makes him a popular figure with today's conservatives.

The age of Jackson represented the pinnacle of presidential power in the first half of the nineteenth century. While his immediate successors might well have been expected to capitalize on Jackson's bold assertion of presidential authority in the face of Congress and the state legislatures, for the most part they did anything but that. From the end of the 1830's through the opening of the 1860's, political direction came not from the men in the White House, but from the Senate, from the newspapers, and even from literature.

At first the country began to drift, and the economic achievements of Jackson's second

term would be offset by a financial panic during the only term of his handpicked successor, Martin Van Buren of New York. Van Buren, who served Jackson as Vice President during his second term, was a New Yorker who had served his home state as a legislator, U.S. Senator, and governor before becoming Secretary of State in the first Jackson Administration. Widely if erroneously rumored to be the illegitimate son of Aaron Burr, he was the first President born in the United States rather than in a British crown colony. His term of office is noted chiefly for the Panic of 1837, which he could do little to stymie, and for his rather awkward efforts to maintain the status quo between the rapidly polarizing regions of North and South.

He was succeeded by William Henry Harrison, who had been nominated by the Whig Party, which was a loose confederation of the old Federalist Party combined with Henry Clay's short-lived New Republican Party. Even more short-lived was Harrison as President, because the old hero of the Battle of Tippecanoe contracted pneumonia while delivering his inaugural address and died a month later in the White House.

Andrew Jackson, the founder of the modern Democratic Party, sketched speaking to a crowd of supporters on his way to Washington for his inauguration in 1833.

Harrison in his turn was succeeded by John Tyler, a distiguinshed Virginia legislator, Senator, and governor who had been elected Vice President in 1840. In his one term, Tyler managed to alienate his own Whig party leaders to such an extent that his entire Cabinet resigned, except for Secretary of State Daniel Webster, and he had to fill the vacancies with members of the Democratic Party.

James Knox Polk, a former Tennessee governor and once the Speaker of the House of Representatives, was elected President in 1844. He was more successful in many ways than any of his three immediate predecessors, largely because of his prosecution of the Mexican War. But history has not judged him kindly, because it seems obvious now that Polk prodded the Mexicans into a war they could not hope to win out of his desire to increase U.S. territory in the Southwest. He was also virulently opposed by the opposition Whig Party, which feared that the pro-slavery Polk intended to spread into the newly won territories in an effort to offset a Northern, anti-slavery imbalance of power. Though Polk chose not to run for a second term, he was upset when his Democratic Party lost the election, feeling it a judgment on his conduct in office.

General Zachary Taylor, hero of the Battle of Buena Vista during the war and Whig candidate for President in 1848, came next, and almost fomented the start of the Civil War during his fifteen months in office. The extension of slavery, rather than its abolition, was the burning issue of the day, and Taylor, anti-slavery, refused to compromise on the issue. Daniel Webster, who worked so hard on the Compromise of 1850, was certain that if death had not come to Taylor when it did, he would have vetoed the Compromise of 1850 and touched off the Civil War. But death did take Taylor, from heat stroke brought on while attending the cornerstone ceremony at the Washington Monument in July, 1850.

Taylor's Vice President, Millard Fillmore, is invariably rated near the bottom of any

Left. John Tyler favored state's rights to such a degree that he would be the only former President to side with the South during the Civil War.

MANIFEST DESTINY: 1812-1856

Above. James K. Polk, pro-slavery, Democratic President who prosecuted the war with Mexico.

Left. Franklin Pierce, Democratic President from 1850-1856. He had an ego to match Aaron Burr's and a drinking problem to rival General Grant's.

William Henry Harrison.
Hero of the Battle of Tippecanoe, he served one month
as President before succumb-
ing to pnuemonia in 1841.

historian's list of Presidents. His defense of the Compromise of 1850 postponed the Civil War for ten years, but his enforcement of the Fugitive Slave Law in the North made the war inevitable. Dumped by his Whig Party colleagues at their convention in 1852, he would accept four years later the nomination of the Know Nothing Party, a xenophobic party of anti-immigrant, anti-Catholic bigots, a decision which would only add to Fillmore's ignominy.

Fillmore was succeeded by Democrat Franklin Pierce, who hoped to emulate Polk by expanding the territory of the United States. But for the $10 million he spent he was able to acquire only a strip of land in the Southwest known as the Gadsden Purchase, which would be used for the construction of the Pacific Southwest Railroad. Pierce's pro-slavery outlook ruined his chances for renomination when fighting broke out in Kansas, and he bitterly watched the nomination go to his eventual successor, James Buchanan.

This series of lackluster if occasionally competent Presidents did not mean that there were not strong political personalities in the country at this time. Quite the contrary is true. But the nation's desire for compromise and delay on the issue of slavery meant that it was almost inevitable that a strong personality could not become President. They were out there, though, in the Congress, in journalism, and in literature, and it is these men—and women—whom we shall examine next, as well as the one great issue that colored their thinking on virtually all other issues. If the North and South were polarizing into two separate camps with the possibility of becoming two separate countries, then it was slavery that had brought them to that point.

4 A House Divided 1856–1877

Slavery began in the United States when the first slaves were brought to the Jamestown settlement in 1619. Throughout the period of British rule of the colonies and beyond, slavery was legal in all the North American territories. It was not seriously questioned as an institution until the debate over the Declaration of Independence during the Second Continental Congress, for Jefferson, himself a slave owner, had inserted a clause which would have emancipated the slaves in the United States. The Southern colonies, dependent on large plantations as their economic base and on slaves as the primary source of labor for the upkeep of those plantations, balked at the provision and would have withheld ratification if it were not removed. Jefferson, not wishing to risk the independence of all Americans, duly removed the controversial clause, though he continued to regard slavery as an abject evil unworthy of a home in the land of freedom and would himself, like Washington, free all of his own slaves.

Near the close of the eighteenth century an abolitionist movement, spurred on chiefly by the mainline Protestant churches, began to gain strength in the North, and by 1804 all of the states north of the Mason-Dixon Line had outlawed slavery. The abolitionists, though, were not content to excise the "pecular institution" from their own states, and turned their attention to the South.

In 1807 the abolitionists were successful in forcing the federal government to outlaw the slave trade, which meant that no new slaves could be imported from outside the United States for sale within its borders. The South, while not particularly happy about the law, was pragmatic enough not to grumble too loudly about it. Southern leaders realized that normal reproduction among the slaves already present would assure replenishment in the years to come, and viewed the law as a bone which would satisfy the Northern abolitionists. Having outlawed slavery in their own territories, and having abolished the importation of slaves from outside, these Northerners would realize that they had done all they could, and their consciences would be soothed—or so went the Southern line of reasoning. Knowing that they could do nothing about slavery in the South, they would savor the victories they had won and would leave well enough alone.

The Southerners could not have been more wrong. The abolitionists, far from satisfied with their victories, were emboldened by them, and determined to push their cause until slavery had been eradicated in every place where the American flag flew. But like the Southerners, they too were pragmatic, and realized that to concentrate on the South, where slavery was deep-rooted and would be fiercely defended, was misguided and would prove ultimately fruitless.

And so the abolitionists concentrated on the new territory of Louisiana. Shortly after its purchase from the French, President Jefferson sent his private secretary, Merriwether Lewis, and the explorer William Clark to survey the land. Their expedition made clear to all Americans the sheer magnitude of what had been bought. It was also clear to the abolitionists that large sections of the land lay south of the Mason-Dixon Line, and any of these sections that organized themselves into territories would expect to be admitted to the Union as slave states.

Their fears were first realized in 1812 when Louisiana proper, which consisted of New Orleans and the surrounding counties, was admitted as a slave state. But the war forced the question to be put off, and it was not until 1815 that the abolitionists were able to regroup in an effort to prevent a recurrence. When Missouri applied for territorial status in 1819, the abolitionists were ready.

Henry Clay was born in Hanover County, Virginia, one year after the outbreak of the American Revolution. As a young man he clerked for the attorney general of Richmond, and was himself admitted to the bar in 1797. Richmond at the end of the eighteenth century was already a prosperous and bustling city, with more than its share of experienced lawyers. Clay found there was little work for a lawyer who was largely self-educated and had never attended law school, so he decided to head west to the new lands being carved out in Kentucky. His innate skill with a jury won him a host of admirers in his adopted city of Lexington, and by 1799 he was a member of the state constitutional convention. There, he quickly lost some support by taking a stand against the perpetuation of slavery, but the fact that slavery was being questioned at all in a Southern territory indicates that he was not alone. At any rate, his decisive stand and bold oratorical attacks against the much-despised Alien and Sedition Act soon put him back in good stead with the people of Kentucky.

In 1806, Clay, then a member of the state legislature, was appointed to fill an unexpired term in the U.S. Senate. Though his term lasted only a few months, his probing mind and power of speech made him famous, and from that time on he was a national figure.

By 1819, Henry Clay had spent eight years as Speaker of the House of Representatives, and was generally acknowledged to be one of the most powerful men in the United States. He deplored the growing factionalism in the country, and while his career record proves that he was no supporter of slavery, neither was he in agreement with the more strident elements in the abolitionist camp. He recognized that slavery was a question that could well pull the country apart, and he was determined above all to preserve the Union.

The abolitionists were equally determined to do everything in their power to prevent the admission of Missouri to the Union as a slave state, while the Southerners demanded that the act be accomplished as quickly as possible. Civil war loomed as a very real possibility if no agreement could be reached, and Clay charted a course to prevent this.

The fruit of his efforts was the Missouri Compromise. Under its provisions, Missouri was to be admitted to the Union as a slave state, but to maintain the balance of power in the Senate, Maine was to be admitted as a free state. As for the Louisiana Territory, slavery was to be forbidden in any area above 36° 30′ north latitude.

It was a quintessential compromise, in that it made no one completely happy, but appealed to enough people on both sides of the question so that disaster was avoided.

It almost fell apart the next year, though, when the Missouri Territory amended its constitution to prevent the migration of free Negroes from the North to Missouri. Congress passed legislation forbidding the President to proclaim Missouri a state unless she agreed to grant full rights to all American citizens under the Constitution. Monroe agreed, Missouri backed down, and was finally admitted in August, 1821.

Both sides may have been placated by the Missouri Compromise, but neither was pacified. In the North, the abolitionists began stringent efforts to appeal to the public conscience to force an end to slavery in America.

Chief among those agitating for abolition was William Lloyd Garrison of Massachusetts. Only fifteen years old at the time of the Missouri Compromise, he was an apprentice at the Newburyport *Herald* and already held deeply rooted anti-slavery views, which were based on his faith in fundamentalist Christianity. By 1829 he was a publisher in his own right, launching a monthly periodical called *The Genius of Universal Emancipation* in Baltimore, then a center of the internal slave trade (which was still very much legal). In 1831 Garrison founded a far more influential newspaper, *The Liberator*, which galvanized the abolitionist movement throughout the North and made Garrison one of the most famous—and feared—men of his day.

Garrison himself cannot be considered a conservative either of his own day or retrospectively of ours. He was a committed pacifist (though he would support the Northern cause in the Civil War), once publicly burned the Constitution, calling it a pact with Satan, favored free trade (then a "liberal" plank), and championed the cause of women's suffrage and prohibition. Yet in one of those anomalies with which history is littered, it was largely through the efforts of this man and other like-minded abolitionists that the Republican Party, today the repository of mainstream conservatism, would come into being.

William Lloyd Garrison was just one of many in his time who found the printed word to be the most effective means of transmitting political ideas to a wide audience. Undoubtedly the most powerful newspaper publisher of the period was James Gordon Bennett, owner of the *New York Herald*. To this day Bennett remains a fascinating character to students of journalism and general history as well. A Scottish immigrant and a Roman Catholic, he was an ardent American nationalist who feared the effects of the rising tide of immigration brought on by repeated crop failures in Ireland and wondered in print whether one could truly be a faithful Roman Catholic and a loyal American.

In literature, several social conservatives of this period are still viewed as giants of American writing. James Fenimore Cooper is best remembered today for *The Last of the Mohicans*, but his literary efforts encompass far more than the novels which made him

James Fenimore Cooper, patrician New Yorker who was a leading conservative social critic in the first half of the nineteenth century.

The writer Nathaniel Hawthorne. An "Experimentalist" in his youth, he drifted toward a neo-Calvinist view of society in his later years, though he himself was bereft of faith.

famous. Born in a well-to-do New York family in 1789, he lived the life of a country squire, making money from his wife's estates until he took up his pen at around the age of thirty. His first successful novel, *The Spy*, published in 1821, made him a literary sensation, and he was able to make his living from his writing for the rest of his life.

Cooper lived and traveled in Europe from 1826 to 1833, and spent a great deal of his time during this period defending the principles of American democracy. Upon his return home, he found America in a political frenzy during the age of Jackson, and felt that the democratic principles he had so ardently defended in Europe were being abused by his less patriotic countrymen at home. He then directed his attention to social criticism, and it is on the basis of the work he produced during this period that his reputation as a conservative thinker rests. Works such as *A Letter to His Countrymen*, *The Monikins*, *The American Democrat*, *Homeward Bound*, and *Home as Found*, all published between 1834 and 1838, survive today as classic examples of conservative social thought in the first half of the nineteenth century. During the next decade, when land disputes would arise in New York State between tenant farmers and large landowners, Cooper would adopt a less egalitarian and more aristocratic—many would say more conservative—view of demo-

Washington Irving, whose
History of Old New York was a
subtle attack on the Jefferson
Administration.

Essayist Henry David Tho-
reau, whose belief in individual liberty over the power of
the state was more suited to
the 18th century than to his
own time, or to ours. His
influence would be felt by
men like Mahatma Gandhi
and Martin Luther King, Jr.

cracy, which is evident in works such as *Satanstoe, The Chainbearer,* and *The Redskins.* In later years, after his death, Cooper would be attacked by literary critics, as much for his wooden dialogue as for his conservative principles. One of his most vociferous critics was Mark Twain (e.g., "Fenimore Cooper's Literary Offenses"), but Twain's own motives are suspect. A man who had more time for European radicals than American democratic conservatives, Twain loathed Cooper because of his admiration for upper-class European and American mores; Twain's own disgust with European society may have had less to do with egalitarianism than with his rabid anti-Catholicism, a taint from which Cooper appears to have been free.

Perhaps the greatest work of conservative social satire was written by another New Yorker of this period, Washington Irving. Like Cooper, the son of an upper-middle-class family and, also like Cooper, chiefly remembered for other works, he made his reputation as a conservative social critic with his *History of Old New York,* whose authorship Irving ascribed to his comic character Professor Diedrich Knickerbocker. Ostensibly a light-hearted look at New York politics during the period of the Dutch occupation, it is in fact a stinging indictment of Thomas Jefferson and his Democratic-Republican Administration. Spending the bulk of his adult life in Europe both as a traveler and a diplomat, Irving would eventually lose touch with domestic American politics and his desire to use literature as a form of social commentary.

Among historians of the era, the most prominent conservative was certainly William H. Prescott, chronicler of the Spanish conquests in North and South America. A close friend of Irving and a recluse due to near-total blindness (he lost the sight of one eye after being hit with a piece of stale bread while a student at Harvard), Prescott peppered works such as *A History of the Conquest of Mexico* and *A History of the Reign of Ferdinand and Isabella the Catholic* with marvelous social criticisms both of sixteenth-century Spain and nineteenth-century America.

If, as noted, political direction was not forthcoming from the men who occupied the White House, there was certainly no lack of it coming from the Congress. Indeed, the antebellum years may well be viewed as the golden age of congressional leadership in the United States. Three men stand out from the rest even in this period, though, and while they represented different parts of the country and often held widely divergent views on how best to deal with the issues that confronted the nation, all three nevertheless are viewed as part of the conservative heritage.

Henry Clay we have dealt with before, and of the three, he is the most readily identifiable as a conservative. After his success with the Missouri Compromise in 1820-21, Clay was a leading candidate for President in 1824. His involvement in the electoral debacle which brought John Quincy Adams to the White House has already been discussed, but its effect on Clay's career was devastating. After serving four years as Adams' Secretary of State, he retired to Kentucky in 1829 and spent the next two years in private law practice. But despite the harm done to his national reputation, he was still the most widely respected figure in his home state. When one of Kentucky's U.S. Senate seats was vacated in 1831, Clay was appointed to fill the unexpired term, and was elected to a full term five years later.

Nominated again by the Whigs for President in 1832, he lost to the incumbent Jackson, but so successful was he in restoring his stature as a national figure that he was able to play a large part in breaking the deadlock between the President and Congress over the issue of nullification. Elected to a full term in 1836, he again retired after serving another six years in the Senate, and was again called back by the Whigs to run for President in 1844. And again, he lost. He went home for another four years, but was returned to the Senate in 1848.

During these, his final years in the Senate, Clay realized that the threat of war between

North and South was even more real and more imminent than it had been in 1820, and he devoted all his energies to finding a compromise that would preserve the Union. The result of his efforts is popularly known as the Compromise of 1850, but in fact it was more than a single measure; the Compromise is actually five separate pieces of legislation introduced by Clay and adopted by the Congress during August and September 1850. Two of the five measures represented concessions on the part of the South to the North; the first abolished the slave trade in the District of Columbia, and the second allowed the admission of California to the Union as a free state. Of the three concessions made by the North to the South, two were by themselves not enough to polarize the nation irreversibly. These entailed payment to Texas of some ten billion dollars in compensation for land in adjoining territories that Texas claimed rightly belonged to her, and the division of land newly won in the recent Mexican War into the territories of New Mexico and Utah, with the provision that they were to be opened to settlement by both slaveholders and abolitionists. This latter measure, which superseded the Missouri Compromise, caused widespread discontent in the North, but it was as nothing compared to the outcry that would be raised over the final measure of the Compromise of 1850.

This was the Fugitive Slave Law, and it was the enactment and enforcement of this law more than any other single factor save the later election of Abraham Lincoln that made the Civil War inevitable.

The first laws providing for the return of slaves who escaped into free territory had been passed by Congress in 1793, but it was left to the individual states to enforce them as strongly or as leniently as they saw fit. The result was that very few law-enforcement officials in the North bothered to do anything about returning runaway slaves in their jurisdiction, despite continuous protestations by the Southern states throughout the years. By 1850, an effective and enforceable Fugitive Slave Law was the price the South

90

Opposite. Harriet Beecher Stowe, author of the abolitionist classic *Uncle Tom's Cabin.*

Above. Harriet Tubman, the escaped slave who led hundreds more to freedom along the Underground Railroad.

demanded for continuing in the Union, and Clay saw no other course but to give them what they wanted. The 1850 version of the law placed the entire responsibility for enforcement on the federal government as a means of circumventing unwilling state officials in the North. In addition, it mandated that the courts refuse to accept evidence provided by fugitive slaves, suspended their right of habeas corpus, imposed penalties on any official from whose custody a fugitive slave escaped, and made the aiding and abetting of an escaped slave an act of treason. The abolitionists howled, and Northern legislatures passed ordinances forbidding federal agents from using Northern facilities for the transport south of captured slaves, but the lines had finally been drawn, and radicals on both sides of the question now moved to center stage. Clay's greatest desire had been to preserve the Union, and largely through his efforts, its dissolution was now completely unavoidable.

John C. Calhoun, the second member of our congressional triumvirate, had been born in Abbeville, South Carolina, in 1782 and, going somewhat against the norm, had been educated in the North, at Yale University. Elected to the House of Representatives in 1811, he joined with Clay as a war hawk, and, like Clay, his eloquent oratory during this period made him a national figure. Calhoun served as Secretary of War under President Monroe from 1817 to 1825, then served the next eight years as Vice President of the United States, under both Adams and Jackson; he is the only man in our nation's history to be Vice President under two different Presidents. (And, to underscore how murky were the political waters of the day, the two Presidents he served under were of different parties and had diametrically opposed policies. To Calhoun's conservative credit, it was the Democrat Jackson, not the Federalist/Whig Adams, who threatened to hang him.)

In 1832 Calhoun, no longer on speaking terms with the President he theoretically served, resigned as Vice President following his election to the Senate from South Carolina. Despite his long record of public service in a variety of offices, it is chiefly for this time spent in the Senate that Calhoun is remembered today. For it was here that he engaged in a series of debates with a senator from the North, in which Calhoun championed the cause of states' rights with more force and power of logic than had been done since the debates in the Constitutional Convention nearly fifty years before. He stoutly defended the right of Southerners to own slaves if they so chose, and set forth the guidelines for secession if the North attempted to abrogate this right either by legislation or by force. It is perhaps ironic that the senator with whom he debated is our third man, Daniel Webster of Massachusetts.

He has come down to us as an almost mythical figure, celebrated in song and story, quoted at length in American history books more often than anyone but Lincoln. He was and is "the Godlike Daniel." Born in Salisbury, New Hampshire, in 1782, Webster was noted for his oratorical skills even as a young lawyer. A Federalist, he was elected to the House of Representatives from New Hampshire and served from 1813 to 1817. It was during these first two terms that he came to know and respect the House Speaker, Henry Clay. Webster returned to private practice in 1818, and the following year earned at least a notch in the history books because of his persuasive arguments before the Supreme Court in *McCullough v. Maryland*. Now famous as a lawyer, he knew his prospects for handling important cases were better in Boston than in New Hampshire, so he moved there in 1820. Three years later he was back in the House, representing his adopted city.

After two more terms in the House, Webster was elected to the Senate from Massachusetts in 1826, and quickly became a shining star in the new Whig Party, successor to the Federalists. Recognized by one and all as the most powerful speaker ever to serve in the Senate, he consistently championed the causes of his native New England and of the Union. But Webster was not an abolitionist. He opposed slavery as a moral evil, and freely supported the Free Soil Movement, but his most ardent desire was the preservation of the Union, not the abolition of slavery. It is interesting to note that while Calhoun's finest hour as an orator came in his debates with Webster, Webster's came in his debates with a lesser-known Southern Senator, Robert Y. Hayne. It was while debating Hayne over the issue of nullification that Webster uttered the immortal words: "Liberty *and* Union, now and forever, one and inseparable!" Because of this and similar speeches, Webster was regarded by his constituents as an abolitionist, but they misunderstood his position. He wanted slavery ended and the Union preserved, but if he could not have both, he was willing to compromise on the former, never on the latter. Thus he shocked many of his New England supporters when he actively supported Clay's Compromise of 1850.

How then did Webster differ from Clay? Perhaps only in the intangibles, in ways that we can never be sure of. If the Compromise of 1850 had failed outright and sparked the Civil War there and then, it is difficult to say with any degree of certainty which way Henry

WEBSTER'S ORATION AT THE CAPITOL.

Webster, "The God-like Daniel" (*inset*). A contemporary sketch shows him speaking from the Capitol steps.

Clay would have gone. Many Southerners in similiar positions to his own—having no great desire to see the perpetuation of slavery and opposing secession—nevertheless felt honor-bound to support the South when the war did come. One thinks here most readily of Robert E. Lee. But with Webster there can be no question. The Union was his lifeblood, and that was why he was willing to compromise in order to preserve it. Had that failed, he would most certainly have been willing to fight for it.

It is difficult to determine precisely the true conservative position on the major crisis during the antebellum years of our nation's history; it is far easier to determine what it was not. It was not forcible abolition, surely, because the active abolitionists like Garrison embraced too many positions that were wholly incompatible with conservative philosophy. And forcible abolition was certain to provoke civil war, the end of order, anathema to conservatives. But to conclude therefore that the conservative position embraced the perpetuation of slavery is not just too simple, it is wrong. Men like Clay and Webster made no secret of their feeling that the "peculiar institution" would have to go, eventually.

Conservatives after the age of Jackson had begun to adopt states' rights, the heart of Jeffersonian democracy, as their own position in regard to good government. Does this, then, mean that the conservatives could accept secession if no further compromise could be reached? For Calhoun, the answer is clearly yes; for Webster, clearly no. Which then was the true conservative? Calhoun understood his position as a Senator to be that of a representative of the people who elected him. He would represent their interests and philosophy to the exclusion of all others. Webster on the other hand viewed the Senate as a deliberative body established to preserve the interests of the nation as a whole, and he

93

would argue for the common good against regional self-interest, no matter how justified that region might believe it was. Thus he was able to oppose slavery against the wishes of the Southern people and reject the argument that the North had no legitimate interest in Southern regional affairs, and later to go against the wishes of his own New England constituents in seeking accommodation with the South rather than force abolition and incite civil war. Webster's aim was the preservation of the Union and the preservation of moral and civil order; Calhoun was willing to sacrifice the Union and bring on a national holocaust for the sake of a chosen few in one region. Clearly, it is Daniel Webster, and Henry Clay, to whom conservatives must look to find their antebellum heritage; Calhoun was merely a regional reactionary.

By the end of 1852, all three of them were dead, and the nation drifted inexorably toward war. More than three hundred years earlier, in 1541, the Spanish explorer Francisco de Coronado had crossed the heartland of what would become the United States searching for a land he had heard of called "Quivira." What he found was a small village of Wichita Indians, and he went away bitterly disappointed. He did not know that he was the first white man to set foot in what we could call Kansas, a land that would be torn apart by white men over the question of what to do about men of color. There was little further interest in this land until after 1803, when the United States purchased it as part of the Louisiana Territory. After that it was explored by Lewis and Clark and the soldier-explorer Zebulon Pike, but there was little or no settlement there, and the Indians roamed free. The region was considered part of Missouri until 1821, when Missouri proper became a state. It remained unorganized territory thereafter until 1854, when Senator Stephen Douglas of Illinois, chairman of the Senate Committee on Territories, proposed legislation organizing this and its neighboring regions into the territories of Kansas and Nebraska. Douglas's major ambition (beside becoming President) was to see completed the construction of a transcontinental railroad starting in the North and running through the South; to accomplish this required the creation of Nebraska as an organized territory. But the South refused to support Douglas's proposal because much of the land lay north of the line of demarcation effected by the Missouri Compromise; those territories would by law have to be incorporated as free lands, with slavery outlawed. Missouri would have none of it, and the South supported Missouri. The transcontinental railroad looked like a dead issue.

But Douglas wanted his railroad, and he wanted the White House, so he set about to find a way to placate everyone. What he devised was the Kansas-Nebraska Act, organizing both territories and stating that it would be left up to the future inhabitants to decide whether slavery would be legal or not. This was clearly repeal of the Missouri Compromise, and it was an invitation to disaster. But with Southern support it passed the Congress, and was enthusiastically supported by the pro-slavery President Franklin Pierce.

Neither side of the slavery issue missed that point about "future inhabitants," and pro-slavery immigrants poured into Kansas from Missouri and Arkansas, while abolitionist societies in the North raised money to send as many anti-slavery settlers there as they could. Elections for territorial representative to Congress brought about the first in a series of armed clashes between the two groups. In 1855, Kansas had an anti-slavery territorial governor and a pro-slavery legislature; in July of that year, the governor in effect broke diplomatic relations with the legislature. Forced out of office, the governor, Andrew H. Reeder, with the backing of the Free Soil Party, organized a rump government which adopted a constitution that prohibited slavery and excluded Negroes from settling in Kansas. This compromise measure was adopted by the whole state in a referendum, and in January, 1856, the Free Soil Party took control of the de facto government.

But the compromise was short-lived as pro-slavery mobs took to the streets, imprison-

"Sun of Intellectual light & liberty,
stand ye still in Masterly inactivity,
that the Nation of Carolina may continue
to hold negroes & plant Cotton till the
day of Judgment!"

Above. James Buchanan, the
ineffective fifteenth President
who did nothing to stop the
nation's drift toward civil
war.

Left. Cartoon excoriating
South Carolina Senator John
C. Calhoun.

ing Free Soil Party leaders on charges of treason and sacking the abolitionist stronghold of Lawrence. In retaliation, an anti-slavery army under the control of a fanatical lay preacher named John Brown armed itself and murdered five pro-slavers at Pottawatomie Creek on May 23, 1856. Guerrilla warfare had begun in earnest; civil war was no longer being spoken of in terms of "if," but rather "when." Stephen Douglas's railroad might not only be intercontinental, but international as well.

Even before Kansas had begun to bleed profusely, conservative politicians began searching for a method to break the Southern stranglehold on national affairs. The Whig Party was tired and ineffective, and many northern Democrats were resentful of Southern domination of their party. In a meeting called in Ripon, Wisconsin, on February 28, 1854, to oppose the Kansas-Nebraska Act, a new party was born in an effort to effect the necessary changes. The host at that Wisconsin meeting, Alvan Bovay, motioned that the new party be called the Republican Party, and so it was. The Republican Party attracted large numbers of Whigs (so many in fact that the Whig Party was shortly out of existence), Free Soilers, disaffected Democrats, and abolitionists. The party platform called for a legislative end to slavery eventually, the prohibition of slavery outright in new territories, a repeal of the Kansas-Nebraska Act, and such conservative staples as a high protective tariff and increased westward expansion by granting free land to settlers.

The new party was able to score several impressive victories in congressional races during its first year in existence, and two key events the following year enhanced its stature immeasurably. In the first, Democratic Senator Salmon P. Chase ran for governor of Ohio as a Republican and won, bringing a major state under the control of the Republicans; in the second, New York publisher Horace Greeley joined the Republicans and made his *New York Tribune* a major party organ. By 1856, the Republicans were clearly the second most powerful party in the country, and were strong enough to hold a national convention and nominate a Presidential candidate.

That man was John Charles Frémont. Born in Savannah, Georgia, in 1813 and schooled as a mathematician and engineer in Charleston, South Carolina, Frémont joined the army in 1838 and was commissioned a second lieutenant in the corps of engineers. The following year the army sent Frémont to accompany the French explorer Joseph Nicollet, who was mapping the area between the upper Mississippi and Missouri Rivers. Frémont led three expeditions into the Oregon Territory between 1842 and 1845, during which he surveyed and mapped all of the Oregon Trail to the Pacific Coast. He also surveyed large parts of Nevada and California.

It was his knowledge of California that brought Frémont to the rank of major during the Mexican War, and he is credited with being instrumental in its conquest. So highly thought of was he by the American naval commander of the area, Commodore Robert Stockton, that Stockton appointed Frémont civil governor of California at the conclusion of the war. But if Stockton thought highly of Frémont, he thought even more highly of himself, because he did not have the authority to appoint anyone to be the governor of California. That power rested with Frémont's commanding officer, Brigadier General Stephen Kearny, who ordered Frémont to relinquish his office and report to his headquarters. Frémont, who very much thought that "governor" had a nice ring to it, refused, citing Stockton as the military commander of the area. No one, not even Stockton, was as embarrassed as Frémont (or in as much trouble) when Washington cabled orders reaffirming Kearny's authority as the supreme military commander in California. For his part, the Commodore loaded a train of burros and marched them to the sea, where he resupplied his ship and sailed away; Frémont was left with the unpleasant task of returning to Kearny's headquarters, where he was arrested and court-martialed for insubordination. Found guilty, he was ordered dismissed from the service, but President Polk granted a remittance of his sentence and he was allowed to resign.

Frémont's luck was to change again swiftly. In 1849, gold was discovered on his California estate, and he was suddenly a wealthy man. His money, coupled with his fame (as the "Great Pathfinder," not the inglorious governor), made him a natural candidate when California was admitted to the Union, and his constituents sent him to Washington as one of their original senators. But Frémont quickly became disillusioned with life as a junior senator, and he went back to California after only a year in office.

Frémont, himself a free-soil Democrat, welcomed the emergence of the Republican Party in 1854, and was instrumental in its organization in California. When the national convention met in Philadelphia in June, 1856, only Chase of Ohio was more highly regarded by the delegates. But Chase felt the time was not yet ripe for a national Republican victory, and he withdrew his name from consideration. Frémont was nominated for President by acclamation.

The Democrats rejected their incumbent President, Franklin Pierce, as he had ridden roughshod over the party during his term in office and had made too many enemies. They also rejected the party's leader in the Senate, Stephen Douglas, because he was too closely associated with the disastrous Kansas-Nebraska Act, and the delegates feared that a Northern backlash would make him unelectable.

James Buchanan was born near Mercersburg, Pennsylvania, in 1791, and had graduated from Dickinson College in 1809. Admitted to the bar in 1812, he practiced law for two years before winning election to the Pennsylvania legislature in 1814. He served two terms there, then left public life in 1816 to return to the law, and he was able to build up a lucrative practice. In 1820 he re-entered politics, winning a seat in Congress as a member of the dying Federalist Party. In the disputed election of 1824, Buchanan actively supported Jackson, and tried to persuade Henry Clay to do so as well. Disappointed though he was by the election of Adams, Buchanan nonetheless remained a Federalist during Adams' term, but when Jackson was elected in 1828, Buchanan switched parties and supported his friend as a Democrat.

Jackson rewarded Buchanan for his consistent support by appointing him Minister to Russia in 1832, a post in which the Pennsylvanian had good success for the almost two years he served. But James Buchanan was politically ambitious, and he feared that remaining too long outside the United States would cause him to be forgotten by the voters; in 1833 he asked Jackson to bring him home.

His move was well-timed, for in 1834 the Pennsylvania state legislature elected Buchanan to the United States Senate, where he would serve for the next eleven years. In the Senate, Buchanan supported Southern slave interests, more out of political pragmatism than from any regard for the institution. His pragmatism paid off, and he was named chairman of the powerful Senate Foreign Relations Committee, making him one of the leading lights of the Democratic Party. In 1845, he again backed the right horse, and President Polk named him Secretary of State, a post he had longed for. But he and Polk clashed repeatedly, and it was probably the lack of Polk's support that cost him the Democratic Presidential nomination in 1848.

Buchanan returned to his estate near Lancaster in 1849, but kept his eye on the nation's political situation. In 1852 he again offered his name for consideration at the Democratic convention, and again he was narrowly defeated, this time by Franklin Pierce. But Pierce wanted Buchanan for an ally, albeit an out-of-the-way ally, and thus appointed Buchanan Minister to Great Britain. Ever resourceful, Buchanan found a way to bring his Minister's post in London to center stage of American politics.

In 1854, Pierre Soulé, U.S. Minister to Spain, was ordered by the President to open negotiations with the Spanish government over the proposed American purchase of Cuba. So high-handed was Soulé in his manner that he managed to offend the Spaniards to the point where they wanted to hear no more about Americans in Cuba. The

97

The "Know Nothing" Convention of 1856 that nominated former President Millard Fillmore as its standard-bearer.

President was equally angered by Soulé's diplomatic blundering, and he ordered his errant Minister to seek advice from the Ministers to France and Britain, John Young Mason and James Buchanan. The three American diplomats met in the Belgian port town of Ostend, and Buchanan quickly made himself the chairman. The result of their meeting was the Ostend Manifesto, which urged Spain to sell Cuba to the United States, implying in not-so-subtle terms that the U.S. would use force to wrest Cuba away if Spain did not comply. The outcry in Spain was as nothing compared to that in New England.

Abolitionists in the North knew that slavery was a well-established institution in Cuba, and feared that the forcible annexation of noncontiguous slave territories would doom their efforts to prevent the spread of slavery to territories the U.S. already owned. Spain was so furious that Pierce had no choice but to repudiate the treaty publicly, which cost him support among his base constituency in the South, while doing nothing to gain him support in the North, where the abolitionists hated him no matter what he did. Buchanan for his part wrapped himself in the flag, declaring that he had acted only in the national interest. Pierce knew he'd been had, but there was little he could do, and James Buchanan came home to a hero's welcome and the Democratic nomination in 1856.

When the Whig Party folded, not all of its adherents drifted automatically into the Republican Party. A group of reactionary Whigs, fearful of the rising tide of immigration from Europe and consumed with hatred for the immigrants' religion, Roman Catholi-

Roger B. Taney, Chief Justice of the Supreme Court, who handed down the *Dred Scott* decision.

cism, founded their own radical party, which was popularly dubbed the Know Nothing Party. This group of xenophobes added to the volatility of American politics in 1856 by persuading former President Millard Fillmore to accept their presidential nomination.

The election returns of 1856 clearly demonstrate how the nation was deeply divided. Democrat Buchanan received about 45% of the popular vote, Republican Frémont about 33%, and the Know Nothing Fillmore about 22%. Buchanan had won, but a majority of the electorate had voted against him. If the Know Nothings had not fielded a candidate, it is likely that a majority of their votes would have gone Republican on the basis of issues other than immigration. Had that happened, it is conceivable that Frémont would have received more than 50% of the popular vote. And he still would have lost the election. Buchanan had carried a solid majority of the electoral votes by carrying every slave state save Maryland, which went to Fillmore.

Buchanan hoped that his election would hold the Union together by convincing the South that they still had a friend in the White House. He himself would take no stand on the burning questions in Kansas, saying that they were matters for the courts to decide, and he as Chief Executive would abide by their decisions. What he was not telling anyone was that Supreme Court Chief Justice Roger Taney had already informed him that the Court was ready to hand down its decision in the explosive Dred Scott case, and further, had informed him what that decision would be.

Dred Scott was a Negro slave owned by an Army surgeon named Dr. John Emerson, who was a citizen of Missouri. In 1836 the army transferred Dr. Emerson to Fort Snelling in the Minnesota territory, where slavery was forbidden by law. Upon Dr. Emerson's death in 1846 the Emerson family returned to Missouri, bringing Scott and his wife, another slave owned by the Emersons, with them. Scott tried to buy his way out of slavery, but when the family refused, he sued them in the Missouri Supreme Court, claiming that his residence on free soil released him legally from slavery. The Supreme Court of Missouri begged the question, ruling only that his return to Missouri reattached the bonds of slavery to him, if they had ever been loosed by residence in Minnesota. Abolitionist lawyers appealed the case to the Federal Circuit Court, which also ruled against Scott. The case went before the Supreme Court in 1855, where it was argued for two years, not being decided until the early part of 1857. The majority of the Court ruled that the government had no power to make citizens of Negroes, slave or free, because at the time of the adoption of the Constitution Negroes were forbidden to become citizens. Thus, Scott was not a citizen of Missouri, and had no right to sue in her courts for redress.

The ruling itself was enough to rouse the wrath of abolitionists and Free Soilers, but the ruling was not all that the Court issued. The Latin scholar Eugene Ehrlich defines the term *obiter dictum* as follows: "A legal phrase, designating a statement made in passing by a judge on a tangential matter in connection with a judicial opinion he is rendering. While an *obiter dictum*—the plural is *obiter dicta*—has no legal bearing on the opinion to which it is appended, it may have considerable effect in later cases since it may be read and considered along with the full opinion, and in some circumstances become even more important than the opinion itself."

Taney, who wrote the majority opinion, also inserted the *obiter dicta*. He expressed his opinion that Scott, a slave, had no more legal standing than any other chattel owned by a free man, and therefore, like any other chattel, could be taken anywhere in the U.S. and would still belong to that man; further, that the Missouri Compromise violated the Constitution; and finally, that Congress could not prohibit slavery in any of the territories of the United States. Legally speaking, the abolitionists and the Free-Soilers were thoroughly beaten, and, short of a constitutional amendment, had no recourse but to acquiesce.

The effect of the Dred Scott decision was to make even centrist Northerners as willing to fight as the Southerners were. The Court had given the South a free hand in regard to slavery, and had left the North without even the right to prohibit its spread to the Northern territories. But as the events unfolding in Kansas would prove, the North was not about to give in.

John Brown, forever linked with Kansas, was actually born in Torrington, Connecticut, in 1800, and grew up in Ohio, where his father had moved the family when Brown was five years old. From an early age he was steeped in a fundamentalist interpretation of the Bible and in a hatred for the institution of slavery, both legacies from his stern and pious father. An itinerant preacher and school master, the younger Brown moved to Pennsylvania, where he fathered a large family of his own. In 1834, he launched a project among his fellow abolitionists to educate the Negro, and he spent the next twenty years in pursuit of this goal. He also took an active part in the underground railroad, which was a network of safe houses set up by abolitionists from the Deep South to the Canadian border to aid in the flight of runaway slaves.

When the Kansas-Nebraska Act was passed in 1854, five of John Brown's sons went to Kansas to aid the abolitionist cause there, and a year later, their father followed them. By the time he arrived, violent skirmishes had already broken out between the pro- and anti-slavery forces, and Brown, long a believer in the Old Testament doctrine of an eye for an eye, was determined to avenge injustice by any means necessary. After a pro-slavery

Dred Scott, the negro slave
who sued for his freedom,
and lost.

mob sacked the abolitionist stronghold at Lawrence and murdered several of the leading townspeople, Brown organized his sons and several of his followers into an armed guerrilla band. They exacted revenge for Lawrence on May 24, 1856, by storming the town of Pottawatomie and executing five pro-slavery settlers. Suddenly famous throughout the territory, his ragtag army swelled in numbers and he moved on to the town of Osawatomie, where he fought and won a pitched battle against pro-slavery Missourians in August.

Not satisfied with small victories in a small war, Brown, his fanatical zeal for abolition now out of control, secretly journeyed north to New England to raise the funds necessary to start a major insurrection. Many Northern abolitionists, happy to have someone else do the actual fighting, gave him the money he required, and Brown returned to Kansas to spell out his plan to his supporters. Picking a force of eighteen men that included several of his sons, Brown made his way to Virginia late in 1858, where he established a refugee for fugitive slaves in the mountains. After months of planning and preparation, he launched his attack on the night of October 16, 1859, marching to and seizing the federal arsenal at Harper's Ferry. Once in charge of the arsenal and the town, Brown dug in for a long defense.

But it was not to be. The local militia surrounded the arsenal immediately after Brown seized it, and the next day authorities in Washington dispatched a company of Marines to reinforce them. The Marines were placed under the command of a seasoned army officer,

Robert E. Lee, pictured at
the end of the Civil War, led
the force which captured
John Brown at Harper's
Ferry.

John Brown, the fiery abolitionist who touched off the
violence that led to the Civil
War.

Colonel Robert E. Lee of Arlington, Virginia. Early in the evening of the 17th, Lee gave the order to attack the arsenal. In the brief battle that ensued, ten of Brown's followers, including two of his sons, were killed. Brown himself was wounded, and was forced to surrender what remained of his company shortly after the battle commenced.

Arrested and charged with treason and murder, Brown was brought to trial in a civilian court in November. He offered as his only defense his fervent belief in the need for abolition now. While many who viewed the trial would cite Brown's passion and elo-quence, his defense was not good enough to save him from the hangman's noose, which claimed him on December 2nd. Brown was viewed as a martyr in the North and a vicious murderer in the South, and his memory would not fade on either side for many years to come.

Stephen Douglas, who had done so much to cause the violence by his desire for a railroad, was up for re-election to the Senate in 1858. He was forty-five that year, having been born in Brandon, Vermont, in 1813, and educated there and in upstate New York. Once he earned admission to the bar, he headed west for Illinois, where he rapidly made a name for himself as a public prosecutor, member of the state legislature, state secretary, and state supreme court judge. He was elected to the House of Representatives when he was thirty, and served two terms there, leaving upon his election to the United States Senate in 1847. A few years earlier, he had courted the socially prominent Miss Mary Todd, but she had rejected him; perhaps she was put off by his small physical stature, for Douglas stood no more than five feet four inches tall. (Perhaps there was another reason, for Miss Todd seems to have been singularly unimpressed by physical appearance; she married another lawyer who by general consensus was considered the ugliest attorney in Illinois, Abraham Lincoln.)

Once in the Senate, Douglas became that body's most ardent proponent of national expansion. He enthusiastically supported the Mexican War, advocated the annexation of Texas, and was among the first to propose the annexation of Cuba. He was rewarded with the chairmanship of the Senate Committee on the Territories, whose counterpart in the House he had also chaired. He worked closely with Henry Clay in formulating the Compromise of 1850, and after Clay's death in 1852, viewed himself as the heir apparent to the political mantle of the Great Compromiser.

His first foray into solo compromising was the Kansas-Nebraska Act of 1854, with all of its disastrous results. Undaunted by that colossal political blunder, he vied for the Democratic nomination for President in 1856, but lost it to James Buchanan. Immediately upon his inauguration, it was Buchanan's turn to blunder, for he announced in his inaugural address that he would serve only one term as President. Viewing Buchanan as a lame duck from his first day in office, party leaders from the North more and more looked to Douglas as the leader who could prevent a Republican victory in 1860.

But first Douglas had to be reelected to the Senate in 1858. Since there was no direct election of Senators then (or until 1913), this entailed receiving the endorsement of his party's state convention, and then insuring that enough Democrats were elected to the state legislature, where they in turn would elect him to the Senate. Douglas was still wildly popular among the Democrats of Illinois, though he had lost considerable support among followers of President Buchanan and Democrats throughout the South. He had no trouble procuring his party's Senate nomination. In July, 1858, the Republicans held their own nominating convention, and endorsed the candidacy of a respected lawyer and former Congressman from Springfield, Abraham Lincoln.

Born in that now-legendary log cabin near Hodgenville, Kentucky, on February 12, 1809, Lincoln spent an uneventful childhood there, the son of a poor dirt farmer. His father moved the family to Indiana in 1816, where Lincoln was sadly affected by the death of his mother three years later. Though he had less than a full year of formal education in his entire life, young Lincoln developed a great love of books and would walk miles to borrow them from more affluent neighbors. When he was nineteen years old, Lincoln hired out as a deckhand on a produce flatboat headed for New Orleans, and it was in that city that he got his first look at the degradation brought to human beings by slavery. It was an experience he could and would never forget.

In 1830, when Lincoln was twenty-one, his father again decided to go further west, and moved the family to Decatur, Illinois. Abraham helped in the move, stayed to put down the first crop, and then decided to leave his family—and farming—to try his luck on his own.

He settled in the small town of New Salem, Illinois, and took a job as a store clerk, where his gregarious personality made him widely popular with the local farmers. The following year, war broke out between the settlers and a band of Indians led by Chief Black Hawk, and Lincoln was elected captain of the militia group formed in his area. His company was disbanded after a month, but Lincoln served for another three months as a private in the regular state militia, though he saw no fighting.

Back in New Salem, Lincoln tasted his first electoral defeat in a race for the state legislature which he had entered before he embarked upon his military service but had not had time to campaign for. Turning his attention to the world of business, he entered into a partnership in a general store, but soon went broke. It took him almost seventeen years to repay all of his debts from that venture.

Counting himself a failure in business and politics, he decided to study the law, often travelling the twenty miles to Springfield on foot to borrow law books, as there was no attorney in New Salem. In 1834, still teaching himself the law, he ran again for the state legislature as a Whig, and won. His first term was uneventful, as Whigs were few and far be ween in the Democratic stronghold of Illinois, and Lincoln thought it best to practice prudence. Still, he distinguished himself well enough among his constituents to be re-elected in 1836, the same year he was admitted to the bar to practice law. When the state capital was moved to Springfield in 1837, Lincoln moved there also, becoming the law partner of John T. Stuart in addition to carrying out his duties in the legislature. He would be re-elected twice more to that body, serving until 1842.

After choosing not to run for another term in Springfield in 1842, Lincoln married Mary Todd (the former sweetheart of Stephen Douglas) and set his sights on Congress. He was unable to win the Whig Party's nomination for the congressional elections in 1844, but after two years in private law practice, he sought the nomination again in 1846, won it, and went on to win the general election in November.

Lincoln's one and only term in Congress might have been as uneventful as his first term in the Illinois state legislature had not war with Mexico broken out a few months before his election. The Whig Party was opposed to the war, seeing it as dangerous adventurism on the part of a Democratic Administration, and the main thrust of Lincoln's congressional tenure was the defense of his party's anti-war position and the chiding of President Polk for having started it. In January 1848, Lincoln delivered his most memorable speech in the House, holding aloft a map and symbolically challenging the President to "show me the spot" where Mexican troops had supposedly crossed into American territory and fired on U.S. garrison troops to start the war. (It was the Whig's contention that the episode had actually taken place on Mexican soil and thus it was the Americans who had violated the border and provoked the conflict.) Pro-war Democratic newspapers in Illinois lambasted the state's only Whig congressman, calling him "Spotty Lincoln" or portraying him as a Mexican named "Ranchero Spotty." They accused him of treason for attacking an American President during wartime. So virulent did the attacks become that even Lincoln's Whig constituents were hard pressed to defend him, and he was not offered renomination.

Returning to Springfield, Lincoln effectively dropped out of politics for the next six years, concentrating his efforts on practicing law with his new partner, William Herndon. But the passage of the Kansas-Nebraska Act fanned the flames of abolition throughout the North, and feelings ran especially high in Illinois, which was represented in the Senate by the bill's chief sponsor, Stephen Douglas. Douglas traveled up and down the state defending his sponsorship of the bill, and was followed wherever he went by Lincoln, denouncing the bill. Lincoln's renewed popularity as the leader of the anti-Nebraska forces won him another election to the state legislature, though he quickly resigned to campaign for the U.S. Senate. But the statehouse was firmly in the hands of the Democrats, and Lincoln had no chance to win. Still, his effective speechmaking on the subject had won him a fair amount of fame throughout the North. Lincoln helped to organize the Republican Party in Illinois, and when the party's first national convention met in Philadelphia in June 1856, the Illinois delegation put forth Lincoln's name as a running mate for Frémont. He did not get the nomination, but he had come to the attention of some of the most prominent and powerful people in the country.

With Douglas facing re-election in 1858 and the Republicans gaining considerable strength in Illinois, Lincoln again decided to try for the Senate. That 1858 campaign has become famous because of the series of debates between the two men, all of which turned on the issue of slavery.

It is true that Stephen Douglas is remembered today chiefly for his adversarial relationship with Abraham Lincoln, but it is equally true that Lincoln's career was made because of his relationship with Douglas. Douglas was, after all, the most powerful Northern Democrat in the Senate and was certain to be nominated by at least one faction of his rapidly splintering party for President in 1860. Virtually the only issue in their Senate race

AMERICAN CONSERVATISM: AN ILLUSTRATED HISTORY

William Henry Seward, Lincoln's able Secretary of State and the man who bought Alaska for the United States.

President Lincoln with son Tad, photographed by Mathew Brady.

was slavery, and the two men held clearly divergent views on the subject. They held seven direct debates, and Lincoln won them. When the votes were counted, his candidates for the state legislature had outpolled Douglas's by more than fourteen thousand votes. But not every seat in the Illinois state legislature was being contested in 1858, and when the new session convened, it would have fifty-four Democrats and forty-six Republicans. Lincoln had won a moral victory through the power of his eloquence; he had lost the election yet again.

But he was now famous nationwide, and many Republican leaders began to view him as a possible Presidential candidate. Lincoln himself shrugged off such suggestions, contending that he was "not fit to be president"; nevertheless between the winter of 1858 and the spring of 1860, Lincoln went on speaking tours throughout Kansas, Ohio, New York, Massachusetts, Connecticut, Rhode Island, and New Hampshire.

The Republican Convention of 1860 was held in Lincoln's home state, opening in Chicago's Palmer House Hotel on May 18. Lincoln remained in Springfield. When the first ballot was held in the morning, New York Senator William H. Seward was in the lead with 173½ delegates. Lincoln, who had only the 22 votes of Illinois pledged to him, received 102, and Chase of Ohio, who now wanted the nomination, was running a distant third. Informed by telegram, Lincoln was stunned by the size of his support but doubted that Seward could be stopped. Indeed, on the second ballot Seward had increased his delegate total by 11 votes to 184½, but Lincoln had gained an incredible 79 delegates following Pennyslvania's switch to his column, and was now running neck and neck with Seward. When he passed the New Yorker on the third ballot, the convention hall erupted into wild pro-Lincoln demonstrations, and Lincoln was nominated by acclamation on the fourth ballot. "Honest Abe" would be the Republican candidate for President. ("Honest Abe" was an appellation Lincoln detested; he didn't mind being called honest, but he hated being called Abe.)

Meanwhile, the Democratic Party had shattered itself at its own convention. The Southern Democrats, who controlled the convention, viewed the Dred Scott decision as a vehicle which prevented the prohibition of slavery anywhere in the United States. Northern Democrats still clung to Douglas's view that any state or territory could prohibit slavery if it so desired. Lincoln and the Republicans wanted to limit slavery to the Southern states where it now existed, prohibit its spread to the territories, and use whatever means were necessary to force the South to eventually accept abolition. The Northern Democrats were completely stymied at the convention, and withdrew to hold their own, as did another group of Democrats who were mostly former Whigs and Know Nothings. The Northerners, as expected, nominated Stephen Douglas; the Southerners nominated Buchanan's Vice President, John C. Breckenridge, and the small third group rallied behind John Bell of Tennessee.

The three-way split in the Democratic Party virtually guaranteed a Republican plurality in the popular vote, but it was by no means sure that Lincoln would carry a majority of the electoral votes. In an effort to prevent such an occurrence, several Southern legislatures adopted resolutions declaring their intention to secede from the Union if Lincoln was elected, thus hoping to scare enough Northerners into voting for one of the Democratic candidates. But when the results were in, Lincoln, garnering nearly forty percent of the popular vote, had carried every Northern free state, along with California and Oregon in the West; he had 180 of the 303 electoral votes. Douglas, who had finished half a million votes behind him in the popular tally, had only 12 electoral votes. Breckenridge carried most of the South, winning six times as many electoral votes as Douglas, though he finished a distant third in the popular vote, and Bell carried the remaining 39 electoral votes while winning a mere twelve percent of the popular vote. Lincoln was President, and the election would not go to the House of Representatives.

HARPER'S WEEKLY.
A JOURNAL OF CIVILIZATION.

VOL. IV.—No. 208.]　　　NEW YORK, SATURDAY, DECEMBER 22, 1860.　　　[PRICE FIVE CENTS.

Entered according to Act of Congress, in the Year 1860, by Harper & Brothers, in the Clerk's Office of the District Court for the Southern District of New York.

KEITT.
BOYCE.　　CHESNUT.　　McQUEEN.
ASHMORE.　　HAMMOND.　　BONHAM.
MILES.

THE SECEDING SOUTH CAROLINA DELEGATION.—[PHOTOGRAPHED BY BRADY.]

The North had elected Lincoln, fully cognizant of the fact that they were in all likelihood voting for civil war. But slavery had had a stranglehold on America's political development for more than forty years, and the protagonists on both sides were determined to settle the question once and for all, no matter what the cost. As Lincoln himself had said to the Illinois state Republican convention in 1858, "A house divided against itself cannot stand." The time had come to sweep away the cause of that division, forever, by force if there was no other way.

Events moved rapidly. Three days after Lincoln's election, South Carolina called a convention to draft a resolution of secession. In response, the government in Washington, still headed by Buchanan, dispatched Major Robert Anderson to take command of the federal forces in Charleston. Anderson, correctly gauging the situation, called for reinforcements. On December 4, Buchanan, in his final State of the Union message to

CHARLESTON
MERCURY
EXTRA:

Passed unanimously at 1.15 o'clock, P. M., December 20th, 1860.

AN ORDINANCE

To dissolve the Union between the State of South Carolina and other States united with her under the compact entitled " The Constitution of the United States of America."

We, the People of the State of South Carolina, in Convention assembled, do declare and ordain, and it is hereby declared and ordained,

That the Ordinance adopted by us in Convention, on the twenty-third day of May, in the year of our Lord one thousand seven hundred and eighty-eight, whereby the Constitution of the United States of America was ratified, and also, all Acts and parts of Acts of the General Assembly of this State, ratifying amendments of the said Constitution, are hereby repealed; and that the union now subsisting between South Carolina and other States, under the name of "The United States of America," is hereby dissolved.

THE
UNION
IS
DISSOLVED!

Opposite. South Carolina's Congressional delegation, pictured on the cover of *Harper's Weekly* after their state seceded from the Union in 1860.

Congress, demonstrated his own confusion and ambivalence by declaring secession unconstitutional but adding that the federal government was powerless to force states to remain in the Union. Five days before Christmas, South Carolina seceded from the Union.

Anderson, fearful of being overrun by the growing Southern militia, removed his troops to the more easily defended Fort Sumter on December 26, and finally, after much hand-wringing, President Buchanan ordered him reinforced on the last day of the year. Toward that end, the naval vessel *Star of the West* set sail from New York on New Year's Day, 1861. When it appeared off Charleston Harbor on the 9th, heavy gunfire from South Carolina militia shore batteries prevented its reaching Fort Sumter. Upon hearing the news that afternoon, the Mississippi legislature announced that that state was seceding. The next day, Florida seceded from the Union; on the 11th, Alabama followed. By the

109

12th, every Southern member of Buchanan's cabinet had resigned and left Washington; so had dozens of congressmen, senators, and Army officers. On the nineteenth, Georgia seceded, followed a week later by Louisiana. Ironically, on the 29th of January, Kansas was admitted to the Union as a free state.

On February 1st, Texas seceded from the Union; the sixth flag to fly over that huge land would be the Confederate Stars and Bars. On the 4th of February, a peace conference proposed by Virginia opened in Washington; it was given lip service in the North, and boycotted by the South. That same day, the seceded states opened a convention in Montgomery, Alabama, to organize the government of what they were calling the Confederate States of America. On the 8th, this convention adopted a constitution for a provisional government, and the next day chose Jefferson Davis, former Secretary of War and senator from Mississippi, as President, and Alexander H. Stephens, an eight-term congressman from Georgia, as Vice President. James Buchanan was now the first President in American history to be confronted with the fact that another man was claiming to be President of a significant portion of the country; he did not respond. On the 11th Lincoln left Springfield by train for the long journey to Washington. On the 23rd, he arrived secretly in the early morning hours after an all-night journey from Harrisburg, Pennsylvania. He had bypassed an expected stop in Baltimore, then a hotbed of secession, because of fears that he might be assassinated there.

Opposite, above, and below. Contemporary sketches show enthusiastic crowds outside the White House, and a company of black troops bidding farewell to their families, at the start of the Civil War in 1861.

March 4, 1861 was the day set by law for the inauguration of Abraham Lincoln as the sixteenth President of the United States. No one was happier when that day arrived than the fifteenth President, James Buchanan. Unlike another former President, John Tyler, who was elected to the Confederate Congress from Virginia, Buchanan would remain loyal to the Union. But he would spend his remaining years defending himself against the charge that his own inaction had helped to facilitate the crisis. Shortly before he died in 1868, he declared, "I have no regret for any public act of my life, and history will vindicate my memory." It would not.

Lincoln announced his Cabinet selections the day after his inauguration. It was top-heavy with prominent Republicans who wished that they were President, and gave Lincoln precious little support as his administration set out to work. Among them were his convention rivals, Seward of New York and Chase of Ohio, Secretaries of State and Treasury respectively, and the devious Simon Cameron, scion of a prominent political family, who was appointed to head the War Department and worked against Lincoln from the start. The President's first major decisions would concern the reinforcement of federal forts in the Southern states. The Cabinet urged him to move slowly, while Lincoln wanted a show of resolve as quickly as possible. Still, he was unsure of himself in his new position, and did not wish to act without the approval of at least a majority of the Cabinet. At first, he was supported only by Montgomery Blair, Postmaster General and another product of a famous political family whom Lincoln had mistakenly distrusted when their relationship was new. After some firm pressure from the President, however, the Cabinet met on the 29th of March and backed Lincoln's plan to reinforce the forts.

Lincoln ordered a relief expedition to assist Fort Sumter, where federal troops were nearing starvation, and it duly set sail from New York on April 8. The Confederate militia soon got word of its impending arrival, however, and rather than wait to fire on the expedition, opened fire on Fort Sumter itself on April 12. The following day, Major Anderson, his men exhausted and near collapse from lack of provisions, realized that the situation was hopeless and surrendered the fort to General Pierre Beauregard of the new Confederate Army. The Civil War had begun.

The story of that bloodiest, cruelest, and most heroic American conflict is better told elsewhere. It is, in fact, the most written-about subject in all of American history. From a political perspective, it is safe to say that conservatives in the North supported the Union

The inauguration of Jefferson Davis as President of the Confederate States of America in Montgomery, Alabama, on February 18, 1861.

and conservatives in the South supported the Confederacy. This was a crisis that transcended political affiliations, with each side feeling that its homeland was under attack by the other. What is more germane to this treatise is to attempt to determine what place Abraham Lincoln, the prime mover in this monumental era and, along with Washington, generally rated as the greatest American President, has in the conservative tradition.

One must first realize that there was still an active political role being played by the President during the war apart from the purely military decisions that were his constitutional burden as commander-in-chief of the armed forces. Lincoln was still the head of his party, still had to deal with an opposition in Congress, still had to direct the purely political affairs of a nation which, torn asunder and plunged into war, still existed.

The thrust of Lincoln's political agenda was the restoration of the Union in such a way that it could never again be divided over the issue of slavery, but would otherwise reestablish the constitutional balance of powers to that of the *status quo ante bellum*; in other words, the Southern states were to be readmitted to the Union on an equal footing

with those states which had not joined in the rebellion. To do this, Lincoln had to accomplish three things: 1) he had to win the war militarily; 2) he had to abolish slavery; 3) he had to set forth a plan for reconstruction of the country that was at odds with many of the leading members of his own party who wanted to see the rebellious Southern states punished for fomenting the war.

As to the first condition, the war would drag on for the next four years at a cost of a million men killed or wounded and billions of dollars spent on war production while billions more were lost in commerce and agriculture. Lincoln would appoint and remove a series of military commanders who, provided with an army and resources far superior to those available to the Confederates, nonetheless almost lost the war by inaction and blundering. The most famous of these was the megalomaniacal George Brinton McClellan, only thirty-four when first appointed to command the Army of the Potomac, viewed by many as the new Napoleon and by himself as what Christ would have been if he'd lived another year. He organized his cadre of volunteers into an efficient, professional army and

Above, top. An unbearded Abraham Lincoln pictured between his election and inauguration as the nation's sixteenth President of the United States.

Above. U.S. Capitol still uncompleted at the time of Lincoln's inauguration.

AMERICAN
CONSERVATISM:
AN ILLUSTRATED
HISTORY

Thomas Nast's patriotic illustrations were the highlight of *Harper's Weekly* during the Civil War.

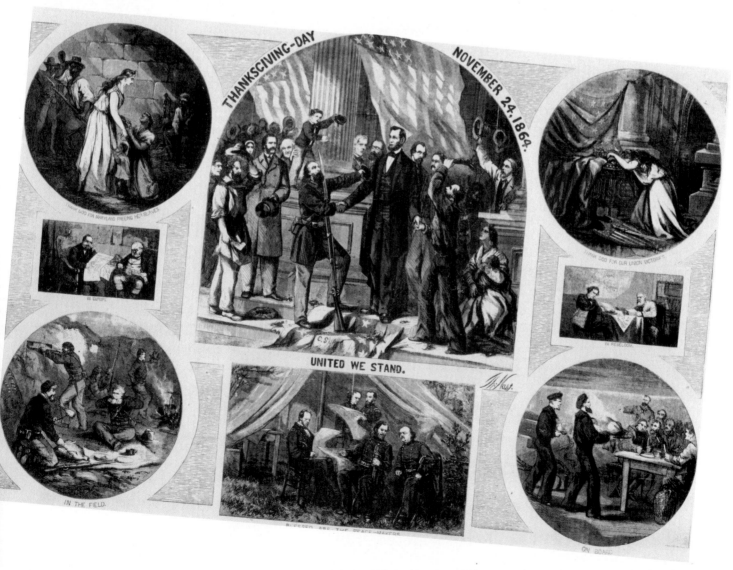

then refused to let it fight. Replaced by lackluster commanders such as Ambrose Burn-side, Joseph Hooker, and George Meade, McClellan would harbor such resentment against Lincoln for removing him that he would accept the Democratic Party's nomination for President in 1864 despite the fact that the convention had adopted a plank calling for an end to the war on Southern terms. It was not until the March, 1864 appointment of General Ulysses S. Grant, an officer who had once resigned from the army to avoid being cashiered for drunkenness but who had returned to win stunning victories in the West as overall commander of the Union forces, that the North finally had a general who knew how to fight and would do so until the war was won. Together with the firebrand General William Tecumseh Sherman, who devastated much of the South and burned Atlanta on his famous march through Georgia to the sea, Grant was able to corner the brilliant Southern commander Robert E. Lee and force the Confederates to surrender in April, 1865.

Long before that, though, Lincoln had to deal with his second plank, the abolition of slavery. On July 25, 1861, Congress had passed the Crittenden Resolution, declaring that the object of the war was the preservation of the Union. While Lincoln agreed with that, one of the implications of the Crittenden Resolution was that there were many in the North, supporters of the Union cause, who not only refused to declare that they were fighting for abolition, but refused to admit that abolition was either wise or necessary. With this Lincoln could not agree. He knew the war would end someday, and despite the early military setbacks, never wavered in his belief that the North would win the war. But to win and leave the slavery question unsettled would have made the whole fight worthless. The President took a series of steps to avoid such an outcome. In August, 1861, he signed the Confiscation Act, which provided for the seizure of any property, including slaves, which was being used to aid the rebellion. In March, 1862, he proposed to Congress a plan for the gradual emancipation of slaves in the border states which had stayed loyal to the Union; this plan included a provision for government compensation to the deprived slave owners. In July, he began to discuss with his cabinet the possibility of issuing a Presidential edict which freed the slaves behind the Southern lines if the South would not end the war. Many in his Cabinet were opposed; obviously, he could not enforce such a decree, and the effect might be to lose some of the border states to the Confederacy.

By September, the President had decided. Emancipation, he declared, was a military necessity; the war was meaningless without it. He would continue to press Congress for the gradual emancipation of slaves in the border states; all slaves in the rebellious states would be declared free on January 1, 1863, if the war had not ended by then. (The implication here is not that Lincoln would forget about emancipation if the South did surrender before January 1; rather, Lincoln was simply saying that he would no longer have the authority to end slavery by Presidential decree if the war ended, because there would no longer be a military necessity for it.)

The reaction throughout the South was predictable, with Southern leaders denouncing Lincoln for attempting to foment a slave insurrection whose victims were women and children while the men were off to war. But reaction in the North was generally enthusiastic, and the border states, though they were not pleased, recognized the inevitability of what was to come and did not join the Confederacy. Perhaps most importantly, by declaring that the North was fighting for abolition as well as the Union, Lincoln prevented Britain and other European states from granting diplomatic recognition to the South, a move they had been considering since the war began. Having abolished slavery in the U.S. territories, the ostensible cause of the war, in June 1862, Lincoln signed the Emancipation Proclamation freeing the slaves in the South on New Year's Day, 1863. In February 1865, Congress would offer to the states for ratification the Thirteenth

A Confederate Army
chow-line.

The C.S.S. *Virginia* (formerly
the U.S.S. *Merrimac*) in
action against Union gun-
boats off Plymouth, North
Carolina.

President Andrew Johnson.
His opposition to radical
Reconstruction led to his
impeachment and near-
conviction by the Radical
controlled Senate in 1868.

Amendment to the Constitution, abolishing slavery everywhere and forever in the United States. It would be ratified in December of that year; by then, the war had been over, and Lincoln had been dead, for seven months.

By 1864, with the emancipation question behind him and a Northern victory assured if not yet in sight, Lincoln turned his attention to reconstructing a postwar United States. In December of the previous year he had proposed to Congress a policy which would restore the rebellious states to the Union when one-tenth of their 1860 voters agreed to form a Loyalist government. Beyond that, he proposed no punitive measures to be taken against the Confederate states, no blame affixed, no reparations demanded. Additionally, and significantly, he also did not propose the enfranchisement of the freed Negro; he had hoped that the former slaves would opt for some sort of colonization, preferably in Africa. He was answered by the radical wing of his Republican Party in January 1864, with the publication of the Pomeroy Circular. In it, a group of liberal Republican senators led by Samuel Pomeroy of Kansas declared that Lincoln's reconstruction policies were a betrayal of Republican principles and that he should be dumped from the ticket in 1864 in favor of Treasury Secretary Chase. The "Chase Boom," as it was called at the time, was short-lived and did little more than cost Chase his job, but the radicals geared up to fight Lincoln on Reconstruction. There was also some conservative opposition to Lincoln's

renomination, mostly based on a lack of faith in him as a military leader. James Gordon Bennett favored Grant for the 1864 nomination, while another group of dissidents met in Cleveland in July and nominated Frémont at a rump convention. Grant refused to be considered, and by September, Frémont had withdrawn from the race in favor of Lincoln.

In June the regular Republicans met in Baltimore, renominating Lincoln and choosing Democrat Andrew Johnson of Tennessee, one of the few Southern senators at the outbreak of the war to remain loyal to the Union, as his running mate on a fusión ticket. But Lincoln's trouble with the Radicals was not over. In July, they pushed through Congress the Wade-Davis Bill, a much harsher plan for Reconstruction than Lincoln had proposed. Risking much of his popularity in an election year, Lincoln employed the pocket veto to kill the bill. By late August, Lincoln was expressing doubt that he could be re-elected. On the 29th of that month, the Democrats convened in Chicago and nominated General McClellan for President, while at the same time declaring that the war had gone on long enough and should be ended by making peace with the South. McClellan accepted the nomination, though he did not publicly endorse the peace plank.

In November, Lincoln was surprised at the size of his reelection victory. He captured fifty-five percent of the popular vote and 212 electoral votes to McClellan's 21. Most surprising was the overwhelming vote he received from soldiers in the field; among them, George McClellan had always been their most popular commander. Lincoln now had a mandate to end the war and reconstruct the nation on the terms he had already laid out.

And that is undoubtedly what he would have done had he not been shot by a deranged

President Andrew Johnson greets a delegation of Indians in the days before such affairs were merely campaign hoopla.

Southern actor on April 14, 1865. His death the next morning served not to aid the Southern war cause, as John Wilkes Booth had intended; Lee had already surrendered and the war was effectively over. Instead, it served the ironic purpose of depriving the South of the one man who could reunite the nation in the manner he had set forth in his second inaugural address—with malice toward none, with charity for all. A Democrat unsupported by either party was now in the White House; the Republicans who would seize control of the nation were of the radical variety, and the South would suffer harshly, more for the death of Abraham Lincoln than for any other reason.

What then do we make of the political legacy of Abraham Lincoln? That he had served conservative causes up to his election to the Presidency is indisputable. Was he a conservative President? All Presidents shift to the center to some degree after taking office; in Lincoln's case, this meant moving somewhat to the left and giving a very broad interpretation to his constitutional powers. He employed political devices that conservatives would resolutely oppose in peacetime: the suspension of *habeas corpus*, the occasional imposition of martial law in some places, the sweeping use of presidential edict to create law. But Lincoln was not called upon to serve in peacetime; rather, he led the nation through a war that, in terms of national survival, was the most dangerous we have ever fought. Conservatives, opposed to a broad interpretation of the powers of central government, nevertheless support strong Presidents, especially in times of crisis. The theory that makes such an apparent anomaly possible is that one man, powerful though he may be, does not an overbloated bureaucracy make (unless, of course, that man is a liberal). Lincoln was elected by conservatives and supported by conservatives. He employed some liberal interpretations of his powers during a time of the most severe national crisis, but he is very much a towering figure in the American conservative tradition.

On May 13, 1865, a relatively small skirmish took place at Palmetto Ranch near Brownsville, Texas. It was to be the last fighting of the Civil War. Two weeks later, General Kirby Smith surrendered all Confederate forces remaining in the field to General Edward R. Canby, and the war was over. After a six weeks' journey through the North, the train carrying the body of Abraham Lincoln finally arrived in Springfield, and he was laid to rest.

Andrew Johnson was born in 1808 in the thriving Southern city of Raleigh, North Carolina. Virtually uneducated in his youth, he was apprenticed to a tailor at the age of fourteen, and worked for two years in a sweatshop, where one of his co-workers taught him the fundamentals of reading and writing. Apprentices were little better off than slaves in the South of the 1820s, and when Johnson was sixteen, he escaped from his master's yoke and traveled to South Carolina, picking up whatever work he could until he made his way to Greenville, Tennessee, in 1825. He, like Lincoln in Illinois, quickly became popular with the local population, who brought their business to the tailor shop he opened, and when he was nineteen, he was elected an alderman. While serving in that capacity, his new young wife, whom he had married in 1827, worked with him to improve his education. So polished did he become that in 1830 the good citizens of Greenville elected him mayor, a post he held for the next three years. Between 1835 and 1843, Johnson served two terms in the Tennessee house of representatives and one in the state senate, and was elected to Congress as a Democrat in 1843. During his five terms in the House he invariably voted with his party, supporting the Mexican War, the Compromise of 1850, and self-determination on the question of slavery. Well-respected and well-liked by his constituents and his party leaders, he was elected Governor of Tennessee in 1853, and overwhelmingly reelected in 1855. At the end of his second term in the Governor's mansion, the state legislature honored him further by electing him to the United States Senate.

Somewhat overwhelmed, Johnson arrived back in Washington, where he became a

GENERAL SHERMAN'S RECEPTION IN THE UNITED STATES HOUSE OF REPRESENTATIVES, JANUARY 29, 1866.—[SKETCHED BY A. M'CALLUM.]

champion of a homestead law that would provide free land in the West to anyone willing to settle there, long a part of the conservative agenda that was supported on both sides of the aisle. But the nation faced far more serious questions than homesteading in Oklahoma, and as Buchanan's term in the White House drew near an end, Johnson as a Southern senator knew he might well be called on to make some hard choices.

General Sherman's reception in the House of Representatives, January 29, 1866.

At the splintered Democratic convention of 1860, Johnson was put forth as a favorite-son candidate by the Tennessee delegation, but he quickly withdrew his name in favor of the candidacy of John Breckenridge. His support of the southern Democrats' candidate seemed natural enough, and when Southern secession became a reality after Lincoln's election, it was simply assumed that Johnson would resign from the Senate and return to Tennessee. But Andrew Johnson, always the loyal party man and native son, shocked the nation in 1860 by declaring that secession was illegal and that the secessionist leaders should be arrested, tried for treason, and upon conviction, executed. When Tennessee voted to go with the South, Johnson elected to remain in Washington. He was held up as a shining example of patriotism in the North, and was reviled as a traitor in his native region.

Union troops quickly occupied most of western and central Tennessee, where there were more anti-secessionists like Johnson among the population than anywhere else in the South with the exception of western Virginia. In 1862, Lincoln appointed Johnson military governor of the occupied portion of the state, and Johnson was well-received by

121

the native population upon his return. While serving as military governor, he implemented two important policies; first, he pushed for the emancipation of slaves in Tennessee, and second, he granted amnesty to captured Confederates who agreed henceforth to remain loyal to the Union. When Lincoln promulgated the Emancipation Proclamation on January 1, 1863, Tennessee was specifically exempted from its provisions because it was not under the domination of the Confederate government; thus under Johnson, it became the only secessionist state to emancipate the slaves of its own accord.

Johnson, a Southerner, a Democrat, and a loyalist, was the perfect candidate to run with Lincoln on a fusion ticket in 1864. Together, they swept the election in November, and Johnson looked forward to serving in his new position. But on March 4, 1865, Inauguration Day, Andrew Johnson committed the worst blunder of his political career. He arrived at the swearing-in ceremony drunk, and had to be stopped by friends midway through his incoherent inaugural address and led away from the podium. Many upright souls in the government urged Lincoln to demand Johnson's resignation, but Lincoln declared that Johnson was no drunkard (which was true) and would not acquiesce. Still, the damage was done, and the President, deeply embarrassed, never spoke to Johnson again during the six weeks he had left to live.

Killing Andrew Johnson was part of the conspiracy that John Wilkes Booth had hatched in his boarding house, but the man assigned to eliminate the Vice President had lost his nerve, and Johnson was sworn in as the seventeenth President shortly after Lincoln's death on the morning of April 15, 1865. Committed to Lincoln's plan for mild terms of reconstruction, Johnson soon found himself opposed by both the Congress and his own Cabinet, all of whom were holdovers from the Lincoln Administration. Johnson wanted the Southern governments to be in the hands of educated men capable of governing; providing that they had not been important government officials or members of the general staff, he was perfectly willing to let repatriated Confederates assume the burden of rebuilding the South. But the Radical Republicans in the Senate and the Cabinet were not about to turn the affairs of Reconstruction over to men who were traitors and, worse, educated Democrats.

Johnson quickly set in motion a plan to allow white Southerners to regain control of their state governments, vetoing a congressional bill which would have instituted military governments throughout the South. Unable to override the President's veto in 1865, the Radicals acquiesced, but after gaining strength in the congressional elections of 1866, they started anew.

Their first act was to vote for the enfranchisement of the freed Negroes, a bill which Johnson vetoed. The Radicals confidently overrode that veto. The motive for granting the vote to the new free men was not as altruistic as it may appear; the Radicals' aim was not the equality of the black man, but the punishment of the Southern white man by turning the affairs of his state over to the men he had formerly subjugated. The Radicals were counting on the black man's gratitude—and his lack of political sophistication—to keep them in power. Equally, it cannot be said that Johnson opposed enfranchisement out of a belief that the former slaves were not yet ready for the vote but someday would be; like most whites of his time, he would never welcome Negro equality, no matter how much he opposed slavery.

From 1867 on, the Radicals could act with impunity, setting their own harsh agenda for Reconstruction. Johnson remained a thorn in their side, though, so much so that they decided to remove him from office if possible. In 1867 they passed the Tenure of Office Act, stipulating that the President could not remove from office any man who had been appointed with the advice and consent of the Senate. Johnson vetoed the measure and, as was becoming a habit, was overridden. Certain nonetheless that the Act was unconstitutional, in August Johnson attempted to fire the Secretary of War, Edwin M. Stanton, and

ANDREW JOHNSON'S

RECONSTRUCTION,
AND HOW IT WORKS. Th. Nast.

123

A Nast "caricaturama" skewering the Republican Party Leadership, including Johnson (who was never really a Republican), Ulysses Grant, and Edward M. Stanton.

replace him with General Grant. So great was the outcry from Congress that in February, 1868, Grant relinquished the office, and, in defiance of the President, turned it back over to Stanton. Furious, Johnson fired Stanton again and replaced him with Major Lorenzo Thomas. Three days later, Congress voted to impeach the President for violation of the Tenure of Office Act.

The two-month trial opened in the Senate on March 13, 1868. Long before all the testimony was taken, it was apparent that the trial was nothing more than a political sham brought about to remove Johnson from office and replace him with the Radical president pro tem of the Senate, Benjamin Wade of Ohio. Well aware of this, every Democrat in the Senate vowed to vote with the President, but it would still take seven Republican votes to keep Johnson from being evicted from the White House. By the time the day of reckoning, May 13, had arrived, six Republicans had declared their intention of siding with Johnson. One other, Edmund G. Ross of Kansas, had not declared for either side and seemed to be genuinely undecided. When the roll call came, though, he voted with Johnson, and it was by that one vote that the President escaped conviction and removal from office. The Radical Republicans may have lost that fight, but they had won the war, as Johnson's effectiveness had been destroyed.

In 1868, Ulysses S. Grant was unquestionably the most popular man in the country. He was the hero of the Civil War, tenacious in battle, magnanimous in victory. And he had become a hero to the Radical Republicans by his actions during the Tenure of Office crisis. But it was his behavior during that period that should have alerted many people to

Ulysses Grant pictured with the Viceroy of China during his post-presidency world tour.

the fact that Grant was more than a little unsure of himself when it came to the conduct of public affairs. By accepting Johnson's appointment to the Cabinet, he seemed to be siding with the President; but later, by not just abandoning the office but turning it back to Stanton, he proved that he had come under the sway of powerful Republicans who had convinced him that they were his friends. In the end, he did nothing to enhance his own historical image, and ended up alienating a President whom he actually liked and admired.

Born in Point Pleasant, Ohio, in 1822, Ulysses Grant (who was born Hiram Ulysses Grant but changed it owing to his displeasure with his monogram, HUG) early in life showed the lack of business acumen that would dog his years before and after the Civil War. Sent out at the age of eight to buy a colt from a neighbor, Ulysses had instructions from his father to offer the man twenty dollars; if he would not sell, to offer twenty-two fifty; and if he could not get the colt for that price, to go as high as twenty-five dollars. Arriving at the neighbor's farm, young Grant announced, "Papa says I am to offer you twenty dollars for the colt, but if you won't take that, I am to offer twenty-two and a half, and if you won't take that, I am to give you twenty-five." As Grant related in his *Memoirs*, "It would not require a Connecticut man to guess the price finally agreed upon." His father arranged an appointment for Grant to the military academy at West Point, and though he hated the life of a cadet, he managed to graduate in 1843. He spent the next ten years in the army, rising to the rank of captain and seeing action in the Mexican War. In 1848 he married Julia Dent, and it was long separations from her that caused him occasionally to drink to excess. In 1854 his commanding officer, after repeated warnings, forced him to resign his commission because of his drinking.

For the next seven years Grant tried to provide for his family as a farmer, woodcutter, and store clerk, and failed miserably. Old friends seeing him in the street took pity on him, fearing he would die young because of the heavy burdens of his life. Salvation came in the form of the Civil War. Between 1861 and 1865, he rose from a volunteer organizer of Illinois militia regiments to lieutenant general in the United States Army, hailed throughout the North as the hero of Vicksburg and the man who beat Robert E. Lee.

He was unanimously nominated on the first roll call at the Republican National Convention in 1868, and won the election against the Democratic Governor of New York, Horatio Seymour, with 214 electoral votes to Seymour's 80. Surprisingly, the popular vote was much closer, with Grant taking only fifty-three percent to Seymour's forty-seven. This may well have reflected revulsion on the part of many voters to the treatment President Johnson had received at the hands of the Radical Republicans, and their disappointment at Grant's part in it. Grant's first term was almost entirely uneventful, but his Cabinet choices did reflect a portent of things to come. He surrounded himself with financial wheeler-dealers and multi-millionaires, one of whom resigned because of a conflict of interest with government contracts and another of whom left because his Cabinet duties were taking too much time away from his business affairs. Legislatively, the Radical Republicans held sway, inflicting deep divisions in the country by their policies of Reconstruction that have not been entirely eradicated to this day.

If Grant did little right in his first term, he also did little wrong, and the personal regard his countrymen felt for him ensured his reelection in 1872.

But corruption and scandal, which had been hinted at during his first term, broke wide open during the second. Cabinet officers, congressmen, federal judges, and executive appointees by the dozen resigned, were indicted, and sent to jail for using their positions to make deals with the Eastern business establishment that illegally enriched everyone concerned. Grant himself never took a penny, but the fact that corruption was so widespread right under his nose tarnished Grant's image as President forever. Still, a case can be made that had he been willing, he might have won a third term in 1876. This is as much a testimony to the faith the American people were once willing to have in their Presidents as it is to Grant's personal popularity.

If there is a lasting legacy of Grant's years in office, it must be the political maturation and new direction gained by the Republican Party. Formed to deal with the growing slavery crisis, the party had to find a new sense of purpose after its original *raison d'etre* had been eradicated. During the 1870s, it found that purpose. Though the phrase would not be popularized for another fifty years, from this point on, when the Republicans were in power, the business of America was business, and the new American hero would be epitomized by Horatio Alger, the boy who started with nothing and became a success—in business.

5 The Triumph of Individualism 1877–1898

When Ulysses S. Grant left office in 1877, America had still not recovered from the national tragedy that was the Civil War. Federal troops still occupied the former Confederate states, economic depression ravaged the South, the Klan made every former slave fear for his life, unemployment swept over the North, and the government was rocked by scandal and incompetence. Before the outbreak of war with Spain twenty-one years later, America would be a different place, almost as unrecognizable to the people of 1877 as if it were a foreign country.

Those twenty-one years would see the advent of the telephone, the bicycle, electric street lights, the Brooklyn Bridge, national labor unions, electric motors to run an incalculable number of new machines, the Kodak camera, and the automobile.

They would also see another President assassinated, national labor strikes, socialists, billionaires, Tammany Hall, a near-war with Britain, seven new states added to the Union, and a Bureau of the Census report claiming that there was no more American frontier, that the nation had been settled from coast to coast.

Perhaps the best way to make a word mean nothing is to first make it mean too much. Take, for instance, the word "community." It once referred specifically to the immediate area in which a person lived and to the other people who lived there. That relatively small parcel of land and that small group of people were one's "community." Nowadays, born out of a feeling of wishfulness, the word can mean anything from two people working together to all of the people in New York to the United Nations to every inhabitant of the planet living and dead. The word by itself no longer means anything because it can mean everything.

The same effect can be worked upon people as well. The actual historical achievements and failures of a man like George Washington are forgotten by almost everyone, though his name is known throughout the world. He is all things to all people, from the most prodigious hurler of a silver dollar this nation has ever produced to the man who was physically incapable of telling a lie and so on. Very few people are acquainted with his foreign policy toward Russia, nor are they terribly interested in finding out. Everyone knows something that was said about him ("father of his country," "first in war," etc.), but very few people can quote anything *he* actually said.

Much the same fate has befallen Thomas Edison. He is variously credited with everything from discovering electricity to inventing everything worth owning. His actual achievements are monumental enough, and his life story is a microcosm of America in the last quarter of the nineteenth century.

He was born in Milan, Ohio, in 1847 to a family that hadn't much money but did not consider themselves poor. Childhood bouts of bronchitis effectively kept him out of school, though he was tutored and developed a quick mind. The bronchitis also adversely affected his hearing, and by the time he became an adult, he was almost completely deaf.

The long enforced absences from school compelled him to develop hobbies that he could participate in by himself, and he became a tinkerer, one who loved to work with any kind of machine or gadget.

When he was twelve, as was the norm for his time and place, he finished with school altogether and went to work, taking a job as a newsboy on the Grand Trunk Railroad. In his spare time, he continued to repair any kind of machinery he could lay his hands on, especially old printing presses. It was only natural, then, that he would combine his two vocations and begin publishing his own newspaper to sell on the train. *The Grand Trunk Herald* made its debut when its publisher was fifteen years old, but it was short-lived. He had set up his printing press in an abandoned freight car at the stockyard where he worked, and this also served as his laboratory for experiments with more complicated types of machinery and for his newly developed interest in electricity.

It was around this time that young Edison found himself in the position to save the life of a young boy who had tried to jump a boxcar but had slipped. Seconds before he would have been crushed under the wheels of the train, he was pulled to safety by the quick-thinking Edison, who had acted with complete disregard for his own safety. The boy turned out to be the son of a stationmaster, and when this grateful man asked Edison what he wanted as a reward, the resourceful Tom replied that he wanted to learn telegraphy. The stationmaster was happy to comply, and within a short time Edison was an expert telegraph operator able to earn his living from it.

Opposite. Thomas Alva Edison, the Wizard of Menlo Park.

But a telegraph was a machine, and more importantly, one that employed electrical impulses in its operation, and Edison could not resist trying to improve it. His desire to experiment while he was supposed to be working, coupled with a thin skin that would not allow him to tolerate reproof from superiors, kept Edison bouncing from town to town and job to job. But while he was still in his early twenties he was able to improve upon the telegraph system then in operation, inventing a system that allowed messages sent over one wire to be picked up automatically by a second wire without the assistance of an operator.

A short time later, he found himself in Boston and, fittingly in that cradle of liberty, invented a machine that would record and tally votes electrically. While the machine had great merit, and was in fact the forerunner of the voting booth, it proved too cumbersome and expensive to win widespread adoption. He next turned his attention to the stock market, though not as an investor. He devised a machine that would print out stock quotations in offices far removed from the actual market site. This was, of course, an early model of what would become the ticker-tape machine. This invention brought him to the attention of the Gold and Stock Telegraph Company of New York, which hired him to make improvements on its telegraphic apparatus. While he showed the company how to upgrade its equipment, it taught him marketing. Within a year, the sale of his improved telegraph devices—and his services—netted him some $40,000, freeing him from the obligation of having to hold down a steady job. He could now turn all of his time and attention to his inventions.

With the money, he opened a major laboratory in New York City, and was even able to employ assistants. While he continued turning out devices to improve the nation's telegraph service, he also spent a great deal of time delving into other areas of scientific endeavor that had caught his interest. Rarely sleeping more than two hours at a stretch, within a year he had invented the carbon telephone transmitter to improve on Bell's invention, which was itself brand new, and then announced the invention of the phonograph.

Edison's first phonograph was little more than two cylinders covered with tin foil. Owing to his deafness, he needed the assurance of his assistants that it actually worked. But it did, and all subsequent machines employing the use of recorded sound—from

dictaphones to tape recorders, from talking pictures to video cassette recorders—can trace their roots to those two cylinders covered with tin foil.

Two years after the phonograph, in 1879, Edison publicly demonstrated the incandescent light bulb, his most important invention, and the one he would spend the most time modifying and improving. The electric light would revolutionize the world, first on its own, and later through the number of other devices that were based on its usage. One of these was Edison's own kinetoscope, the first motion-picture projector.

Thomas Edison spent the rest of his life creating new inventions and improving on old ones. With his phonograph he produced the first disc records, played with a diamond stylus. Combining the phonograph and the kinetoscope, he produced the first talking picture, fourteen years before *The Jazz Singer*. He invented the alkaline battery, and at his death in 1931, held over 1,000 other patents as well. He was honored by all the major governments of the world, including his own. He was honored by the people of the world in 1929, the fiftieth anniversary of the light bulb, and again two years later, when electric lights were dimmed all over the world during his funeral.

What the world would be like today had not Thomas Edison lived when he did is hard to imagine. What is certain is that he was able to achieve the things he did because of the time and place he lived in. The America of Thomas Edison's early manhood was a country where achievement was celebrated and rewarded with fame and fortune, and where it was believed that *anybody*, no matter how humble his station in life when he started or what the odds were against him, could go on to greatness. Thomas Edison and others with a similar spirit proved that, and they were the heroes of the age. Though he would later be criticized for his commercialism (Edison did little or nothing without charging a fee), that too was seen as right and natural in his own time. Americans wanted to be like Thomas Edison— successful, celebrated, powerful, and rich. After nearly a century of political upheaval, war, devastation, and depression, the country was eager for triumph. And it would honor the men who could bring it—men like Thomas Edison. The triumph of the individual was the triumph of the nation.

As noted previously, Ulysses S. Grant, despite his inability to prevent his political appointees from robbing the U.S. Treasury blind, still carried enough personal prestige with the American people to be considered a shoo-in for a third term as President if he decided to run. But Grant, citing the example of General Washington, said that Presidents should not serve more than two terms and declined to seek the Republican nomination in 1876.

Rutherford B. Hayes was fifty-four years old in the year that his country celebrated its 100th birthday, having been born in Delaware, Ohio, on October 4, 1822. His father died several months before the boy was born, but he had been a successful merchant, and bequeathed a large enough estate to allow his widow to live comfortably and send his sons to college. Accordingly, young "Rud," as he was called, attended Kenyon College and graduated with honors at the age of twenty. He had done so well, in fact, that upon his graduation he was accepted as a student at the Harvard School of Law, earning his degree three years later, in 1845.

Returning to Ohio, Hayes was admitted to the bar and practiced law in Lower Sandusky before moving on to Cincinnati, which was then a center of the underground railroad for runaway slaves. Hayes met and was greatly influenced by the leading abolitionists of that city, and he helped to form the Ohio Republican Party in the mid-1850's.

When he was thirty Hayes married Lucy Ware Webb, a college-educated teacher who headed up the local chapter of the Women's Christian Temperance Union. After that, Hayes never took another drink in his life, and when Lucy was around, neither did anyone else.

In 1858 Hayes entered politics, winning an appointment to fill the unexpired term

of the city solicitor in Cincinnati. He won the office in his own right in 1859, but was defeated for reelection in 1861.

By that time, though, Hayes had other things on his mind. With the coming of the Civil War, he organized a company of Ohio volunteers from the literary club he belonged to, and was elected captain of the bookworms. It may sound like an inauspicious start for a military career, but in fact, Hayes distinguished himself as one of the finest soldiers in the Union Army. At the battle of South Mountain, in Maryland, Hayes won acclaim for leading a charge up the mountain in the face of a murderous barrage of enemy gunfire. He continued the charge despite the fact that the bones of one arm were shattered by a bullet, and went on even after a third of his company lay dead or wounded on the hillside. Promoted to lieutenant colonel, he was sent to Virginia late in 1864 to take part in the Wilderness Campaign. Before April of 1865 he had been wounded four more times and was a brigadier general.

So impressed were the folks back in Ohio with the accounts of his heroism that they nominated him for Congress in 1864, and he won the election without ever leaving his

Henry Ford, whose assembly-line method of production revolutionized American industry.

WOMANS HOLY WAR.

Grand Charge on the Enemy's Works.

THE DRUNKARD'S PROGRESS.

Opposite, and left. Temperance
Crusades, often led by
women, sought the end of
the sale of liquor in the
United States.

post in Virginia. When the war ended, he returned briefly to Ohio to thank his constituents, then went to Washington to take his seat in Congress.

Though he remained a party regular, he often voted with the Radical Republicans on Reconstruction issues. Hayes wanted no soft peace for the South. He was re-elected to Congress in 1866, and his ability as a representative, coupled with his natural intelligence and his hard-won reputation as a war hero, made him one of the most prominent men in Ohio. His party nominated him for the governor's office in 1867, and, resigning his seat in Congress, he ran for the job and won. He was an honest and capable administrator, and was elected to a second term in 1869.

Samuel I. Tilden, winner of the election of 1876 and the rightful nineteenth President of the United States. He was robbed of the office by Radical Republicans in Congress.

After leaving the governor's mansion, he ran for Congress again in 1872, but there was a resurgence of the Democratic Party in Ohio that year and he was defeated. Retiring to his estate, he assumed he would practice law for the rest of his life. But in 1875 the Republicans again turned to him and nominated him for governor. His victory in the fall made him the first three-term governor in the history of Ohio.

After Grant's disavowal in 1876, the national bosses of the Republican Party expected to sew up the Presidential nomination for James G. Blaine, political kingmaker and former Speaker of the House of Representatives. But although nothing could be proven against him personally, Blaine was too close to too many people who had been brought down in the scandals of the Grant Administration, and the party regulars, fearing that Blaine was unelectable, refused to nominate him and threw the convention wide open.

On the seventh ballot, Hayes, who had been nominated by the Ohio delegation as a favorite son, won the nomination. He was the ideal candidate. A teetotaler, a Harvard man, an experienced and competent legislator, and thrice governor of Ohio, he was untouched by scandal and had a brilliant war record. If anybody in the United States in 1876 *deserved* to be elected President by the people, it was Rutherford B. Hayes, but the people refused to do their part.

Samuel I. Tilden was eight years older than Hayes, and he was a Yale man. A railroad lawyer since 1841, he was also active in Democratic Party politics in his native New York State. Named the party's state chairman in 1866, he set about to fight the corruption that emanated from the New York City Democratic machine headed by William Marcy "Boss" Tweed. It was largely through his efforts that the Tweed ring was broken and many of its leading members, including the Boss, were sent to jail. On the strength of his reputation as a corruption-buster, he was elected governor of New York in 1874, and continued to weed out and prosecute lawbreakers in government and politics. Knowing that corruption would be a major issue in the campaign, the Democratic Party nominated Tilden for President in 1876. And he won the election, fair and square.

The day after election day, fair and square went out the window, and foul play was immediately suspected in their demise. The leaders of the Republican Party in the South claimed that Negro voters had been prevented from casting their ballots in droves, or, in places where they were allowed to vote, that the ballot boxes had mysteriously disappeared. There was no doubt a great deal of truth to the charges, but the fact remains that Tilden had outpolled Hayes by more than a quarter of a million votes, surely more than enough to cover any irregularities. But the Republican leadership challenged the returns from South Carolina, Florida, Louisiana, and Oregon. If these states were taken out of the Democratic column and awarded to Republicans, it would change the electoral vote count from 203-166 in favor of Tilden to 185-184 in favor of Hayes.

For three months the country waited while the two parties bickered over who would be inaugurated in March. The vote could not be thrown to the House of Representatives because there was no constitutional question involved (and besides, the Democrats controlled the House and the Republicans were too smart for that). Instead, a deal was worked out between the two parties' leadership to settle the matter. A special electoral commission would be formed, made up of ten congressmen—five from each party—and five justices of the Supreme Court, supposedly impartial. They would pass judgment on the disputed returns from the states in question and award the electoral votes accordingly.

It was all a publicity stunt. Three of the five justices chosen were Republican appointees, and neither party had any delusions about which way they would go. But in conceding the White House to Hayes and the Republicans, the Democrats had exacted a price. If he was going to be President, Hayes would have to agree to remove federal troops from the South, leaving the governments there in the hands of white Southern Democrats. The Republican leadership, and Rutherford B. Hayes, agreed. The whole flap had begun over claims that the Negro in the South was being disenfranchised by the Democrats; now he would be disenfranchised with the blessing of both parties.

Rutherford Hayes wanted very much to be a good President, and there is no doubt that he was as well qualified to do the job as almost any man who had ever become President. But the Congress felt he owed it his election, and cared little about what he had to say. The people angrily resented the way that he had gained the office, and they too would not support him. To ease the economic depression in the country, Congress voted to issue dollars redeemable in silver. Hayes, a conservative believer in "sound money" and the gold standard, vetoed the bill, urging austerity instead. His veto was easily overridden. He still showed flashes of the general he had been, however, as in 1877, when railroad workers went out on strike nationwide. Riots broke out at strike sites all across the country, and Hayes called out the troops to quell the violence and end the strike, thus earning the enmity of organized labor.

He was the first President to urge reform of the civil service, wanting to cut back on the patronage system that bloated the federal bureaucracy. Like sound money, this issue would become a fundamental plank in the conservative platform, and remains so to our own day. To underscore his seriousness about reform, he fired the Collector of the Port of New York, despite the fact that the man was a major leader of the New York State Republican Party. Two years later, that man, Chester Arthur, would be President. When Hayes's term ended, virtually everyone was glad to see him go, an ironic ending for a man so eminently qualified to govern. His parting shot was to ban the sale of liquor at army installations. It pleased Lucy. The reaction of the general staff is not recorded.

James Garfield was also from Ohio, having been born there in November, 1831. Though his family was left destitute by the death of Garfield's father two years later, his mother managed to save enough money to have the boy educated in school. When he was seventeen he attended Geauga Seminary, and learned enough to drop out and become a teacher. When he had earned enough money from teaching, Garfield entered Hiram College, studying Latin and Greek. A friend loaned him the funds to journey to Williamstown, Massachusetts, and he enrolled in Williams College there as a junior. To support himself in New England, he spent one winter teaching at a small schoolhouse in Vermont, replacing the previous teacher, Chester Arthur. After graduating from Williams College in 1856, Garfield returned to Hiram College as a professor of classical languages. When he was only twenty-six, the faculty elected him president of the school. Two years later, he entered politics, winning election to the Ohio state senate as a Republican.

When the Civil War came, Garfield organized the students of Hiram into a brigade, and they elected him lieutenant colonel. Within a short time he received an army commission as a full colonel and was placed in charge of the regiment to which his brigade was attached. He led the campaign which drove the Confederates out of eastern Kentucky, was promoted to brigadier, saw action at Shiloh and Corinth, and in 1863 was appointed chief of staff to Major General William Rosecrans.

By then, word of his military success had reached the people of Ohio, and like Hayes, he won a seat in Congress while he was still in the field. For bravery at the Battle of Chickamauga he was promoted to major general. Then, at the height of his military fame, which might have brought him command of all the Union armies, he bowed to the wishes of Abraham Lincoln, resigned his commission, and took his seat in Congress. As much as he needed fighting generals, Lincoln also needed men who would fight for him in Congress, and he could count on Garfield.

Garfield would serve in the House of Representatives for the next seventeen years, a record of unbroken congressional service unmatched by any President up to that time. But his career in the House was not uncheckered. He was implicated in the Credit Mobilier scandal during the Grant Administration, though no charges were ever brought

and nothing was ever proved. He also served on the electoral commission which may well have rigged the Presidential election of 1876 in favor of his friend Rud Hayes. But he was a political powerhouse, and after serving as the House minority leader he decided he wanted to go to the U.S. Senate. The Ohio state legislature duly elected him in January 1880. He never took his seat.

In July of that same year the Republican National Convention opened in Chicago. With the renomination of Hayes out of the question, the party had split into two factions, the "Half-Breeds" led by New York Senator Roscoe Conkling, who were determined to draft Grant whether he wanted the nomination or not (in fact, he did, but would not say so publicly), and the "Stalwarts," followers of Senator Blaine, determined to win for their man the nomination he had been denied four years earlier.

For thirty-three ballots the convention was deadlocked between Grant and Blaine. On the thirty-fourth, Wisconsin decided to float a trial balloon by giving its votes to Garfield, who had not even gotten the favorite-son endorsement from Ohio. The ploy worked, for on the next ballot Blaine swung all his votes to Garfield, and the Ohioan was nominated on the thirty-sixth roll call.

The Democrats had nominated a Civil War hero of their own, General Winfield Scott Hancock. (For about twenty-five years after Appomattox, it was almost impossible to gain major elective office if one had not been a war hero. There were exceptions.) Hancock tried to revive the scandal charges against Garfield and the Republicans, but if Hayes had performed one great service while in office, it was to restore a sense of dignity to the government. The people had forgotten about scandals, and the election turned on the issue of the protective tariff. It was still a conservative doctrine to support American manufacture by supporting the tariff, and the more conservative Garfield won, squeaking by with a plurality of 9,500 votes out of nearly nine million cast. He did better in the electoral voting, carrying 215 of those to Hancock's 155.

What kind of President Garfield would have been can never be known with certainty, but in conservative terms, he did not start off well. He appointed Blaine as Secretary of State in a blatant political payoff, and went back on Hayes's plan to reform the Civil Service, restoring the patronage office of Collector of the Port of New York.

On July 2, 1881, the President and the Secretary of State were about to board a train in Washington bound for Massachusetts, where Garfield was going to attend his twenty-fifth class reunion at Williams College. A man named Charles Guiteau, who had previously sought a patronage apppointment from Garfield but had been rebuffed without ever seeing the President, stepped from a crowd of well-wishers and shot Garfield twice in the back. The President lingered on until September, with doctors unable to locate one of the bullets, though they even tried listening to hear an interruption of the blood flow with a telephone pressed against the President's body. Early in that month the heat of Indian summer in Washington made Garfield so uncomfortable that he asked to be removed to the seashore, and he died in a summer cottage at Elberon, New Jersey, on September 19.

He was succeeded by the Vice President, Chester A. Arthur, who had been living in a state of nervous anticipation since the President was wounded in July.

On the day that Garfield died, Andrew Carnegie was one of the richest men in America, lagging behind only the oilman John D. Rockefeller and the banker J.P. Morgan. But some thirty years before, he was a penniless immigrant from Scotland, holding down a job as a bobbin boy at a cotton mill in Allegheny, Pennsylvania, for $1.20 a week. He had been born in Dumferline, Scotland, in 1835, and emigrated to the United States in 1848. After his stint in the cotton mill, he took a job as a messenger in a telegraph office and, as Edison would later also do, learned the art of telegraphy well enough to earn a living. His skill as a telegrapher brought him into the employ of the Pennsylvania Railroad, where he soon became private secretary to one of its top officials, Thomas Scott. Carnegie's willingness

to work doggedly marked him as a young man on the rise, and Scott soon made him superintendent of the Pittsburgh division of the railroad.

When the Civil War came, Simon Cameron called Scott to the War Department and put him in charge of transport and telegraphy for the Union Army. Scott tapped Carnegie to be his assistant, and Carnegie delivered yeoman's service to the Union throughout the war. It was during his time in Washington that Carnegie came to grips with just how immense a country the United States was and how integrally its future was tied up with the railroad. When the war ended, Carnegie politely turned down Scott's offer of his old job. He wanted much more from railroading than he could get as a superintendent in Pittsburgh.

Carnegie formed a company to produce iron railroad bridges, and it was this that would lead him to his fortune. His most expensive overhead payment was the purchase of scrap iron, so he founded a steel mill in Pittsburgh to produce it for him. It soon became apparent that steel and iron were going to be used in much more than the building of railroad bridges, and he set about to produce as much steel and scrap iron as he could sell. When he was thirty-three years old, he had the then-astronomical income of $50,000 per year. When he died in 1919, his fortune could not be accurately measured, but it was estimated that he had given away more than $350 million.

Deeply patriotic and conservative to the core, Andrew Carnegie had a fundamental understanding of the function of government and the stewardship of private wealth that is the basis of conservative politico-economic philosophy. In a capitalist society, wealth is in the hands of the private sector, and the government should be empowered to collect enough money to perform the obligations it is constitutionally charged with carrying out. These obligations include providing for the national defense, the building and maintenance of roads and canals, the protection of the citizenry from crime and their relief

The mortally wounded President Garfield is removed from the White House for the trip to Elberon, New Jersey. He was dead within a fortnight.

139

IN DANGER.
PUCK: "What are you going to do about it?"

"Monopoly" entwined around Congress and threatening Liberty in a panel from the renowned 19th century political cartoon "Puck."

if needed from disasters natural or man-made, and a host of other duties specified by law that will, if carried out properly, promote the general welfare of the people. Nowhere in the Constitution does it stipulate that the government is formed to *provide* for the general welfare. This is not to say that the government is prohibited from being compassionate, merely that compassion is more effectively transformed into concrete action which will achieve desired results when it proceeds from the private sector, where the wealth is. Government is not structured to provide long-term relief for private individuals from economic setback. Thus, when it attempts to do so, it does not do it well, neither providing relief for the individual nor promoting the general welfare.

Where, then, does a person seeking such relief turn, if not to his government? Carnegie demonstrated, and conservatives believe, that such relief must and will come from the private sector in the form of philanthropies, charities, lending institutions, and private individuals who are in a position to help. Liberals consider this a naive view, insisting that the government is the best conduit of relief, because it can be forced to act by legislation. But the government has no money of its own, and earns none. To produce the necessary funds, it must levy taxes, so that the money comes from the private sector *anyway*. The argument is then reduced to who is in a better position to distribute such funds and provide more effective relief, the government or private-sector philanthropies? This question would come into much sharper focus after the advent of the New Deal and the Great Society programs in the twentieth century, and forms a large part of the basis of difference between liberals and conservatives today.

There are some modern historians, and especially that most irritating breed of the entire species, the "psycho-historian," who contend that Andrew Carnegie gave away huge sums of money to ease a conscience made guilty by his wealth because he had so much while others had little. This view is nonsense. Wealth in the latter part of the nineteenth century was not a cause for embarrassment among those who had it, nor a cause for violent resentment among those who did not, at least in America. Neither did Carnegie act out of a sense of *noblesse oblige*. He never forgot his start as a penniless Scottish immigrant, and he was too imbued with republicanism to consider himself a part of any aristocracy. Rather, he believed in the "stewardship of wealth," a common conservative philosophy among men in every economic class. According to this view, if a man has just enough wealth to provide for his family, that is what he must do. If he has a little extra and a neighbor is in need, he is obliged to help. If he can aid in providing a better life for hundreds of thousands, then, like Carnegie and Rockefeller, he is bound to set up the machinery to do so. This philosophy went out of fashion after the government nationalized the compassion industry following the Great Depression, and was not revived until the 1980's.

In our day, for a variety of reasons (among them misunderstanding and deliberate distortion of ideals), the words "compassion" and "conservative" do not roll trippingly off the tongue together. But in the nineteenth century, many conservatives were in the forefront of the fight for social reforms, again believing that such reform was better effected when it was instigated by the private sector. Charles Francis Adams, Jr., scion of conservative Presidents and son of the American minister to Great Britain during the Civil War, sought better labor relations and, as chairman of the Board of Railroad Commissioners and later president of the Union Pacific Railroad, promulgated that industry's regulations in regard to railroad workers. Charles Loring Brace, member of a wealthy and distinguished New York family, founded the Children's Aid Society. Conservative philanthropist Henry Bergh launched the American Society for the Prevention of Cruelty to Animals. Richard Watson Gilder, ancestor of the modern conservative philosopher George Gilder, was the first president of the Kindergarten Associates, which urged free education for toddlers, and was the founder of the Society of American Artists and the Free Art League. One of the earliest consumer advocates was Josephine Shaw Lowell, who had married into the famous Lowell family of Massachusetts and shared their conservative outlook. Adding to these accomplishments the work done by the foundations begun by Carnegie, Rockefeller, and Henry Ford, and remembering that the Republican Party was formed to combat slavery, one can lay to rest the idea that compassion and social justice lay in the private domain of liberals and Democrats.

A hundred years before Ronald Reagan would attempt to revive the "stewardship of wealth" philosophy, at a time when it was still very much in vogue, one Republican senator was informed of the death of James Garfield and exclaimed, "Chet Arthur is President! Good God!" The son of a Baptist minister, Arthur was born in Vermont in October 1830. His father was a roving preacher, and Arthur was educated in a number of schools in New England and upper New York State. An excellent student, he entered Union College when he was fifteen, made Phi Beta Kappa, and graduated in three years.

He was an ardent abolitionist, and after his admission to the bar in 1853, he often defended accused blacks without charge. He was one of the earliest members of the Republican Party in New York, and campaigned hard for Frémont in 1856 and New York gubernatorial candidate Edwin Morgan in 1858 and 1860. When the Civil War began, Morgan appointed Arthur quartermaster general of New York State, and in 1862 made him inspector general of militia, with the rank of brigadier. Though he kept the post for only a year and never saw any combat, Arthur introduced himself to people as "General Arthur" for the rest of his life. After a Democratic victory in New York in 1863, Arthur returned to private practice, and devoted much of his time to rebuilding the fortunes of his party.

He was soon recognized as the most powerful behind-the-scenes Republican in the state, and after supporting General Grant for president, was able to wrangle an appoint-

141

Right. John D. Rockefeller, oil billionare and founder of the politically powerful Rockefeller clan, in a uncharacteristically docile pose.

Opposite, above. Andrew Carnegie, industrialist, wrote "The Gospel of Wealth" and expressed his opinion that wealth should be used for the benefit of all humanity.

Opposite, below. J. Pierpoint Morgan, the financier who made New York the financial capital of the world.

ment as Collector of the Port of New York. This gave Arthur control over more than a thousand patronage jobs in the New York Customs House, and he made a fortune from it. President Hayes held Arthur up as a model of what was wrong with the civil service when he fired him and abolished his office in 1879.

At the Republican Convention in 1880, Arthur was a "Stalwart," supporting Grant to prevent Blaine from being nominated. When the "Half-Breeds" switched their support to Garfield, it was obvious that a "Stalwart" would be needed to balance the ticket. New York was an important swing state in the 1880's, and the Republicans hoped to kill two birds with one stone by nominating a "Stalwart" from New York for Vice President. Arthur, despite being embarrassed nationally by Hayes two years before, was the man they chose.

Garfield was only forty-nine years old when he took office, and no one expected that he would not live out his term in anything but cheery good health. But an assassin's bullet

ensured that he would not live out his term at all, and Chester Arthur was indeed President.

Conservatives were wary enough of the bureaucratic Garfield, but they viewed the succession of Arthur as nothing short of an unmitigated disaster. The man had used the hated civil service as the means to his own enrichment, and he'd also been too close to the radical fringe of the abolitionists before the war. There was just no telling what he might do now.

As it turned out, their fears were unwarranted. Arthur as President produced a record that a conservative today would be very happy to run on. Arthur pushed for recognition of America's new eminence in the world by encouraging scientific and political exchanges with other nations. He reduced the confusion caused in intercontinental travel and communications by establishing the standard time zones. He sought to broaden America's ability to trade on the open market by suggesting that all of the nations of North and South America adopt a uniform currency. He negotiated a treaty to build a canal through the Isthmus of Darien with the government of Nicaragua, a treaty that was rejected by the Senate. In perhaps the most incongruous of all his accomplishments, he re-instituted the reform of the civil service that had been initiated by President Hayes with his firing in New York. And in a move guaranteed to endear him to the hearts of conservatives for all time, he pushed for abolition of internal-revenue taxes on all products except tobacco and alcohol. Finally, reflecting the state of uncertainty that he had had to endure for two months, he urged the Congress to lay out specific regulations for the assumption of power by the Vice President when the President is incapacitated.

It is unfortunate that Arthur brought with him to the Presidency the unwanted baggage of being tainted by earlier corruption, because it hampered his relations with the Congress and the people, and left him little regarded by historians. Yet, he was an excellent President, too much forgotten not only by conservatives, but by all Americans today.

From 1860 until 1912, only one Democrat was elected President. But he managed the feat twice, becoming our twenty-second *and* twenty-fourth Presidents, and he may well have been the most conservative of all the Presidents in the post-Civil War era.

Like his immediate predecessor, Grover Cleveland was a New Yorker who was born outside the state. His birthplace was Caldwell, New Jersey, and he came into the world on March 18, 1837. Also like Arthur, Cleveland's father was a minister whose work took him from place to place, finally settling in Clinton, New York. His father died when Cleveland was sixteen, and the young man took odd jobs to help support his family. Two years later, he decided to head west to seek his fame and fortune. But he stopped first to visit with an uncle in Buffalo, and reviewing his situation, agreed to stay and work on the uncle's farm. Not long after that, his uncle secured a position for the boy as a clerk with a local law firm, and Cleveland was able to study for the bar.

He was admitted to the bar in 1859, and was promoted to chief clerk at the firm, where he earned a steady salary to help in his family's support. Buffalo was a Democratic stronghold then, and Cleveland campaigned for Horatio Seymour in the gubernatorial election of 1862. Like Seymour, Cleveland opposed the Civil War, and paid the $300 necessary to buy an exemption from active military service. With Seymour's victory, Cleveland was appointed assistant district attorney of Erie County, New York. Three years later he ran as the Democratic candidate for district attorney, but lost to Republican Lyman K. Bass. The two remained on good terms, though, as much from necessity as anything else. They were roommates.

Cleveland returned to private practice after that election, and stayed out of politics for five years, until he ran for sheriff of Erie County in 1870 and won. His tenure in that office won him the distinction of being the only future President ever to have hanged a man. He gave up the office, though, at the next election.

Opposite. Andrew Carnegie, pictured as the general public saw him, on the cover of *Life*.

ALBERT
LEVERING

ANDREW
CARNEGIE

LIFE
COPYRIGHT, 1905

145

Grover Cleveland's business-like management of his Administration was saluted in this cartoon entitled "Call on a Man of Business."

For nine years Cleveland led the life of a prosperous attorney in upstate New York, until he was approached by the reform wing of the Democratic Party in 1881 and asked to run for mayor of Buffalo. He accepted, and won the election handily. His reputation as a reformer got him the Democratic nomination for governor of New York the following year, and he won in a landslide, helped by the fact that his Republican opponent was so corrupt that reform Republicans bolted from the party and endorsed Cleveland.

His meteoric rise over the previous three years and his reputation for toughness and honesty made Cleveland the darling of the Democratic Convention in 1884, and despite Tammany Hall's objection to another reformer heading the ticket, he was nominated on the second ballot. On the Republican side, James G. Blaine had finally won his party's nomination, despite the objections of some reformers to having a reputed crook head the ticket. But Blaine had been around for so long and survived so much innuendo that he was the odds-on favorite to win in November.

Ten days after Cleveland's nomination, a story broke in the newspapers that made Blaine a lead-pipe cinch. Cleveland was publicly accused of having fathered an illegitimate child eleven years earlier, and he did not deny the story. He very well couldn't, because it was true and the newspapers had the goods. About all Blaine had to do was stay alive and reasonably sober until November, and he would be elected President.

But the Democrats refused to lay down and die. They hit back with an equally true story that Blaine's oldest child had been born only three months after the wedding. As the

146

Left, and below. Horatio
Alger, chronicler of the
American Dream, and two of
his most popular books.

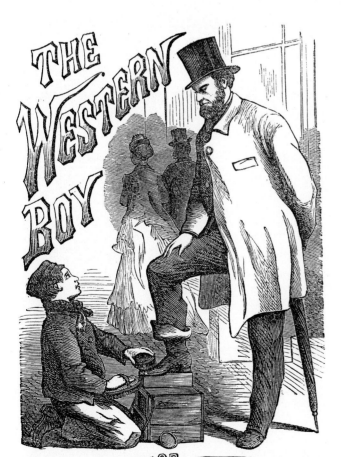

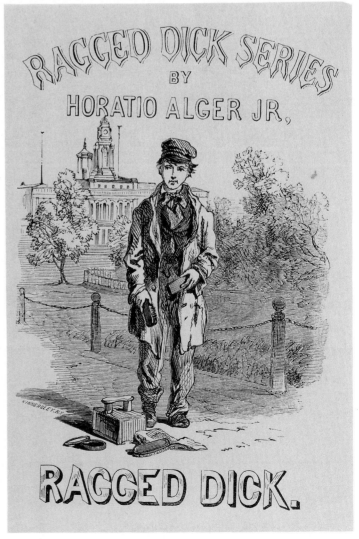

Opposite. President Grover
Cleveland confers with
tycoon J.P. Morgan in an
effort to bolster the federal
reserves following the Panic
of 1893.

Left. Cleveland sketched near
the end of his life, is still
greatly admired by conservatives today.

campaign wore on, the furor over Cleveland's child subsided and the race tightened up, but Blaine still led in New York, and without his home state, Cleveland could not win.

Six days before the election, Blaine was campaigning in New York City when he received a delegation of Protestant ministers making a courtesy call. He thanked them for their visit, and with reporters present, gave a little campaign speech in which he denounced the Democrats as the party of "rum, Romanism, and rebellion." His slap at the Irish Catholics was printed up and distributed by Democratic volunteers outside every Catholic Church the following Sunday, and the Irish swung *en masse* from the Blaine camp to Cleveland. On election day, Cleveland carried New York by less than 1200 votes out of a million cast, and won the election by a whisker.

Cleveland's first term in office established his solid conservative credentials. He continued with the reform of the civil service, called for an end to the coinage of silver dollars and a return to "sound money," vetoed a $12-a-month pension for unemployed soldiers who had not been disabled in the war, and recovered more than eighty million acres of public land grants to the railroads and powerful cattle ranchers. Perhaps the only President who read every word of every piece of legislation that came before him, Cleveland used his veto power more than 300 times in his first term, or about two and half times more than all of his predecessors combined. Opposition from conservatives came with his creation of the Department of Labor and his signing of the Interstate Commerce Act, setting the precedent for direct government regulation of industry.

Cleveland was renominated by acclamation at the Democratic Convention in 1888, but again the election would ride on the outcome in New York. This time, Tammany Hall geared up to defeat the conservative reformer. When the election results were in, the President had outpolled his Republican rival, Benjamin Harrison of Ohio, by more than 100,000 votes, improving on his 1884 showing by nearly a million. But he had lost New York, and Harrison had a majority of the electoral votes, and the White House.

Benjamin Harrison was fifty-six years old when he came to the Presidency in 1889, and the only previous election he had won by popular vote had been for the job of reporter to the Indiana Supreme Court a year before the outbreak of the Civil War. An attorney by trade, he organized a regiment of Indiana volunteers in 1862 and was commissioned a colonel. He and his regiment saw heavy fighting near the end of the war, and Harrison marched to the sea with Sherman. He was deservedly promoted to brigadier general a month before the war ended.

Returning to Indiana, Harrison opened a law practice with a former governor of the state, and his fortunes prospered. In 1876, the Republican Party asked Harrison to run for governor. He was a natural choice, having been a member of the general staff during the war, and coming as he did from one of the most prestigious families in America—his great-grandfather, the first Benjamin Harrison, had signed the Declaration of Independence, and his grandfather, William Henry Harrison, was the hero of Tippecanoe and the ninth President of the United States, if only briefly. Harrison lost the gubernatorial election by a hair, but had become an established figure in Indiana politics.

In 1881, the Indiana state legislature elected him to the U.S. Senate, where he generally voted with his party leadership. Returning to his law practice after his term was completed, Harrison was happy to have served but considered his political career finished. He did, however, lead the Indiana delegation to the Republican convention in 1888, where a deadlock developed between John Sherman of Ohio and William Q. Gresham of Indiana. Pressured to withdraw, Gresham refused to release his delegates to anyone but Harrison. Sherman would not withdraw if Gresham would not. Apprised of the situation at his vacation retreat in Scotland, party boss Blaine (who had apparently sworn off conventions) sent a famous two-word telegram: "Take Harrison." The general was nominated on the next ballot.

When Harrison took office, the Republicans controlled the House of Representatives by a majority of 173 to 156. It is axiomatic in American politics that the party which controls the White House will lose congressional seats in the off-year election. When the 1890 returns were in, the Democrats controlled the House by a margin of 235-88, one of the greatest off-year debacles for a ruling party in American history.

The major cause had been the McKinley Tariff Act, which sent prices skyrocketing. In addition, government spending was way up. The Treasury was purchasing large quantities of silver and paying for it in notes backed by gold. This drain on the nation's gold reserves made the dollar unstable and eventually sparked the Panic of 1893. Harrison had also increased government expenditure by signing a bill that granted pensions to unemployed war veterans, putting thousands on the dole. In his first term, the normally conservative Cleveland had advocated a free-trade policy and a reduction in tariffs, but only because there was a surplus in the Treasury and Cleveland did not want excess money coming into the government coffers for Congress to waste. Within two years of taking office, Harrison had authorized sufficient legislation to squander the entire surplus. The government was operating from a deficit position and the national economy was on the rocks.

To his credit, Harrison did pursue a vigorous foreign policy, pushing American claims to Samoa and presiding over the first Pan-American Conference. In addition, six new states were added to the Union during his term of office. But his deficiencies far outweighed his achievements, and he was beaten by Cleveland in the election of 1892. Still, he made a decent showing, pulling in forty-four percent of the vote to Cleveland's forty-seven percent. The remaining nine percent went to General James Weaver, candidate of a western populist party. Many of Weaver's votes were siphoned off from the Republicans, despite the fact that Harrison's disastrous silver policy was put in place to please western farm owners and mine operators.

Upon his return to office, Cleveland realized that his first priority was to deal vigorously with the nation's economic problems. He immediately sponsored legislation to terminate the Treasury's obligation to buy silver, but the measure was too late. Within a few months of his second inauguration, the Panic of 1893 set in and Cleveland, who did not cause it, was powerless to do anything to stop it. Banks foreclosed on mortgages to preserve liquidity, investors panicked and caused runs on banks, unemployment was rampant, savings were wiped out. But Cleveland held firm, realizing that the economic life of a country runs on a course of its own, and refused to involve the government in any "quick-fix" schemes that would so appeal to later Presidents. In May 1894, an "army" of 400 unemployed veterans marched on Washington, under the command of the self-styled "General" Jacob Coxey. They demanded that Congress pass a bill authorizing $500 million to be spent on a road-building program, with themselves as the builders. When they went to demonstrate at the White House, Cleveland had Coxey arrested for trespassing. Later that month, the Pullman Company laid off 500 workers who refused to accept a pay cut, and the American Railway Union went out on a sympathy strike. Violence broke out, and Cleveland called out the troops to keep order. He also saw to it that Eugene Debs, the socialist leader of the union, was tried for conspiracy to commit violence. Convicted, Debs served six months in prison.

Although the cupboard was now bare, Cleveland again turned to tariff reduction as a means to reduce prices and stimulate the economy. But the Congress was reluctant to go along, though it did eventually send up a tariff reduction bill which Cleveland considered vetoing because the reductions were negligible. By January of 1895, the American gold reserves were threatened, with the government now able to back only about $40 million of paper money with gold. To go off the gold standard, as the western progressives were demanding, would ruin American credit abroad and lead to devaluation of the dollar and the printing of cheap, if not worthless, money. Cleveland would have none of it.

THE TEMPERANCE CRUSADE.
FOUR HOURS IN A BAR ROOM.

1ST HOUR
CYNICAL INDIFFERENCE.

2ND HOUR
MOCKERY AND DEFIANCE.

A. J. FISHER 98, NASSAU St. NEW YORK.

3RD HOUR
RAGE AND DESPAIR.

4TH HOUR
UNCONDITIONAL SURRENDER.

Entered according to Act of Congress in the year 1874 by A. J. Fisher, in Office of the Librarian of Congress at Washington

Opposite, and left. These contemporary sketches indicate the vehemence of the Temperance Crusaders in their feelings about the saloonkeepers they fought and the police who often broke up their demonstrations.

153

Opposite. William McKinley,
who with Grover Cleveland,
was the most conservative of
Presidents in the latter part
of the nineteenth century.

He arranged with a syndicate of New York bankers led by J.P. Morgan to purchase a new issue of government bonds and to pay for them in gold. The bankers, with as much to gain from a "sound money" economy as the government, agreed, and the deal brought an infusion of more than $65 million in gold to the Treasury. Still, while the government was on a sounder footing which could only help the economy in the long run, economic depression continued to grip the nation.

While he had precious little time to devote to foreign policy, Cleveland further impressed conservatives with his defense of the Monroe Doctrine. In 1895, Venezuela and Great Britain entered into a dispute over the boundary of British Guiana, with the Venezuelans claiming that the British were infringing on their territory. Britain announced that it would decide where the proper boundary lay, and would inform the Venezuelans of her decision. In response, Cleveland sent word to Congress that he wanted a commission sent to South America, and in consultation with the other parties involved, the United States would decide where the boundary was. After the commission was appointed, Cleveland announced that the U.S. would "resist by every means in its power, as a willful agression," any attempt by Britain to ignore the findings of the American commission and decide the matter unilaterally. After some consideration of the matter, and while the U.S. was swept by war fever, the British foreign office announced that it would "welcome" American mediation of the boundary dispute.

By 1896, the liberal, progressive wing of the Democratic Party was in the ascendancy. When the convention opened in July, the delegates overwhelmingly adopted a provision calling for an end to the gold standard and the implementation of a free-silver economy. In an attack on the conservatives who favored "sound money" and the gold standard, William Jennings Bryan of Nebraska railed that "we will answer their demand for a gold standard by saying to them: You shall not press down upon the brow of labor this crown of thorns! You shall not crucify mankind upon a cross of gold!" His speech stampeded the convention, and Bryan was nominated for President. Cleveland, feeling that his efforts had been repudiated by his own party, refused to support Bryan, and was glad to see William McKinley, the Republican candidate, win the election.

Cleveland left office shouldering the blame for an economic depression that he did not cause and, when the economic pendulum swung back toward prosperity a few months later, he got none of the credit he deserved. It is perhaps for that reason that future Presidents did not look to his example in times of economic crisis. His method of staying calm, keeping government expenditure on a sound footing by refusing to involve it in "quick-fix" social programs, and accepting the political backlash while waiting for the private sector economy to straighten itself out as he knew it inevitably would, was the wisest course to follow in terms of what was best for the country in the long run. But it was not politically expedient, and many of his successors would knowingly choose the expedient over the wise.

From the end of the Civil War through the turn of the century, every Republican President with the exception of Chester Arthur was born in Ohio and served as an officer in the Civil War. William McKinley fit the mold. Born in Niles, Ohio, in 1843, he showed an early inclination toward the Methodist ministry and polished his homiletic skills by joining the local debating society. When the Civil War broke out, McKinley, who had dropped out of college after a year due to illness and was working as a postal clerk, joined the 23rd Ohio Volunteers as a private. During the regiment's training period, McKinley was promoted to mess sergeant. His regiment was at Antietam on September 17, 1862, the day on which 22,000 men were shot. The battle went on for so long that the troops had to be served meals while they were still under fire, and McKinley so distinguished himself getting hot food to his regiment that he was given a battlefield commission as a second lieutenant. He was made brigade quartermaster on the staff of General Rutherford Hayes,

155

Samuel Langhorne Clemens,
better known as Mark Twain,
was a liberal social critic,
political gadfly and satirical
writer with a biting wit.

Henry Wadsworth Longfellow, poet, was part of an
intellectual triumvirate that
included Oliver Wendell
Holmes and James Russell
Lowell.

and his gallantry under fire won him successive promotions to captain and major, the rank he held when the war ended. He was twenty-two years old.

Returning to Ohio, he clerked in a law office for two years, then entered law school in Albany, New York, and was admitted to the bar a year later. Settling in Canton, Ohio, he won election as district attorney of Stark County, normally a Democratic stronghold, though he lost the race for reelection two years later by forty-five votes. In 1876, he won a seat in Congress, coming in on the coattails of his former regimental commander Hayes, who was elected President that year. With his political philosophy not yet settled, in his first term McKinley voted with the liberal Democratic majority on free-silver legislation, and voted with them again to override Hayes's veto of the measure.

McKinley would remain in Congress for fourteen years, during which time he became increasingly more conservative. His major theme was the need for a high tariff to protect American industry. Here he differed with Cleveland, who, well in advance of most conservatives, had been converted to a free-trade philosophy during his first term in the White House. McKinley's advocacy of the tariff culminated in the McKinley Tariff Act of 1890, which drove up the price of consumer goods so much so fast that fully two-thirds of all the Republicans in the House of Representatives, including McKinley, lost their seats in the November elections.

Although he had lost the affection of his own constituency, McKinley was still highly regarded by the Republican Party in Ohio, and the following year he was nominated to run for governor. He traveled the length and breadth of the state, defending his policies in every county, and on election day he won a narrow victory over his Democratic opponent. His skillful handling of the governor's office served to rehabilitate McKinley in the eyes of the national Republican leadership, and at the 1892 convention he received 192 delegate votes for the Presidential nomination that eventually went to the incumbent President Harrison.

The death of James G. Blaine in 1893 left a vacuum in the power structure of the Republican Party, one that was filled by a millionaire industrialist from Cleveland, Marcus Hanna. Hanna greatly admired McKinley, and was determined that he should win the Republican Presidential nomination in 1896. Accordingly, he financed a seventeen-state speaking tour for the Ohio governor, and McKinley's oratorical skill effectively knocked the competition out of the race. At the convention in St. Louis in June 1896, McKinley was nominated on the first ballot.

He was prepared to run a defensive campaign because of the McKinley Tariff Act of 1890, but Bryan's surprise nomination after his electrifying "Cross of Gold" speech at the Democratic convention put a new face on the campaign. Seeing that the opposing party was now dominated by economic extremists who were demanding fundamental changes in the nation's financial structure, the man who had authored the most disastrous tariff legislation in American history could now offer himself to the American people as the candidate of fiscal responsibility.

And in many ways he was. He still believed in the protective tariff, but he had long since been converted from the free-silver notions of his youth and campaigned vigorously as the champion of the gold standard and "sound money." His stance won him the support of President Cleveland and the conservative "Gold Democrats." Progressive Republicans, descendants of the Civil War-era Radicals, found a new home in the Democratic Party with Bryan as the nominee. Previously, liberals and conservatives permeated both parties, frequently fighting with each other in intra-party squabbles as much as they did with the opposition party. Though it hardly became iron-clad, 1896 marked the beginning of the national identification of the Republican Party as the "conservative" party and the Democrats as the "liberal" party in the modern sense of those words.

McKinley rolled up seven million votes in November, handily defeating Bryan. It was a victory for "sound money," the gold standard, and conservative economics. The win was especially gratifying to Grover Cleveland, who felt that his policies had been vindicated by the American people after they had been repudiated by his party.

Within months of McKinley's inauguration, the economic depression eased and the economy went on an upswing, further confirming the rightness of Cleveland's policies and making McKinley the most popular President in the hearts of the people since Ulysses Grant. After four years of depression, the mood of the people was buoyant. The end of the century was rapidly approaching, and the people, spurred on by American achievements in science, technology, exploration, medicine, literature, finance, and a host of other endeavors, were anxious for the new age to begin. The close of the century was a period of great patriotism, of parades, banquets, conventions, and speeches all extolling the virtues of America and her people. The Americans were marching headlong into the twentieth century, ready to take center stage in world affairs. And they were marching behind their flag. They had planted that flag from one end of their wild continent to the other. They were proud of that flag, they loved that flag, and they were going to show it to the world.

6 Stars and Stripes Forever 1898–1929

In May 1895, a revolution broke out on the island of Cuba, a Spanish colonial possession ninety miles off the coast of Florida. The American people, always ready to back a revolution that would throw off the yoke of monarchy and bring democracy, overwhelmingly supported the Cuban insurgents. President Cleveland, already embroiled in the controversy with Britain over the Venezuelan boundary dispute, carefully avoided involvement in the Cuban uprising for fear that events might move so swiftly that the United States could find herself at war with two major European powers. By 1898, America's two most influential newspaper publishers, William Randolph Hearst and Joseph Pulitzer, were trying to outdo each other printing lurid tales of Spanish atrocities against the Cubans. Between them, they stirred war fever in America to such a pitch that when Cleveland's successor McKinley also resisted American involvement in the war, his own Assistant Secretary of the Navy said publicly that the President had "no more backbone than a chocolate eclair." Luckily for the young Assistant Secretary, the remark was not picked up by the newspapers, and McKinley was not compelled to fire Theodore Roosevelt.

But two events in the early months of 1898 forced McKinley's hand. The Hearst newspapers had gotten hold of a private letter written by the Spanish ambassador to a friend that was personally insulting to the President and the American people. A week later, the battleship *Maine* mysteriously blew up and sank while it was anchored in the harbor at Havana. The newspapers immediately blamed the explosion on Spanish saboteurs, and though the charge was never proven, it was widely believed by the American people, who now demanded war. In March, McKinley requested a congressional appropriation of $50 million to put the Army and Navy on a war footing. When the President felt that the armed forces were sufficiently prepared, he asked Congress for a declaration of war against Spain, and it was overwhelmingly approved the same day, April 25.

By August it was over. The major battle of the war occurred on May 10, when Commodore Dewey and the U.S. Navy destroyed Spain's Pacific fleet at Manila Bay. On June 10, the Marines landed at Guantanamo Bay, Cuba, and on July 25 in Puerto Rico. Spain's Caribbean fleet had been decimated at Santiago on July 3. With the fall of the Philippines on August 15, the Spanish government asked for peace terms. The United States took possession of Cuba, Puerto Rico, and the Philippine Islands. During the war, the United States had annexed Hawaii for use as a naval base for her Pacific fleet. After the war, McKinley signed an executive order making the annexation permanent.

Militarily, the Spanish-American War was a minor conflict. Less than 300 Americans had been killed, though some 5,000 succumbed to tropical diseases. But it threw America into a state of almost frenzied elation. The United States had defeated a European power, and now had to be considered a world power herself. Isolationism, which had been the major thrust of conservative foreign policy since Washington was President, was now as dead as the venerable Founder was. McKinley's last speech before dying would address that very subject, when he said that "isolationism is no longer possible or desirable."

Once he had tasted the fruits of victory, McKinley continued with his newly vigorous foreign policy. In 1800, he sent American Marines to join in the international expedition to quell the Boxer Rebellion in China. When Filipino insurgents refused to accept American domination of their country in place of Spain, he ordered General Arthur MacArthur to use whatever means were necessary to put down the revolt.

One of the heroes of the war with Spain was Theodore Roosevelt, who had left the Navy Department when fighting commenced and helped organize a cavalry unit dubbed "The Rough Riders." On the basis of his exploits in Cuba, he was elected governor of New York in 1899. When the Republican Convention of 1900 met in Philadelphia, the dashing young Roosevelt was chosen to run on the ticket with McKinley, who was unanimously renominated for President.

The Democrats again nominated Bryan, who stayed with his demand for an end to the gold standard and added new charges that the Republicans were making the United States into an imperialist country. But the American electorate, flushed with victory and proud of their new prominence in world affairs, rejected Bryan even more desicively than they had in 1896, giving McKinley nearly a million-vote plurality in November.

William McKinley was greatly loved by the American people, and left a legacy to be greatly admired by the conservatives who came after him. His adherence to the conservative principle of "sound money" was rewarded with the great prosperity the American people enjoyed during his Administration. Though he is often accused of having allowed himself to be dragged into a war he did not want, his subsequent foreign policy indicated that he had become a true believer in the end of American isolationism. He forcefully brought conservative philosophy to bear on the problems of the new twentieth century, and much of its response to those problems was due to McKinley's example and influence. The entire nation was plunged into grief when, on September 6, 1901, he was shot by an anarchist at the Pan-American Exposition in Buffalo, New York. After pleading with his attendants not to tell his invalid wife what had happened and then cautioning the police not to harm his assassin, he was removed to a private home, where he died eight days later.

The adjectives that could be employed to describe his successor, Theodore Roosevelt, are limited, perhaps, only to the extent that there are not an infinite number of such words in our language. Conservative, liberal, progressive, reactionary, reformer, agreeable, obstinate, charming, and boorish—all could describe Theodore Roosevelt at a given time

Theodore Roosevelt, the
youngest President in the history of the United States, in
his two favorite roles—
politician and naturalist.

in his life, and at some of those times, on a given day of the week. He was Roget's *raison d'etre*, and his worst nightmare.

Teddy, as he was called boy and man, was born in New York City to a patrician family that could trace its roots to the days when their fellow Dutchmen ruled New York. Scrawny and sickly as a child, he entered upon a drastic regimen of physical exercise and weight training to build up his body in a gymnasium his father had built for him in their home. By the time he was a young man, and ever after, no physical description could be made of him that did not include the word "robust."

Entering Harvard at eighteen, he specialized in the study of natural science, which keenly interested him throughout his life. He was elected to Phi Beta Kappa, and graduated in 1880, at the age of twenty-one. After marrying that same year, he and his wife traveled through Europe, where he completed work on his first book, *The Naval War of 1812*, which met with favorable reviews when it was published. In 1881, he returned from Europe and entered a race for the New York State legislature, winning the election as the candidate of the reform wing of the Republican Party. In the three years that Roosevelt served in the state legislature, he voted more often than not with the conservatives in his party, opposing labor legislation and pay raises for government employees.

In one of the most striking tragedies ever to befall an American historical figure, Roosevelt's beloved wife and his mother, to whom he was devoted, died of separate causes on the same day, February 14, 1884. Nearly paralyzed by grief, he finished his third term in Albany, then retired from public life and headed west. For two years, he lived the life of a cowboy and cattle rancher, torn between periods of joy at being surrounded by nature and renewed periods of grief and remembrance of things past.

He returned to New York in 1886, and threw himself back into politics with his characteristic vigor. He agreed to run for mayor of New York on the Republican line, but was badly defeated by the conservative Democrat Abram S. Hewitt. He even finished behind Henry George, who was running as an independent but was in fact a well-known socialist.

Joy returned to his life when he remarried late in 1886, and he spent many more months traveling in Europe with his bride. Upon his return, he campaigned actively for Benjamin Harrison in the election of 1888, and was rewarded when Harrison appointed him to the commission overseeing the reform of the civil service. He kept the post for six years, being re-appointed by Cleveland in 1893.

When his friend and fellow reformer William Strong was elected mayor of New York in 1895, Roosevelt was appointed police commissioner, a job he truly loved. Donning a black cape, he prowled the streets of Manhattan late at night, searching out derelict policemen not found at their posts. His nocturnal strolls made a hit in the newspapers, but not so his insistence on enforcing the Sunday blue laws closing saloons. His appointment as Assistant Secretary of the Navy by President McKinley in 1897 was a welcome relief to saloonkeepers all over New York, not to mention drowsy policemen.

It was while he was in the Navy Department that Roosevelt made his caustic remark about McKinley's spine, but the President had a forgiving nature and made nothing of it. When the war in Cuba finally came, Roosevelt resigned from the Navy Department and accepted a commission as second in command of the Volunteer 1st Cavalry under Brigadier General Leonard Wood. Colonel Roosevelt did most of the organizing, drafting many of his polo-playing fellow patricians into service. The outfit shipped out for Cuba, and on July 1 Roosevelt became the hero of the war when he led his "Rough Riders" in the famous charge up San Juan Hill. To the end of his days, Roosevelt always maintained that "San Juan was the greatest day of my life."

Certainly, it was the most fortuitous. San Juan assured Roosevelt of the Republican nomination for governor of New York, and he squeaked by his Democratic opponent in

Abram S. Hewitt, a distinguished conservative, and the man who defeated Teddy Roosevelt in a race for Mayor of New York.

November. While governor, he began to display some liberal bias toward big business that he had not demonstrated in the legislature. To increase state revenue, he forced a tax on corporate earnings, and began to lay the plans for statewide anti-trust laws. When the Republican Convention tapped him to be McKinley's running mate in 1900, Wall Street was as happy to see him leave New York as the saloonkeepers had once been. Not everyone greeted his nomination with such alacrity, or at least relief. Mark Hanna, now a senator from Ohio, stood on the convention floor after the balloting had put Roosevelt over the top and shouted at his fellow delegates, "Don't any of you realize that only one life stands between this madman and the White House?"

But like Garfield before him, McKinley was·in perfect health, and no one expected assassination. When McKinley was shot, Roosevelt rushed to Buffalo, but doctors there assured him that the President would recover. He rejoined his family on vacation in the Adirondack Mountains, only to be summoned back to Buffalo a week later by the news that the President had taken a bad turn and was dying. Roosevelt was at a railway station, preparing to board a train for Buffalo, when he learned that he was President. He completed the journey, and took the oath of office in the house where McKinley's dead body lay.

Above. Isolationists loathed Roosevelt for his interventionist policies. Here he is depicted as the world's policeman, carrying his famous "big stick."

Opposite. Sketches of Roosevelt and his "crowning" glory, the Panama Canal, and T.R. the cowboy taming the conservative leadership of the Republican Party, including Senator Joseph Benson Foraker and New York Governor Charles Evans Hughes, after putting his brand on William Howard Taft.

Roosevelt as President again manifested the liberal bias toward big business that had marked his year as governor of New York. He created the Department of Commerce and had Congress invest it with powers to directly regulate business and industry in the United States; he vigorously enforced the Sherman Anti-Trust Act, breaking up monopolies controlled by J.P. Morgan and John D. Rockefeller. When the United Mine Workers went out on strike, Roosevelt, who had taken such an anti-labor stance as a young legislator, threatened to call out the troops—not to break the strike, as several of his predecessors had done, but to seize control of the mines unless the owners reached accommodation with the workers. (This tactic would later be employed by Harry Truman, and held to be unconstitutional.)

Still, there is much in the Roosevelt Administration for conservatives to admire. In foreign policy, Roosevelt continued the trend begun by McKinley away from isolationism. He negotiated with Colombia for the right to build a canal in Panama, and when the Colombians tried to renege on the deal they had made with him, Roosevelt supported an uprising among Panamanians and recognized their claim to sovereignty. (The Panamanians, in turn, agreed to the original bargain for the building of the canal.) He successfully mediated the war between Russia and Japan, winning the Nobel Peace Prize for his efforts. When Japan, now a major power, made some angry noises about American immigration policy, Roosevelt assembled a fleet of battleships and sent it on a world tour, with specific instructions to make a port call in Tokyo Bay. In 1904, he promulgated the Roosevelt Corollary to the Monroe Doctrine, saying that in extreme cases the United States had the right not only to prevent outside encroachment in the Western Hemisphere, but to intervene in the internal affairs of her neighbors to prevent "flag-

165

At least one cartoonist thought that Roosevelt's policies would come crashing down on the head of his successor, William Howard Taft. Instead, it was Teddy himself who came crashing down on Taft, running against him in 1912 and preventing his reelection.

rant...wrong-doing or impotence." He then became the first President to exercise this right, sending the Marines to Santo Domingo to force the government there to make good on its foreign debt payments.

In the last two years of Roosevelt's administration, he was able to push relatively little legislation through Congress, despite the fact that the Republican Party held large majorities in both houses. His fellow Republicans were of a far more conservative nature than he and, viewing him as a lame duck, were unwilling to legislate his progressivist domestic policies. Still, Roosevelt had enough influence left to secure the Republican nomination for his hand-picked successor, William Howard Taft.

Taft was fifty when the Republican Party nominated him for President at the behest of Theodore Roosevelt, and his life's experience made him far better suited to be the Supreme Court Chief Justice he eventually became than President of the United States.

Born in Cincinnati in 1857, he graduated from Yale in 1878, and received his law degree from Cincinnati College in 1880. He worked in the local prosecutor's office for a year before receiving his first political appointment, as tax collector for the first Ohio district. Resigning after two years on the job, he went into practice with his father for four years, until the governor of Ohio appointed him to the state superior court in 1887. He won election to the court in his own right two years later, and his impressive record as a jurist brought him to the attention of President Harrison, who made Taft Solicitor General of the United States in 1890.

Taft was very successful in winning the government's cases, and in 1892 Harrison rewarded his efforts by appointing him to the Sixth Circuit Court of Appeals. During his tenure on the bench, he established a reputation for strict interpretation of the Constitution.

When the United States took control of the Philippines after the Spanish-American

War, President McKinley sent Taft there as part of the U.S. Philippine Commission in 1900, and the following year made him the islands' first American civil governor. During his time in the Pacific, Taft had some notable run-ins with the American military commander of the Philippines, Major General Arthur MacArthur, whose son Douglas had just graduated from West Point. Eventually Taft won out, and MacArthur went home.

President Taft and his sons. The older boy at right is Robert Taft, who would go on to become a distinguished Senator from Ohio and leader of the conservative wing of the Rupublican Party.

During Taft's tenure as governor, President Roosevelt, who had known him since he was Solicitor General, offered the Ohioan an appointment as associate justice of the U.S. Supreme Court, which for Taft would have fulfilled a lifelong dream. But Taft reluctantly turned the offer down, citing the work still to be done in the Philippines.

By 1904, however, he was ready to come home, and accepted Roosevelt's offer to join the Cabinet as Secretary of War. He was loyal to Roosevelt, assisting him in carrying out his foreign policy and sharing his progressivist outlook on the domestic front. Roosevelt in turn considered Taft to be the best choice to succeed him as President.

Taft as President initiated few of his own policies, merely content to carry on where Roosevelt had left off. Thus it was surprising, to no one more than Taft, when Roosevelt began to publicly denounce his administration in 1910.

Taft was justifiably angry and mystified by Roosevelt's new stance. On domestic policy, Taft was perhaps even more of a progressive than Roosevelt himself, yet Roosevelt was attacking him as a tool of big business. The simple fact was that, to Theodore Roosevelt, an approaching election caused the same reaction as the sound of a bell did to a firehorse or a boxer. When T.R. announced in 1912 that "my hat is in the ring," Taft immediately took steps to secure his own renomination at the Republican Convention. By refusing to seat many delegates pledged to Roosevelt, Taft was able to win renomination on the first ballot, but the Roosevelt delegates bolted from the convention and, to hear Teddy tell it, begged their chief to run on a third-party line. Thus the Bull Moose or American Progressive Party was born.

The Democrats in 1912 nominated New Jersey Governor Woodrow Wilson for President. Wilson's campaign was being managed by none other than William Jennings Bryan, indicating that this was a race between three progressives, without a conservative in sight. But two of these progressives were Republicans, and the split in the ranks assured Wilson and the Democrats of victory. When the votes were counted, Taft had run third, and he never forgave Theodore Roosevelt.

Woodrow Wilson was a lawyer and college professor who had made a national reputation for opposing the trustees of Princeton University and bringing much-needed educational reform to that venerable institution during his tenure as president there. He had in fact gotten such wide acclaim as a battling progressive that the Democratic Party nominated him for governor of New Jersey on the first ballot at the state convention in 1910. Like Cleveland before him, much of his appeal to the national party leadership lay in the fact that he was a newcomer who had risen quickly, and nobody had very much against him. Thus, at a raucous national convention in June 1912, Wilson defeated the conservative Speaker of the House of Representatives, Champ Clark of Missouri, on the forty-sixth ballot to win the nomination for President. He owed his nomination in great part to the support he'd received from William Jennings Bryan, and he asked Bryan to manage his campaign. After defeating the two progressive Republicans in the general election, Wilson appointed Bryan Secrtetary of State.

In his first term, Wilson pushed through the new Democratic Congress much liberal legislation, including the creation of the Federal Trade Commission to further regulate American business, the reduction of protective tariffs by twenty-five percent, the introduction of the income tax, the creation of the Federal Reserve System, the Clayton Anti-Trust Act, child labor laws, and government subsidization of farmers.

His foreign policy was somewhat more unbalanced, alternately threatening war with Mexico over territorial violations and issuing the Neutrality Proclamation in regard to the massive conflict which had broken out in Europe in August 1914, despite repeated menacing acts by Germany which had Theodore Roosevelt demanding intervention.

Wilson's implementation of his liberal philosophy cost him a great deal of support among the centrist electorate, and his reelection in 1916 looked doubtful. The Republicans rejected yet another bid by Theodore Roosevelt and nominated instead a true conservative, Charles Evans Hughes, associate justice of the Supreme Court and former governor of New York. The race was tight, and as it drew to a close it became apparent that the outcome would hinge on the returns from California, where conservatives and progressives held about equal sway. On Election Night, with the returns from the West coming in slowly, both candidates went to bed believing that Hughes had been elected. But California had gone for Wilson by less than 4,000 votes, and her 13 electoral votes made the President the winner, 277-264. Had there been a swing to the Republicans of less than 10 votes in each of California's electoral districts, Hughes would have carried the state and won the election.

Even before Wilson's second inauguration in March, 1917, American involvement in the European war appeared to be inevitable. On February 1, Germany announced unrestricted submarine warfare that could result in the sinking of any ship, including American ships, involved in trade with the Allies. On the 3rd, Wilson responded by severing diplomatic ties with Germany, and on the 1st of March, he revealed the existence of the Zimmermann telegram, a German diplomatic cable from their foreign office in Berlin to their minister in Mexico City, instructing him to urge the Mexican government to join in a German attack on the United States in return for the recovery of lands lost to the U.S. at the conclusion of the Mexican War seventy years before.

Delivered! Copyright, 1916, by The Press Publishing Co. (The New York Evening World.) 6 By J. H. Casse

Teddy Roosevelt wanted the Republican nomination again in 1916, and promised to bring the Progressives back with him. But by then, most of his followers had defected to Wilson and the Democrats, and T.R. had no chance at the convention.

The American public, whipped into a frenzy by Theodore Roosevelt and others, clamored for war. On March 18, German submarines sank three American merchant ships, and Wilson called for a special session of Congress to meet on April 2. Addressing both houses of Congress, Wilson asked for a declaration of war against Germany and her allies.

American entry into the war broke the stalemate that had existed since the conflict had gotten bogged down in the trenches in 1915. Aided by growing dissatisfaction with the war among the German people, the allies brought the conflict to a successful conclusion in November 1918. The war had bled Europe nearly to death, and had swept away the old order on the continent as completely as the American Civil War had destroyed the planter aristocracy in the South. The Tsar and the Kaiser were gone forever, and so was the notion of European supremacy in culture, diplomacy, and power. The United States was from that moment the most powerful and influential nation in the world, her President the leader of mankind. And he knew it.

Months before the armistice, Wilson addressed Congress to spell out America's war

aims and the conditions under which he would make peace with Germany. His "Fourteen Points" included an end to secret treaties between nations, global disarmament, freedom of the high seas for all nations, and the establishment of a "general association of nations" to settle disputes before they dissolved into war.

When the war ended, Wilson wanted to make sure that the Fourteen Points formed the basis of the peace accord, so he personally led the American delegation to the peace conference at Versailles. Once he was there, he found that dealing with long-time diplomatic horse-traders like Clemenceau of France and Lloyd George of England was not as easy as he thought it was going to be, and he had to bargain away point after point in order to preserve the one that was most important to him, that "general association," or League of Nations.

The trouble he had convincing the Europeans to join the League was nothing compared to the trouble he had trying to convince the Republicans to do it when he returned to the U.S. with the Treaty of Versailles.

Henry Cabot Lodge was born in Boston in 1850, scion of two of the oldest, wealthiest, and most politically powerful families in Massachusetts. Together, they were the subject of a famous New England toast that ran, "Here's to Massachusetts/Land of the bean and cod/Where Cabots speak only to Lodges/And Lodges speak only to God." Educated at Harvard College and Harvard Law School, Lodge was a lecturer in political science at his alma mater for three years before becoming editor of the conservative journal *International Review.* He served two years in the Massachusetts legislature before joining his family's law firm in 1881. He returned to politics six years later, winning a seat in the House of Representatives in 1887. Lodge remained in the lower house until 1893, when the state legislature elected him to the U.S. Senate.

Opposite. Edith Bolling Galt, the second Mrs. Woodrow Wilson, who was suspected by many of wielding inordinate power after her husband's debilitating stroke in 1919.

Above. Woodrow Wilson (*far left*) and his Cabinet, including Secretary of State William Jennings Bryan (*center*).

The Russian Revolution, led
by Lenin, would have a far
greater impact on conservative social philosophy than
anyone would have thought
possible in 1917. After the
rise of Stalin, opposition to
the expansion of Commu-
nism became an obsession
with conservatives.

"Wilson's Baby," the League of Nations, imperiled by conservative "bloodhounds" from the Senate. The bloodhounds won.

In 1918 the Republicans won control of the Congress back from the Democrats, and Henry Cabot Lodge, now one of the most senior Republican senators, was chairman of the Foreign Relations Committee. No treaty could go to the full body without first being reviewed and voted on by his committee. A pre-McKinley isolationist, Lodge was having nothing to do with any League of Nations or anything else that smacked of "one-world" government. Wilson expected Lodge's opposition to the League, but the thunderous cheers he had heard everywhere he went in Europe convinced him of the rightness of the thing, and he intended to bring his case to the American people, certain that they would put enough pressure on the Senate to force ratification. (The differences between Wilson and Lodge went far beyond the merely political; they hated each other. Wilson considered Lodge an anti-democratic patrician living in the wrong country and

His mind and body ravaged by a series of strokes, Woodrow Wilson returned briefly to the spotlight in 1921 when he attended the dedication of the Tomb of the Unknown Soldier.

the wrong century. Lodge thought Wilson was a megalomaniac who had completely lost his mind in Europe and wanted to use the League to become president of the world.) Accordingly, Wilson embarked on an 8000-mile speaking tour through the Midwest and Far West shortly after his arrival home in an effort to drum up support for the League. American honor was at stake, he thundered. The League had been his idea, and for the Senate to reject it now would not be an embarrassment for him personally, but for the President of the United States as the leader of the world. But a wave of isolationism affects every country after every foreign war, and the response to his plea was not nearly what Wilson had hoped for. He was agitated, upset, and exhausted, but he continued with the trip, hoping to find the spark that would ignite the people and rally them to his cause. On September 25, 1919, after delivering a speech in Pueblo, Colorado, he collapsed in his hotel room. The remainder of the trip was cancelled, and Wilson returned to Washington. On October 3, while shaving in his bathroom, he suffered a stroke that left him paralyzed and unable to speak.

His recovery was slow and agonizing. For the first weeks he saw no one but his wife and doctor. Legislative bills sent up to the Presidential sickroom came back signed in a shaky and unfamiliar hand. No one was sure whether it was actually Wilson signing the bills, or his wife, or his doctor. No one was certain that the President was even conscious. Each day brought new rumors that he was dead, or dying, or had been dead for weeks. When he finally reappeared in public, he was but a shell of the man that the country remembered. Still, he fought for the League.

In the Senate, Lodge succeeded in adding amendments to the treaty placing strict limitations on American participation in the League before releasing the treaty for a vote. Wilson instructed the Democrats to vote it down, and in November they did so. It would be his League or no League. He resubmitted the treaty. Lodge added new amendments. Wilson instructed the Democrats again, and in March 1920, they voted it down again.

Despite his crippled condition, Wilson actually hoped to be nominated again at the Democratic Convention in 1920, though he would do nothing in his own behalf. The mention of his name brought tumultuous cheers on the convention floor, but the nomination went to Governor James Cox of Ohio, with young Franklin Roosevelt of New York as his running mate. When the two made a joint visit to the invalid in the White House after the campaign began, Wilson extracted a pledge from Cox to make the League the central issue of the campaign. In November the Republican candidate, Ohio Senator Warren G. Harding, rolled up sixty-four percent of the popular vote to thirty-six for Cox. It was and remains the worst defeat ever suffered by a major-party candidate for President. Wilson was crushed, and the League was dead.

Many people are surprised to learn that Warren Harding gained a greater percentage of the popular vote than any other candidate in history. (Excepting, of course, General Washington, who ran unopposed. Popular vote totals are unknown for the first nine presidential elections, and electoral vote returns indicate that in their reelection campaigns, both Jefferson and Monroe may have won bigger percentages than Harding, but this can not be determined with any accuracy.) Harding ranks at or near the bottom of everyone's list of presidential achievers. His short term in office was riddled with graft and corruption reaching to the highest levels of the government. But in 1920, and in retrospect, Harding may well have been the perfect choice to kick off that period known ever after as "The Roaring Twenties."

During Wilson's time in office three amendments had been added to the Constitution which would affect the political life of the nation to varying degrees. The seventeenth amendment provided for direct election of United States senators by popular vote instead of election by the state legislatures; it was ratified in 1913. The eighteenth amendment, ratified in 1919, banned the manufacture and sale of alcoholic beverages in the U.S. and was popularly known as the Prohibition Amendment. The nineteenth, ratified in 1920, extended to women the right to vote in all elections. This last amendment would have the most profound and far-reaching effects on America's political development, but in ways that were subtle and not easily defined, at least at the outset.

Prohibition was as subtle as a tommy gun. The ban on the legal sale of alcohol gave rise to an entire criminal industry, and its violence and corrupting effect on society concurrently plagued and thrilled the nation for the next twelve years. With Prohibition came the mob, the speakeasy, bathtub gin, wholesale murder in the streets, the FBI, and F. Scott Fitzgerald. Prohibition was twentieth century America's adolescent fling, and it affected the life of every citizen, wet or dry.

Left. A cartoonist's impression of Massachusetts Senator Henry Cabot Lodge.

Below. The end of World War I brought about the formation of one of the nation's most enduring—and conservative—veteran's social organizations—the American Legion.

The irrepressible Al Smith, Governor of New York.

In Paris, a group of self-exiled American writers and artists led by Ernest Hemingway entered their period of "disillusionment" following the end of World War I and produced a body of left-wing though highly successful work that has come to characterize the art and literature of the age. At home, some writers lesser known then and now, most notably Willa Cather and Edith Wharton, continued in the tradition of Cooper, Irving, Hawthorne, and Robert Louis Stevenson by turning out works of conservative social commentary that were not overtly political. Certainly Cather's *A Lost Lady*, *My Antonia*, and *Death Comes to the Archbishop* can stand alongside of the great liberal works of the Paris group in the twenties.

Among those (and there were many) who gave public lip service to the noble ideals of Prohibition and then went home to wash their mouths out with bourbon was Wilson's successor in the White House, Warren G. Harding. Born in Morrow County, Ohio, a few months after the close of the Civil War, he graduated from Ohio Central College at the age of eighteen and the following year scraped together enough money to buy a failing newspaper, *The Marion Star*. A good newspaperman, Harding turned the *Star* into a financial success, and his consistent editorial support of Republican candidates and policies brought him into the highest echelons of the state party hierarchy. In 1899, he was nominated for a seat in the state senate, and won it easily. Four years later he was elected lieutenant governor of the state, but declined to run for re-election, returning instead to manage the *Star*. In 1909, however, he campaigned for the Republican

nomination for governor and won, but was badly defeated in the general election. He determined to stay out of politics after that, returning to the limelight only briefly at the 1912 national convention to place in nomination the name of his friend and fellow Ohioan President Taft.

In 1914 he was urged by friends to run for the U.S. Senate, but he was reluctant to face another defeat. His friends pressed him, however, and their pressure, combined with his own antipathy toward the liberalism of the Wilson Administration, convinced him to make the race. A nationwide Republican gain in that off-year election helped carry him into office.

Once in the Senate, Harding enthusiastically joined "the club" of conservative Republicans who dominated the Party, and was rewarded for his loyalty by being named keynote speaker and then permanent chairman of the 1916 convention that nominated Hughes. Had they not both been from the East, Hughes might well have chosen the handsome, silver-tongued Harding as his running mate. Still, Harding had made enough of an impression on the delegates to warrant remembrance.

In 1920 Harding's campaign manager, Harry Daugherty, bluntly informed his boss that his reelection campaign for the Senate could very well be in trouble. During his first term in the Senate, Harding had missed almost half of the roll call votes, introduced no important legislation, and had voted for Prohibition after previously stating that he was

Clarence Darrow, the liberal attorney who supported William Jennings Bryan three times for President, and opposed him in the Scopes Monkey Trial in 1925.

Opposite. Warren G. Harding, whose silver tongue and handsome countenance propelled him to the White House, where he presided over the most corrupt administration in American history.

opposed to it. The people of Ohio were beginning to wonder whether they were getting the kind of representation they deserved. To avoid disaster, Daugherty convinced Harding to capitalize on the good will he had built up at the 1916 convention. The surest way to be reelected to the Senate, he reasoned, was to make Harding appear to be a national party power. To do that, he convinced the Senator to enter several Presidential primaries. A decent showing would impress the folks back home.

Harding entered three primaries, winning the one in Ohio. Though finishing far behind in the other two, he did well enough to believe that the strategy had worked and his reelection was assured. He wanted to drop out of the Presidential race, but Daugherty convinced him that he had nothing to lose by controlling the Ohio delegates at the convention, and so he remained a nominal candidate. On the first day of the convention, a deadlock developed between the two leading candidates, General Leonard Wood (who had been Teddy Roosevelt's commanding officer in Cuba) and Illinois Governor Frank Lowden. Both refused to withdraw, and after the first session recessed, party leaders held a meeting at which it was decided that all of the uncommitted delegates would vote for the third candidate in the race, Warren Harding. On the tenth ballot the next day, Harding was nominated.

Surprised as he was by the turn of events, Harding threw himself into the race with renewed vigor. When his Democratic opponent Cox announced that he was making the election a referendum on the League of Nations, the election of Harding and his running mate, Massachusetts Governor Calvin Coolidge, became a certainty. What no one expected was the size of the victory, as the American people went to the polls in droves and rejected Cox, Wilson, and the League by giving Harding sixteen million votes to only nine million for the Democrats. Eight million more people voted in the election of 1920 than had voted four years earlier, and Harding garnered eight million more votes than his Republican predecessor Hughes, while the Democratic vote in the two elections stayed virtually the same. The difference was women, and it would seem that every woman who voted in 1920 voted for Warren Harding.

His administration, as noted previously, was a disaster, but no one knew it while Harding was alive. His Cabinet included such distinguished men as Hughes, who was given the State Department, Andrew Mellon at the Treasury, Herbert Hoover—who had done so much to relieve the suffering of refugees in Europe during the war, now Secretary of Commerce—and Henry C. Wallace of Iowa, a leading farm expert, as Secretary of Agriculture.

Unfortunately, it also included Daugherty as Attorney General and several old cronies from Harding's Senate days, most notably Albert Fall of New Mexico, who took over the Interior Department. Among the few things that Harding had time to accomplish in office was the appointment of the first director of the budget, and here he made another fine choice, naming Charles G. Dawes of Illinois, who would go on to become Vice President of the United States and win the Nobel Peace Prize for his work on the Locarno Treaties. Harding did show solid conservative tendencies while in office, increasing the protective tariff and vetoing a pension bill for World War I veterans that would have put a huge strain on the budget. Harding would have signed it, he said, had the bill made some provision for locating the necessry revenue.

During a speaking tour in the West in the summer of 1923, Harding was felled by what appeared to be a severe case of indigestion. He recovered within a couple of days and tried to go on with the tour, but after he arrived in San Francisco, pneumonia set in, and he died on August 2. Medical historians have since argued about whether the indigestion was a heart attack, or whether someone had tried to poison Harding to prevent him from investigating the rumors of irregularities in his administration that were just beginning to reach his ears. Speculation was fueled by the fact that the pneumonia seemed to be passing

President Calvin Coolidge, apparently smiling.

and that his death came as a surprise to his doctors, who suspected then that a blood clot may have killed the President. They would never know for sure, because Mrs. Harding refused to allow an autopsy to be done.

Whatever the cause of the President's death, it soon became apparent that there was a great deal of shady activity going on in his Administration. Contract fraud and stock manipulations at the Interior Department and outright theft at the Veteran's Bureau would send Fall, Daugherty, and Veteran's Bureau chief Charles Forbes to prison, and would cloud forever the memory of Harding, who had appointed them.

Calvin Coolidge succeeded to the Presidency on Harding's death, sworn in by his father, at whose home he was staying when he was awakened after midnight on August 3rd and informed of the tragic event that had occurred in San Francisco. He was fifty-one years old in 1923, a graduate of prestigious Amherst College, and a former state senator,

TRIM
WHEREVER
YOU CAN
C.C.

One cartoonist's version of Coolidge's approach to government expenditures.

lieutenant governor, and governor of Massachusetts. During his term as governor, the police in Boston went out on strike because they had not been allowed to form a union and join Samuel Gompers' American Federation of Labor. With the mayor of Boston unable to restore order, Coolidge called out the state militia to patrol the city and threatened to have all of the strikers fired if they did not return to work. Gompers complained publicly that the policemen were being treated unfairly, and Coolidge replied to him in a telegram stating, "There is no right to strike against the public safety any time, anywhere." The remark made Coolidge a hero to a nation that had had its fill of violent labor unrest, and it gained him the Vice Presidential nomination at the Republican convention the following year.

Easily the most conservative President since McKinley, Coolidge kept the scandals that were rocking the nation from affecting the dignity of the office of President itself by his own upright behavior. He ended the drinking parties and card games that had become a staple of White House life since Harding's inauguration, and ordered every government official to cooperate fully with the law enforcement agencies that were investigating corruption in the government.

In April of 1924 Coolidge vetoed a bonus bill for veterans, again because the Congress was making no provision for the revenue needed to pay for it. His veto was overridden, but

NEW YORK LIFE ~ In this issue
25 29F
Life
March 1, 1929
10¢
CC
Good-Bye, Old Pal!

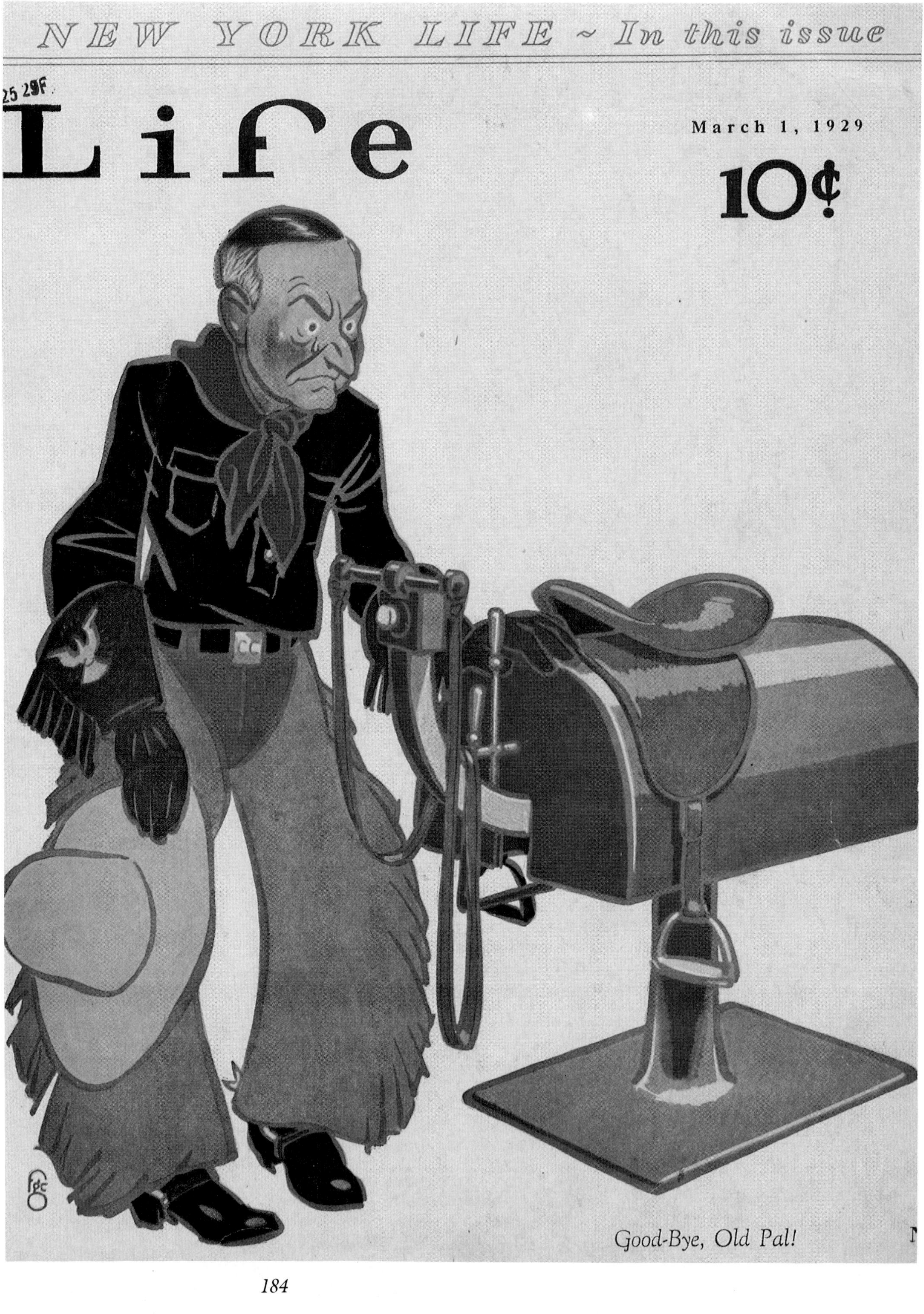

Opposite. Calvin Coolidge says goodbye to the rodeo of American politics, and *Life* says goodbye to Coolidge, shortly before the conservative President's term drew to a close in March, 1929.

Left. William Gibbs McAdoo, trying to shake his image as a Wall Street lawyer during the 1924 primary campaign.

when he vetoed another bill that would have raised the pensions for all war veterans, he did some congressional arm-twisting to make sure it was upheld.

The Republican convention nominated Coolidge for President in his own right in the summer of 1924, and a few weeks later, the most cantakerous, bitter, and divisive Democratic National Convention ever opened in New York City's Madison Square Garden.

The issues were Prohibition, Protestantism, the rise of the Ku Klux Klan, oil, Wall Street, and the League. The principal players were New York Governor Al Smith, William Gibbs McAdoo, Alabama Senator Oscar W. Underwood, and, as ever, William Jennings Bryan. For ballot after ballot, with the temperature in the Garden estimated to be 120° Fahrenheit, the convention was deadlocked between Smith, a Roman Catholic who opposed Prohibition and who denounced the Klan, and McAdoo, former Secretary of the Treasury, oilman, and son-in-law of the late President Wilson, who was supported by the

Klan, endorsed Prohibition, and hated Smith. In the months before the Convention it appeared that McAdoo would be the certain nominee. But after the Harding scandals broke, McAdoo was linked to business deals with E.L. Doheny, who stood accused of bribing Interior Secretary Fall to the tune of some $400,000. The western progressives and farmers who had supported him now feared that McAdoo might be a tool of big business and "the East," as they called Wall Street. The Klan, whom McAdoo refused to repudiate, would not abandon him, believing that he was the only man who could stop Smith and prevent a despised Roman Catholic from heading the ticket. Underwood hoped to be a compromise candidate, supporting Prohibition but denouncing the Klan. And Bryan was in New York offering himself not as a candidate but as the conscience of the party, which he determined would be dry, pro-farmer, fundamentalist, anti-Catholic, anti-oil, and ignorant of the Klan.

When the balloting had gone on for two weeks and no candidate was any closer to a majority than when they'd begun, there was serious talk of adjourning the convention and re-opening it somewhere else, perhaps when cooler heads (and afternoons) prevailed. Finally, after sixteen days and 103 ballots, the Convention nominated John W. Davis of West Virginia, former ambassador to Great Britain, for President. Though nominally from the South, he was anti-Klan, not a fundamentalist, had been a Wall Street lawyer, and had no strong feelings about Prohibition, though he approved of the platform plank supporting it. In a bid for party unity, the convention nominated William Jennings Bryan's brother Charles for Vice President.

Under other circumstances, Davis might have been a very effective candidate, but as it was, the Democratic Party was so divided and dispirited that Coolidge coasted to victory in November, rolling up fifty-six percent of the popular vote to less than thirty percent for Davis. The remainder of the votes went to Robert La Follette, Republican senator from Wisconsin who was so disillusioned with the conservatism of the two major candidates that he revived Teddy Roosevelt's Progressive Party and presented himself as the only liberal in the race.

During his second term, Coolidge directed most of his efforts toward economics, having declared in 1924 that "the business of America is business." He substantially reduced the national debt, kept tariffs at a reasonably high level, and refused to grant subsidies to farmers in the West or to permit the government to buy surplus crops for sale abroad. The government was not in the grocery business, he reasoned.

In foreign policy, Coolidge was not afraid to invoke the Monroe Doctrine or its Roosevelt Corollary, keeping a contingent of Marines in Haiti and sending them into Nicaragua to fight the rebel leader Augusto César Sandino. During his Administration, two of his highest officials, Vice President Charles Dawes (the former budget director) and Secretary of State Frank B. Kellogg, won Nobel Peace Prizes for their work in easing international tensions. (The normally unflappable "Silent Cal" had once become enraged at Dawes when Democrats and progressive Republicans blocked the President's appointment of a conservative, Charles Warren, as Attorney General. Warren lost on a tie vote, while Dawes, who as Vice President could have broken the tie and given Warren the office, slept through the roll call in his Washington hotel room.)

Coolidge surprised everyone in 1927 when he issued his "I do not choose to run for president in 1928" statement, sending a field of candidates scrambling to put together campaign staffs. The most effective was Commerce Secretary Herbert Hoover, whom President Coolidge had dubbed "the wonduh boy," indicating his dislike of the man. Hoover had nearly enough delegates to win the nomination before the convention opened in Kansas City, but not quite enough, and a determined "Stop Hoover" movement formed on the floor before the first vote was taken. It was led by old-guard conservatives who perceived Hoover as being too liberal in his social policies. They hoped to draft

Left. "Economy Is Idealism in
Its Most Practical Form."

Below. Political cartoon savaging Coolidge's interventionist policy in Nicaragua.
He would not be the last
conservative President to find
that small Central American
country a political quagmire.

COOLIDGE CROSING THE GULF

Drawing by Art Young

"This government has felt a moral obligation to apply its principles in order to encourage the Central American States in their efforts to prevent revolution and disorder . . ."
"There is no question that if the revolution continues American investments and business interests in Nicaragua will be very seriously affected, if not destroyed. The currency, which is now at par, will be inflated. American, as well as foreign bondholders will undoubtedly look to the United States for the protection of their interests. . . ."

"I am sure that it is not the desire of the United States to intervene in the internal affairs of Nicaragua or any other Central American Republic. Nevertheless, it must be said, that we have a very definite and special interest in the maintenance of order and good government in Nicaragua at the present time, and that the stability, prosperity, and independence of all Central American countries can never be a matter of indifference to us. . . ."
Cal Coolidge, President, U. S. A.

"Blah, they'll soon forget him! He's only a hero!"

Coolidge despite his disavowal, which was ambiguous at best. But Hoover's floor managers kept his pledged delegates in line, and picked up enough unpledged delegates to put Hoover over the top on the first ballot.

Herbert Clark Hoover was born in West Branch, Iowa, in August 1874, and went west to Oregon to live with relatives after the death of both his parents before his tenth birthday. He attended the then-new Stanford University in California, gaining his engineering degree in 1895. Engineering would take Hoover all over the world, and make him a wealthy man at an early age. He managed a British gold-mining operation in Australia for two years, then accepted an offer from the government of China to become chief of that country's bureau of mines. He was in Tientsin when the anti-Western Boxer Rebellion broke out, and Hoover personally directed the construction of barricades for the besieged foreign quarter. He next accepted an offer of a partnership in another British mining company, and he lived in London until the outbreak of World War I.

When the war came, Hoover organized the evacuation of the 100,000 Americans living in Europe, and came home himself to direct relief operations for war-torn Belgium, where famine had broken out. In 1917, after the United States had entered the war, President Wilson appointed Hoover Food Administrator of the United States, empowering him to set food prices and limit production of certain foodstuffs in favor of others. The following year, Hoover hit the campaign trail with Wilson, ostensibly to support the war effort, but in reality hoping to reelect certain key Democratic congressmen favorable to the administration. This was something that conservative Republicans would never forget nor forgive, and Hoover briefly considered switching parties when it appeared that his chances of gaining higher office might be better with the Democrats.

In 1920, Hoover announced that he intended to remain a Republican, and his name was offered to the convention as a possible nominee by the progressive wing of the Party. When Harding won the nomination, Hoover supported him in the belief that Harding favored entry into the League, but after Cox's manifesto, Harding reaffirmed his opposition to the League. Too late for Hoover, who was already committed. Harding genuinely admired Hoover, though, and after his election offered him the Interior Department, but Hoover preferred Commerce. Harding had to fight and then compromise with conservatives to get Hoover into the Cabinet, promising to bring Andrew Mellon in to head Treasury if they would accept Hoover at Commerce. After Harding's death, Coolidge retained as many members of Harding's Cabinet as he could (those not packing for the trip to Leavenworth), and Hoover remained at his post for the duration of Coolidge's adminstration.

Still, the conservative Coolidge loathed Hoover, and went out of his way to see as little of him as possible. After the President dropped his "I do not to choose to run" bombshell, Hoover travelled to the White House to personally ask Coolidge if he, Hoover, could enter some of the Republican primaries. Why he felt he needed the President's permission is unclear, but most likely Hoover believed that Coolidge was still hoping to be drafted by the convention. At any rate, Coolidge probably believed that Hoover's liberalism would alienate him from the country at large, and certainly he foresaw a strong enough conservative element within the party to deny Hoover the nomination. And so like other men who see things that never were, Coolidge said (literally), "Why not?"

The Democrats in 1928 nominated Al Smith for President, and that "happy warrior of the political battlefield," as Franklin Roosevelt called him in his nominating speech, made the repeal of Prohibition the centerpiece of his campaign. It obviously had not kept people from drinking (alcoholism was at a higher peak in the country than at any previous time), it had turned crime into an organized industry, and it deprived the government of needed revenue from excise taxes, Smith argued. Hoover, on the other hand, referred to Prohibition as a "noble experiment" and pledged to keep the law on the books. Beyond

Opposite. Life's view of the fickleness of American society in 1927.

Hail to the Chiefs. With this group, Coolidge looks downright animated.

Prohibition, the two differed little on social issues or foreign policy, and the election might reasonably have been expected to be closer than it was. But Al Smith was a Roman Catholic, and bigotry against Catholics in this country was as strong in the 1920s as it had been in the time of the Know Nothings, especially in the South, where the Ku Klux Klan was at the height of its political power. In November, Hoover garnered nearly sixty percent of the popular vote, and took a greater percentage of the electoral votes than any candidate since Grant beat Horace Greeley in 1872. (In point of fact, Greeley didn't get any of the electoral votes available that year, since he died before the electoral college could meet. The sixty-six votes pledged to him were divided among four of his supporters.)

In the thirty years since the Spanish-American War, conservatism had shaken off much of the "gentility" that had marked its formation in the nineteenth century. No longer a philosophy that appealed mainly to the well-born and wealthy, conservatism now attracted adherents from all social classes who believed that the essential roles of government were to ensure the stability necessary for the continued expansion of commerce, and to aggressively assert American predominance in world affairs so as to discourage other nations from taking action to disrupt that stability.

Through the machinations of party politics, the American people had not been offered a conservative choice in the election of 1928, but the ascendancy of the liberal Hoover should not be viewed as a rejection of conservatism by the people. Had Coolidge run, there is every reason to believe that he would have won the election by as wide a margin as he had in 1924, if he did not better that showing. Conservative leaders, while disappointed, were not discouraged, believing it would be only a short time until they re-established their dominance of the American political scene. Had they been gambling men, they would have bet on it. And like so many other people in a short time to come, they would have lost their money.

7 On the Outside Looking In 1929–1952

Herbert Hoover had been in office for seven months when the stock market crashed on October 24, 1929. But the market had crashed before, and despite the well-publicized suicides of several speculators who had lost their fortunes, no immediate panic set in. Hoover set out to work with the business community to bolster the nation's confidence, even orchestrating an appearance by Henry Ford at the White House. Ford emerged from lunch with the President and announced that he was so confident of the economy's imminent recovery that he was giving Ford Motor Company workers a raise. But Ford's confidence was misplaced, and the economy did not recover. It continued to sag, and within a year thousands of businesses large and small had closed, and more than twelve million people were unemployed.

Hoover asked Congress for substantial cuts in the income-tax rate, and though Congress complied, the measure did little to stimulate the economy. So many people suddenly had no income that a reduction in taxes they could not pay anyway was meaningless. Though he did authorize a massive public works program, beyond that Hoover followed the example of Grover Cleveland for Presidential action during a depression. He would not refashion the function of the American government, and refused to institute direct federal relief funds for the unemployed. He also vetoed the Bonus Act of 1931 giving almost a billion dollars to veterans, but in February Congress passed the measure over his veto. Like the public works program, it was a short-term answer to a problem that now had all the makings of becoming a long-term disaster.

Though a conservative response to an economic depression always has and always will sound cold and heartless, even the liberal Hoover, whose political career had been launched by his effective and compassionate response to the pleas of the starving people of Europe during World War I, realized that he could not follow the course being urged on him by liberal leaders of the labor movement and the Congress without rejecting what the Constitution said was the purpose of American government, and replacing it with a new, socialist mandate. That he would not do.

And so he was replaced by a man who would. Franklin Roosevelt campaigned for the Presidency in 1932 offering the American people a "New Deal" and a way out of the crisis. What he was offering them was not just a new deal, but a new system of government and a new system of economics. He was offering them a kind of socialism, but he was careful not to call it that, and the people were so desperate for an end to the Depression that they might not have cared if he had.

Franklin Delano Roosevelt was born in Hyde Park, New York, on January 30, 1882. He was a distant cousin to Theodore Roosevelt, but he did not get to know the Republican Roosevelt until the latter was in the White House and Franklin was marrying Teddy's niece (and another of his distant cousins) Eleanor. After attending the prestigious Groton School as a boy, Roosevelt went on to graduate from Harvard University in 1903 and the

Columbia University Law School in 1907. After serving a term in the state legislature in New York, he followed in his famous cousin's footsteps by accepting President Wilson's offer of an appointment as Assistant Secretary of the Navy. He kept the job throughout Wilson's two terms, and was considered a Democratic Party "star" at the 1920 convention, where he was nominated for Vice President on the ticket with Cox. But his star seemed to set when the ticket was swamped by Harding and Coolidge in November, and his political career seemed surely to be doomed when he was crippled by an attack of polio in 1921. Political campaigning was a business for vigorous men, and it was inconceivable in 1921 that anyone could be vigorous from a wheelchair.

But Franklin Roosevelt was not yet forty years old, and he refused to believe that his life, political and otherwise, was over because he could no longer walk. After years of painful rehabilitative therapy, Roosevelt was able to maneuver so well on crutches that many people watching him could not tell that his legs were useless and that he was getting around on the sheer strength of his upper body. By 1924 he was active in politics again, managing Al Smith's unsuccessful campaign for the Democratic nomination. In 1928 he again placed Smith's name in nomination at the convention, and when Smith this time won the nomination, Roosevelt went back to New York and campaigned as the Democratic candidate to succeed Smith as governor. In November, Roosevelt won the election, but Smith failed to carry his home state against Hoover. In large measure Smith blamed Roosevelt for that, believing that Roosevelt deliberately distanced himself from Smith during the campaign because he believed that Smith was a sure loser. The charge was true, but Roosevelt could not be blamed. What he realized, and Smith did not, was that many New Yorkers loved having the brash and cocky Al as their governor, but could not in good conscience inflict him on the nation.

As governor during the first years of the Depression, Roosevelt saw the ravaging effect it was having on the people of New York and underwent a political metamorphosis. Though always a liberal progressive, he had always been a capitalist as well. Now he rejected pure capitalism as being unable to deal with "breaks" in the economy other than to let economic nature take its course and wait for the pendulum to swing back toward prosperity. That was unacceptable to Roosevelt, because the suffering of the people was very real and he believed that many would not survive if they had to wait too long. And so he developed a philosophy of capitalism diluted by a heavy dose of socialism. As governor he instituted the first direct payments of relief money to the unemployed and advocated the implementation of a social security system to guarantee pensions for the aged. To explain his new philosophy he chose very old words, words that could be found in the Constitution itself. "The first duty of a state," he declared, "and by state I mean Government, is to promote the welfare of the citizens of that state." But Roosevelt was giving the word "promote" a meaning that had not been intended by the men who framed the Constitution, a meaning that far better suits the phrase "provide for." And if a government is to provide for the welfare of its citizens, that government *must* reject a *laissez faire* stance toward commerce and industry, and appropriate unto itself either the means of production through direct ownership, or the fruits of production through massive taxation of profits. And that is socialism, no matter how you cut the cards.

Roosevelt called his philosophy the "New Deal" and offered it to the people, and the people enthusiastically accepted. He beat Hoover in the 1932 Presidential election by a larger margin than that by which Hoover beat Smith, and carried more states in the process. In his inaugural address he put Congress on notice that if it would not act to alleviate the crisis by implementing his program, then he would demand that it vote him "broad Executive power to wage a war against the emergency, as great a power as would be given me if we were in fact invaded by a foreign foe." Roosevelt's brash assertion that he as President would be granted what he stopped just short of calling dictatorial power in a

Franklin Delano Roosevelt, thirty-second President of the United States. After him, "conservatism" and "liberalism" would have entirely new meanings.

time of national invasion by a foreign country is questionable at best, but his assertion that he would be within his constititutional rights to request such power in peacetime was, to conservatives, dangerous heresy. It was also unnecessary, because the Democratic Congress had every intention of adopting his program wholesale.

In Roosevelt's first hundred days as President, Congress enacted or created the Agricultural Adjustment Act, giving government the right to decide what crops should be planted in an effort to eliminate surpluses; the National Industrial Recovery Act, bringing American industry under direct control of the government; the Tennessee Valley Authority, bringing hydroelectric power to the poorest part of the country; the Homeowners' Loan Corporation; the Federal Relief Administration to distribute money to the states for relief of the unemployed; and the Civilian Conservation Corps to provide work for unemployed youth.

Roosevelt's first foreign policy act was to establish diplomatic relations with the Soviet Union.

193

Right. Campaign sewing kit from the unsuccessful reelection bid of President Herbert Hoover in 1932.

Opposite. Conservative political cartoon savaging F.D.R.'s New Deal.

Before his first term was over, Roosevelt would push Congress to enact bills creating the Social Security System, federal unemployment insurance, the Securities and Exchange Commission, the Federal Housing Authority, and a host of other boards, commissions and agencies with the power to establish regulations affecting nearly every aspect of America's commercial, industrial, economic and political life.

The Depression continued. In 1936 Roosevelt ran for reelection on a platform admitting that there was no quick cure for a depression as pervasive as this one, but that his social programs would bring relief if they were given the time to take root and grow. Again the people responded, giving Roosevelt an even greater margin of victory than he had received in 1932. His record tally of 523 electoral votes would stand until it was surpassed by Ronald Reagan in 1984. The hapless victim buried under this electoral avalanche was Kansas Governor Alf Landon, who received 8 electoral votes by carrying only Maine and Vermont.

Though Congress gave him virtually everything he asked for and the people stood behind him, Roosevelt ran into a bloc of opposition in the form of the Supreme Court. In 1935 it had struck down the NIRA and the AAA as unconstitutional, and with his second term mandate so large Roosevelt felt powerful enough to deal with the Court. Six of the nine justices were over seventy years old, so Roosevelt proposed legislation that would require a mandatory retirement age for Supreme Court justices, with that age to be coincidentally set at seventy. Even his most ardent supporters refused to go along with Roosevelt on this one, pointing out the Constitution guaranteed justices lifetime appointments. But what the Constitution did not do, Roosevelt reasoned, was set the number of justices who could sit on the Court. So he proposed different legislation which would allow the President to appoint a new justice for every justice who reached the age

VOICE OF THE PEOPLE

Governor Alfred E. Landon of Kansas, one of the biggest losers in presidential election history.

of seventy and did not retire. This would have brought the number of Supreme Court justices in 1937 to fifteen. Roosevelt took the plan to the people, discussing it during one of his radio broadcasts known as "Fireside Chats." But the Court itself made further confrontation unnecessary. Shortly after the President made his "court-packing" scheme public, the Court began to rule favorably on New Deal legislation that, based on its own precedents, it had been expected to strike down. It may have been coincidence, but it was more likely appeasement, not from cowardice, but to prevent Roosevelt from making the Court a permanent tool of the Executive.

Despite all of his efforts, none of Roosevelt's social programs brought an end to the Depression. It ended, as all economic depressions do, by the passage of time and the swing of the economic pendulum. This depression, the "Great Depression," took longer than most to expire because it came about with more force than most and was part of a worldwide depression in the 1930's. But in the meantime, Franklin Roosevelt had fundamentally changed the structure and function of the government, and with it the political agenda of both liberals and conservatives. True conservatism went out when Calvin Coolidge chose not to run in 1928, and from the rise of Franklin Roosevelt until the rise of Ronald Reagan, conservatives in politics were engaged not in setting forth their own agenda, but merely limiting the excesses of the liberal society America had become.

In 1940, Roosevelt did choose to run again, for an unprecedented third term in the

White House. He was opposed by Wendell Willkie, a liberal industrialist in the mold of Herbert Hoover who had not sought previous political office. In the popular vote totals, Willkie did better than the previous two Republican predecessors by taking forty-five percent of the vote, but Roosevelt swamped him in the electoral vote column. With the economy having stabilized by 1939 (though it was nowhere near as healthy as it had been in 1928), Roosevelt in his third term was able to devote more attention to foreign affairs. War had broken out again in Europe in 1939, and though Roosevelt, like Wilson before him, hoped to avoid direct American intervention, he pushed legislation through Congress enabling the American government to materially aid the Allied war effort.

Above. Franklin Roosevelt and his wife, Eleanor. After his death in 1945, she carried on his work, becoming perhaps the foremost spokeswoman for liberal causes in the country.

Many liberals in the United States favored American participation in the war, some to counter the rising tide of Fascism in Europe and others, after the German invasion of Russia in June 1941, to come to the aid of the Soviet Union. In an effort to counter the influence of liberal interventionists with the administration, a group of mainly conservative national figures formed a committee called America First, espousing the principles of neutrality and non-intervention. Though the group did attract some well-known liberals and Progressives such as Burton K. Wheeler and Philip La Follette, son of the late Progressive Party leader, in the main it was comprised of conservatives who were unwilling to fight Germany to save the Soviet Union, though they were concerned about Great Britain and urged that country to negotiate peace with Hitler for herself and the Western European nations that had been overrun by the Nazis. The most prominent spokesman for America First was the aviation hero Colonel Charles Lindbergh.

America First came to an abrupt end on December 7, 1941, when the Japanese Navy and Air Force launched a devastating sneak attack on the U.S. naval installation at Pearl Harbor, Hawaii. The next day, Roosevelt asked for and received a declaration of war against Japan, Germany and Italy from Congress.

197

Benito Mussolini, the Fascist dictator of Italy. He made the trains run on time, then plunged the rest of Italian civilization into chaos.

American entry into the war would eventually turn the tide in favor of the Allies, though there were serious military setbacks for the U.S. during the first two years of the war. In consultation with British Prime Minister Winston Churchill and Soviet Premier Joseph Stalin, his two principal allies in the war effort, Roosevelt agreed that the war in Europe should take priority, and only enough American forces to prevent a Japanese victory were committed to the war in the Pacific. It was a bitter decision for General Douglas MacArthur, who had overall command of the forces fighting the Japanese, as he watched the United States lose the Philippine Islands and other possessions in the South Pacific to the barbaric Japanese Army, while he remained in his Australian headquarters, virtually helpless to do anything about it.

During the course of the war several summit conferences were held among the Allied leaders, at Cairo in November 1943, at Teheran in December of that year, and most significantly, at Yalta in the Crimea from February 4 through 11, 1945. After the Allied invasion of the European continent in June 1944, the defeat of Germany became only a matter of time and attrition. By the time the Yalta Conference opened, the Nazi armies were crumbling and staggering back into Germany, and complete German capitulation was less than three months away. The Allied leaders were thus able to turn their attention to the defeat of Japan. Until this time, Russia had not declared war on Japan and took no part in the Allied defense of Asia and the Pacific. In return for a Soviet declaration of war against the Japanese, Roosevelt (over Churchill's initial objections but with the Briton's

JOSEPH V. STALIN   FRANKLIN DELANO ROOSEVELT   WINSTON SPENCER CHURCHILL

Three Great Leaders

Conservatives would hotly disagree with the assessment that these three were "great leaders." Understandings between Roosevelt and Stalin, with the reluctant acquiesence of Churchill, made Soviet Russia a super-power at a time when she was militarily most vulnerable to American military pressure.

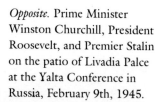

Opposite. Prime Minister
Winston Churchill, President
Roosevelt, and Premier Stalin
on the patio of Livadia Palce
at the Yalta Conference in
Russia, February 9th, 1945.

Above. Roosevelt and Churchill in a "private" moment at
Yalta.

201

eventual consent) agreed to Stalin's demands for a Soviet "sphere of influence" in the nations of Eastern Europe that had been "liberated" by the Red Army, and for a decisive role in determining the political affairs of the Far East as well.

To conservatives, it was a complete sellout of the nations of Eastern Europe to the Communist dictator Stalin. Since the Russian Revolution in 1917, conservatives had viewed the worldwide Communist movement as directed by Moscow to be the greatest threat to democratic liberty in the history of mankind, and they had not changed their opinion simply because the United States found itself temporarily allied with the Soviet Union in the fight against Fascism. (A digression: it is fashionable among political analysts to think of Fascism as "right-wing" and Communism as "left-wing" in much the same way that conservatives are said to be "on the right" and liberals "on the left," thereby implying a relationship between Fascism and conservatism and between liberalism and Communism. The notion is fatuous. Conservatism and liberalism are opposite diffractions of the democratic political spectrum; Fascism and Communism are both anti-democratic offshoots of socialism, and as such have more in common with each other than either has with the two mainstream philosophies. Thus it is no more accurate for a liberal to hurl the epithet of "Fascist" at a conservative than it would be for a conservative to call Joe Stalin a "liberal.")

In the end, the Soviets were not needed to defeat the Japanese, because the advent of the atomic bomb ended the war much sooner than an invasion of the Japanese islands could have. Roosevelt's pledges to Stalin were thus rendered unnecessary, but no less binding. FDR's defenders have argued that he had no choice but to make the agreements he did at Yalta, because he could not have foreseen how the war in the Pacific would turn out, and that he could not have prevented Stalin from holding on to all of Eastern Europe in any event. But conservatives have contended that Roosevelt certainly should have known that a joint Soviet-American invasion of Japan might well be avoided by the deployment of the atom bomb, the development of which he was keenly aware of, and that once the bomb did become available, he would then have a million American men under arms on the European continent *and* the most powerful weapon ever invented at his disposal, surely enough to persuade Stalin to withdraw the Red Army to the pre-war Russian boundaries.

It has since come to light that by the time of the Yalta Conference Roosevelt knew he was dying, and thus he could not be sure that the bomb would ever be made workable if he died before its deployment (which he did, on April 12, 1945). It would appear that he truly believed he was acting in the best interests of his country. But conservatives point out that with all the intangibles involved, a dying man should have removed himself from the position of making such a monumental decision. (There is even evidence that Roosevelt knew before the 1944 elections that he could not live too much longer, and if that is true, then his decision to run for a fourth term is open to vigorous, and perhaps ominous, question.) Other conservatives, seeing more sinister forces at work, point to the fact that one of Roosevelt's leading State Department advisers at Yalta was Alger Hiss, who it would later be confirmed had been a member of the virulently pro-Soviet American Communist Party at least into the late 1930's and possibly beyond.

In September, after the use of atomic weapons to bomb the cities of Hiroshima and Nagasaki, the Japanese surrendered and the war was over. In Europe, Communist governments were emplaced in eight countries west of the Soviet Union stretching from the Baltic to the Adriatic. Included in the eight is East Germany, severed from the western half of that country at Soviet insistence. In addition, the Soviets maintained a military presence in Berlin, and began the process of neutralizing the pro-Western foreign policy of Finland. The Soviets tried to impose a military presence in Japan as well, but their assertions toward this end were effectively rebuffed by General MacArthur, now the military governor of Japan. MacArthur would rule Japan almost single-handedly for the

next four and a half years, ending the feudal political system in the country and replacing it with a liberal democracy based on the American Constitution. In the process, he would win the undying gratitude of the Japanese people, so recently his enemies; even today his name is revered among them.

At the Potsdam Conference that lasted from July 17 to August 2, 1945, the new American President, Harry Truman, affirmed his government's intention to honor the promises made by Roosevelt to Stalin, even though he knew then that Soviet military assistance against the Japanese would not be necessary. The bomb was nearly ready, and four days after the conference ended, the first one was dropped on Hiroshima.

Harry S Truman was born in Lamar, Missouri in 1884, and as a boy moved with his family to nearby Independence. He served as an officer in World War I, rising to the rank of major. Upon his return to Independence he entered into a partnership in a men's clothing store, but the business went bankrupt. In 1922 Truman sought out Tom Pendergast, boss of the Kansas City Democratic Party machine. With Pendergast's help, Truman was elected a "judge" of Jackson County, though the job was not judicial in nature. He was in charge of granting permits for road and bridge building. He was defeated for reelection in 1924, largely because he was opposed by the Ku Klux Klan, which was then politically powerful in the South and in border states like Missouri. (The Klan mistakenly thought that Truman was part Jewish.) Returning to the business world, Truman tried his hand at a number of different ventures, none any more successful than the clothing store had been.

In 1926 Truman's political fortunes were reversed again and he won election as the presiding "judge" of Jackson County, controlling patronage positions in Kansas City that he dispersed in consultation with Pendergast. He held the job for eight years, and was rewarded for his loyalty to the "Boss" by winning the machine's endorsement in the 1934

Henry Wallace, perhaps the only man Franklin Roosevelt considered "too liberal."

Opposite. Alger Hiss, who
through the wiles of nature,
looked innocent. He wasn't.

Left. Test of an atomic bomb,
the single most important
military and political factor
in the world after 1945.

Democratic Senate primary. Truman won the primary, and was elected to the Senate in November by landslide proportions.

During his first term in Washington he was an ardent supporter of Roosevelt and the New Deal. His chances for reelection looked dim when in 1939 his friend and mentor Pendergast was sent to prison on a bribery charge. But Truman was able to separate his own reputation from Pendergast's, and in 1940 held on to win a narrow victory for a second term. During the war, Truman gained national stature as chairman of the Senate committee investigating war profiteering, saving the government some $15 billion by its diligent scrutiny of contracts. When Roosevelt had decided to run for a third term in 1940, his Vice President, John Nance Garner, had refused to support his decision and would not run with him. Roosevelt had chosen his Agriculture Secretary, Henry Wallace (son of the man who had served as Agriculture Secretary under Harding), to replace Garner on the ticket. In the course of his life Wallace consistently drifted further to the left, having started out as a Republican. By 1944, some Democratic Party leaders were afraid that Wallace, who had become enamored of the Soviet Union during the war, had become too liberal and pro-Soviet to be palatable to the American people. Roosevelt agreed that Wallace's criticisms of the Administration for not doing enough to aid the Soviets had placed him in an untenable position as Vice President, and so informed him that he would not be on the ticket in 1944, but would head up the Commerce Department instead. Roosevelt then told the party leaders that he would be happy to run with either Senator Truman or Supreme Court Justice William O. Douglas, whom he had appointed to the bench in 1939. (Again, it is highly likely that Roosevelt knew already that his next running mate would succeed him as President within a short time, and that knowledge may have played a large part in his decision to dump Wallace.) But Douglas was only a shade to the right of Wallace, and the convention chose the centrist Truman, nominating him on the second ballot. (The events at the 1944 Democratic convention would later prompt one conservative critic to remark that the best thing that could be said about Harry Truman was that he kept William Douglas out of the White House, and the worst was that he had kept William Douglas on the Supreme Court.)

Truman was presiding over the Senate when he was called to the White House on April 12, 1945 and told by First Lady Eleanor Roosevelt that the President was dead. His first presidential decision was to affirm that the organizing meeting of the United Nations, also agreed to by Roosevelt at Yalta, would go ahead as planned for the 25th of April. The man who would preside over that meeting was the State Department's Alger Hiss.

Truman's first term was a mixed political bag, reflecting the President's own fiercely independent nature. In the field of labor relations, he alternately alienated and attracted organized labor. He outraged union leaders by seizing control of the railroads during a nationwide strike in May 1946, and asking Congress to draft the strikers into the Army so he could force them to work. The union capitulated before the Congress could act. He employed the same tactic later when the coal miners went on strike, seizing the mines and operating them under the control of the Department of the Interior. His actions in these and related matters were later held to be unconstitutional by the Supreme Court.

In 1947, Truman sided with organized labor by vetoing the Taft-Hartley Act. Taft-Hartley (named for its two principal sponsors, Senator Robert Taft of Ohio and Representative Fred Hartley of New Jersey) was a conservative measure designed to correct perceived abuses by the labor movement. Among the practices it outlawed were the closed shop and automatic deduction of union dues from paychecks, while requiring a cooling-off period before strikes and a declaration of loyalty (later repealed). The measure was passed over Truman's veto, and was considered a major conservative victory.

In foreign relations, the President promulgated the Truman Doctrine, which recognized the monolithic aims of the Soviet Union and provided money to governments in

The conservative wing of the GOP was led by "Mr. Republican," Senator Robert Taft of Ohio. He would surely have been the party's nominee for President in 1952 had not Dwight Eisenhower finally decided that he, too, was a Republican.

danger of Communist takeover. The Truman Doctrine was hailed by conservatives, whose enthusiasm was dampened somewhat when it was widened to include the Marshall Plan, which provided billions of dollars for the rebuilding of Europe.

Harry Truman was widely expected to be defeated in the Presidential race in 1948. Conservative Democrats, mainly from the South, would not support him because of his liberal views on civil rights; labor wasn't sure what to make of him; progressives were rallying around former Vice President Wallace (whom Truman had fired from the Cabinet in 1946) and the Republicans, sensing victory for the first time since 1928, were going all out to win this one.

They nominated Thomas E. Dewey, the Governor of New York, who'd become famous in the 1930's for prosecuting major figures in organized crime. Though himself a liberal who had supported much New Deal legislation, Dewey had been nominated by the

Republicans to run against Roosevelt in 1944, and had made a better showing than any of FDR's other opponents, taking forty-six percent of the popular vote. His sacrificial run against Roosevelt earned him the right to run against Truman in the view of the Republican Party leadership.

Truman was aided in the campaign by his refusal to back down to the Soviets during the Berlin Crisis in July, when West Berlin, wholly surrounded by Communist East Germany, found that all ground transportation in and out of the city was cut off on orders from Moscow. Truman ordered the Air Force to fly provisions into the beleaguered city over East German air space, in effect daring the Russians to shoot down one of the planes and provoke war. The airlift continued for eleven months without incident, until the Soviets backed down and reopened ground routes.

Still, Truman was expected to lose badly, especially after the Democratic Convention when the Southern conservatives, known as the Dixiecrats, bolted from the Party and nominated Senator Strom Thurmond of South Carolina for President. The Progressive wing also bolted, nominating Henry Wallace. But Truman went on a nationwide "whistle-stop" train tour, giving hundreds of speeches between Labor Day and Election Day. For his part, Dewey seemed more concerned with making strategy for his first term as President than with campaigning for the job, and in the most stunning upset in the history of presidential politics, Truman won the election, taking just about fifty percent of the vote in a four-way race.

The four years of Harry Truman's second term saw a major regrouping of conservative forces in the country to oppose both the policies of the man in the White House and the growing threat from Communism, both internal and external. Some conservatives, notably Wisconsin Senator Joseph McCarthy, believed there was definite connection between the Truman Administration and the Communist threat.

In 1948 a man named Whittaker Chambers, then an editor for *Time* magazine, went before the House Un-American Activities Committee, the congressional group probing Communist infiltration into American life, and told what was to say the least a startling story. He told the congressmen that in the 1920's and 1930's he had been a Communist, a member of the party, and a courier of secrets to Soviet agents. The secrets he turned over to the Soviets, he went on, came from the State Department, given to him by a high-ranking official of that Department whom Chambers knew was also a Communist. That man was Alger Hiss, adviser to Roosevelt at Yalta, chairman of the first organizational meeting of the United Nations, and now president of the Carnegie Endowment for International Peace.

To recount all of the facets of the Hiss-Chambers case here would be simply impossible, and has been done extensively elsewhere. Briefly, Chambers said that he had met Hiss in the 1930's, had lived for a time in Hiss's Washington home, had been given a car by Hiss when the two parted, and had received copies of sensitive State Department documents from Hiss which he then passed on to his Soviet counterparts. Chambers further claimed that he had grown disillusioned with Communism in 1939, and had given the names of his contacts and people in government whom he knew to be Communists several times to several government agencies over the past nine years, but that no action was ever taken. Now he brought his story to HUAC, whose most aggressive anti-communist member was a second-term congressman from California, thirty-seven-year-old Richard Nixon. Hiss was called before the committee to answer the charges, and at first vigorously denied that he had ever known Chambers and challenged his accuser to repeat his accusations outside the Congress so that he might bring a suit for libel. Later, in private sessions with Nixon and other committee members, Hiss would back away from his original disavowal of Chambers, saying first that he "might" have known Chambers, and later that he did, but that he knew him simply as a man named George Crosley and that he had no

Governor Thomas Dewey of
New York, who opposed
F.D.R. in 1944, and Truman
in 1948. He led the liberal
arm of the Rupublican Party.

knowledge of Crosley/Chambers' Communist affiliations. Hiss would also deny that he had ever given State Department documents to Crosley.

In the meantime Chambers had gone on the radio to repeat his accusations, forcing Hiss to bring suit. In his defense of the libel charge, Chambers produced microfilm of copies of State Department documents that he had kept since he said they were given to him by Hiss. These documents had been copied on a typewriter that was later found to be in the possession of Alger Hiss, and on the basis of this evidence a charge of perjury was brought against Hiss by the Justice Department for lying to the congressional committee. No charges of espionage could be brought because the statute of limitations had run out. In 1950, after two trials, Hiss was found guilty of perjury and sentenced to five years in prison.

The charges against Hiss reflected badly on the Truman Administration, both because of Chambers's assertion that he had tried to tell his story before and would not be taken seriously, and because in the midst of the controversy Secretary of State Dean Acheson had declared that he would not "turn his back" on his friend Alger Hiss if he were indicted for perjury. Before the jury brought in the guilty verdict on Hiss, another blow fell on Truman's reputation as an anti-Communist. In a speech in Wheeling, West Virginia, in February 1950, Senator Joseph McCarthy of Wisconsin held a sheaf of papers over his head and announced that it was a list of 205 known Communists currently holding high-ranking positions in the Truman administration.

The Red Scare swept over the United States, gripping the nation as no other issue ever had before because of the advent of television. For the next three years McCarthy continued making accusations against the Administration, occasionally changing the number but always hammering away at the same basic theme: the Truman Administration, and especially the State Department, was riddled with Communists. He would not name them, saying that that would come in due course after a thorough Senate investigation.

In 1950 Truman had an even more pressing problem to deal with than Joe McCarthy or Alger Hiss. In June, troops from Communist North Korea swarmed over the border into South Korea intent on reuniting the country that had been partitioned after World War II, under a Communist regime. The United Nations, with the Soviets absent for the vote, condemned the aggression and called on its members to mobilize an army to repel the invasion. Made up largely of U.S. Army troops and placed under the command of General Douglas MacArthur, the U.N. forces were successful in driving the North Koreans back over their side of the border by October. But in that month, the Chinese entered the conflict and inflicted heavy casualties on the U.N. contingent. MacArthur repeatedly urged Truman to turn the conflict into a full-scale war and strike at the Chinese mainland, but Truman refused to widen the hostilities beyond the scope laid down by the U.N. So bitter did the disagreement become that in April 1951, Truman relieved MacArthur of command and ordered him home.

Douglas MacArthur had not been in the United States since 1937, when he'd left to take command of the U.S. forces in the Philippines. His reception when he arrived in Hawaii was nothing short of tumultuous, and it continued everywhere he went, culminating in the largest ticker-tape parade ever held in New York City, and then in his address to a joint session of Congress in which he uttered the immortal words "Old soldiers never die, they just fade away." There could have been no worse public relations move for Harry Truman than to fire the nearly worshipped MacArthur, but to the end of his life Truman maintained that his only regret over the incident was that he had not done it earlier.

Harry Truman announced in April 1952 that he would not run again, for although he enjoyed being President and feared a Republican victory in November, he knew that the combination of recent events insured that he could not be the man to stop it.

Opposite. President Harry Truman decorates General Douglas MacArthur on Wake Island, shortly after the outbreak of the Korean War. Later, after firing Mac-Arthur, Truman would claim that the General kept him waiting half an hour before this meeting and then treated him disrespectfully. No other witness backed the President's claim, and several disputed it.

John Dos Passos, one of the
"disillusioned" writers of the
twenties, who eventually
moved to the right.

The conservatives in Congress were getting most of the press in the early 1950's, though it was by no means a favorable press, but they were not yet strong enough to assert their domination in national party politics. In the Democratic Party, in fact, their influence would steadily wane with the rise of the civil rights movement. Conservatives trained their eyes on the Republican Party, which they had last controlled when Calvin Coolidge was President. Liberalism was still in the ascendancy in both parties, but new groups of conservative writers, philosophers, journalists, and politicians were just beginning to make their presence felt. First they would need to coalesce their ideas into a modern, cohesive conservative concept that could deal effectively with the problems of the postwar world. When they accomplished that, they could then translate their new conservatism into concrete political action that would bring them into a dominant position on the American political scene. At least, that was the plan.

8 Conservative Renaissance 1952–1969

Robert Taft campaigned hard to win the Republican nomination for President in 1952, but the liberal wing of the party had controlled the national apparatus since the days of Herbert Hoover and was determined that Taft not be the nominee. Known as "Mr. Republican," Taft was the son of former President William Howard Taft, but had rejected his father's progressivism in favor of a more conservative political outlook.

When World War II ended in 1945, leaders of both parties had looked favorably upon a possible presidential bid by General Dwight Eisenhower, hero of the war in Europe. But Eisenhower made no effort to enter politics, and was not entered in any primaries in 1948. As late as the end of 1951, people still did not know whether Eisenhower was a Republican or a Democrat. (And it is entirely possible that Eisenhower had not made up his own mind on the subject until then. It is an ongoing tradition among the American officer corps in all branches of the service never to register or to vote while on active duty, and to avoid as much as possible the formulation of partisan political opinions.) In January 1952, Eisenhower finally announced that he was a Republican, and Thomas Dewey immediately endorsed him for President. By the time the convention opened, Eisenhower had won enough delegates to win the nomination on the first ballot. The dejected Taft supported him, but never really recovered from the disappointment before he died the next year.

Eisenhower chose as his running mate Richard Nixon, who had been elected to the Senate from California on the strength of the reputation he had won as an anti-Communist during the investigation of the Hiss affair. During the campaign Nixon would face charges from the Democrats that he maintained a secret "slush fund" supplied by wealthy friends from California in return for his influence in Washington. Nixon went on television to deny the charge, and was so effective in what came to be known as his "Checkers speech" (he admitted that a friend had given his children a dog named Checkers) that Eisenhower kept him on the ticket. In November Eisenhower coasted to an easy victory over the ultra-liberal Governor Adlai Stevenson of Illinois.

During the campaign Eisenhower had dramatically announced that if elected "I will go to Korea," and so he went in December 1952 to get a firsthand look. On his way back he conferred with MacArthur in New York, though he stayed only long enough to tell the General that he agreed with Truman's plan not to widen the war. (There was never any love lost between MacArthur and Eisenhower. Ike had been MacArthur's chief of staff in the Philippines, and had been amused by his superior's military posturing. When a British woman asked Eisenhower during the war if he had ever met MacArthur, Ike replied, "Met him? I studied dramatics under him for seven years.") MacArthur gave the keynote address at the 1952 convention which nominated Eisenhower, and was rankled by the fact that it was his former underling who would go on to the White House instead of himself, a fact which rankled many conservatives as well. While watching Eisenhower's inauguration

Opposite. General Eisenhower's triumphal parade in New York after the end of World War II. Seated behind Ike is New York Mayor Fiorello La Guardia.

Left. General Dwight Eisenhower, Supreme Commander of the Allied Forces in Europe, conferring with General George S. Patton.

Below. In June, 1954, President Eisenhower (*center*) and Secretary of State Dulles (*left*) meet with Prime Minister Churchill and Foreign Secretary Anthony Eden of Great Britain on the White House lawn.

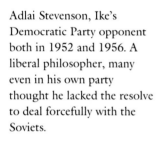

Adlai Stevenson, Ike's Democratic Party opponent both in 1952 and 1956. A liberal philosopher, many even in his own party thought he lacked the resolve to deal forcefully with the Soviets.

on television, Mrs. MacArthur asked her husband if he thought Eisenhower would make a good president. "I'm sure he will," replied the General. "He was the best clerk I ever had." Within seven months of taking office Eisenhower had agreed to a truce which would end the hostilities in Korea.

The new President called his domestic policy "Dynamic Conservatism," and it was neither. He signed legislation expanding the social security system and raising the minimum wage to a dollar an hour. Far more serious problems that confronted Eisenhower on the home front were the burgeoning civil rights movement and Joe McCarthy.

Since his original speech in Wheeling, McCarthy had continued his tirade against Communists in government, and after the 1952 elections gave Republicans a majority in the Senate he became chairman of the Senate subcommittee on investigations. From this lofty position he expanded the probe from the State Department to every government department, and to the armed services as well. But despite his dramatic statements and his sometimes vicious badgering of witnesses, McCarthy never produced the evidence to support his claims of massive Communist infiltration of the government. His downfall began during hearings in which he was investigating the Army, when he accused the Secretary of the Army of concealing Communist espionage activity. During his rebuttal the Secretary made it known that staff members of the McCarthy committee had threatened Army personnel with investigation if they did not give preferential treatment to another former staffer, named David Shine. Such treatment was not forthcoming and that, claimed the Secretary, was the real reason behind McCarthy's latest probe. A Senate Ethics Committee investigation ensued, and though McCarthy was cleared of any wrongdoing, he was censured by his colleagues for his treatment of witnesses and for his abusive treatment of other Senate committees. Eisenhower was happy to see the fall of McCarthy, because he had never forgiven the Senator for calling former Secretary of State George Marshall, a five-star general and a friend of Ike's, a Communist.

Left. Cartoonist's rendering
of Senator Joseph McCarthy.

Below. A 1950's matchbook,
and a campaign flyer, give a
different view of McCarthy.

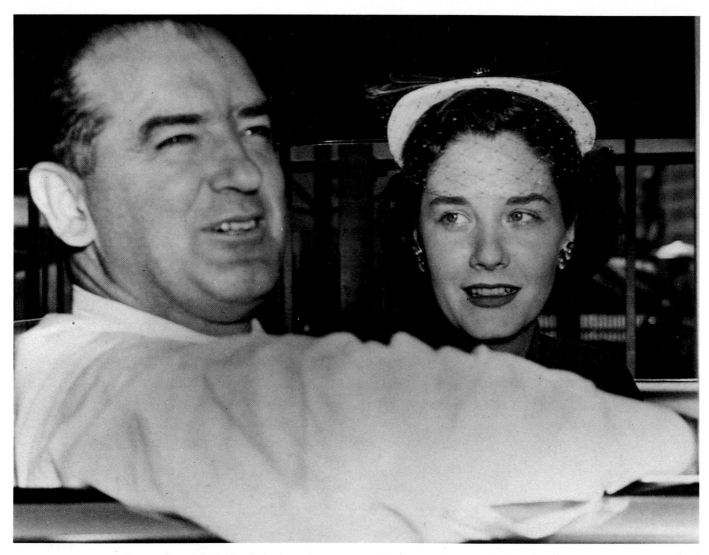

In private, Senator McCarthy, shown here with his wife, was a charming man with a wide circle of friends, including Massachusetts Senator Jack Kennedy. In public, McCarthy rarely smiled, and he sank deeper into a state of sulleness after his censure by the Senate. It is believed that alcoholism caused his death at the age of 48 in 1957.

Joseph McCarthy died in 1957, only forty-eight years old. After his censure he had remained in the Senate, but never wielded anything approaching the power he had before the Army-McCarthy hearings. Today, McCarthy still has defenders among conservatives, many of whom view him as another victim of the plots he endeavored to expose. But other conservatives, among them Whittaker Chambers, viewed McCarthy as the worst thing that could happen to the anti-Communist movement in America. By stirring up fear and passion and then failing to deliver the goods (what he held in his hand in Wheeling was a copy of his speech), he made it too easy for Communists who may well have been in the government to stay where they were, undetected. Any subsequent charges of infiltration were dismissed as mere "McCarthyism." After McCarthy, believing that there were Communists in the government was considered akin to believing that there were monsters under the bed, and that is the disservice that many conservatives feel McCarthy did to the cause, because the Alger Hiss case had strongly indicated that there was a planned Soviet infiltration of the American government. Whoever they may have been, those Soviet agents were never found out, and no charges of spying for the Soviet Union were brought against any government or military personnel until the 1980's.

In 1955 a new publication was launched that would serve as a forum for conservative thinkers and writers down to the present. *National Review* would grow from a small journal of conservative polemics into what is now perhaps the most influential political magazine in the country. The growth of the magazine coincided with the rise in public stature of its founder and editor, William F. Buckley, Jr.

To attempt any kind of worthy discussion of all of the important conservative writers who have proliferated over the last thirty years would expand the boundaries of this undertaking far beyond its intended parameters. But to gain insight into the philosophical formation of "New Conservatism," one need only become familiar with *National Review*.

A Visit to the China Shop

Buckley was born in New York City in 1925, one of ten children of a wealthy Irish-American oilman who was deeply involved in the tangled politics of Mexico in the early part of this century. After graduating from Yale University in 1951, the younger Buckley first gained prominence with the publication of his *God and Man at Yale*, a scathing and witty indictment of the entrenched liberalism in American education. Four years later he founded the *Review*, and since then has become the best-known spokesman for conservative ideology in the country through his magazine, books, and syndicated television program, *Firing Line*. An early and enthusiastic supporter of Ronald Reagan, Buckley never hesitated to disagree with the President (or with anyone else) on matters of public policy when he deemed it necessary.

Though Buckley was also a supporter of Senator McCarthy (and with his brother-in-law, Brent Bozell, wrote a 1954 defense of the Senator's actions entitled *McCarthy and His*

William F. Buckley, Jr., the founder of *National Review* and one of the principal architects of modern conservatism.

Enemies), one of the earliest editorial board members of *National Review* was the anti-McCarthyite Whittaker Chambers. In 1952 Chambers published his autobiography, entitled *Witness*, which dwelt heavily on the Hiss affair and on the tortuous intellectual struggle that had led Chambers to reject Communism and embrace conservatism. For many Americans, *Witness* was a revelatory work that changed the way they viewed their country and the world. The conservative columnist George Will has compared *Witness* to *The Education of Henry Adams*, a 1906 work by a descendent of the famous conservative family that served much the same purpose for readers at the start of the twentieth century.

Among the other major conservative writers who contributed to the development of *National Review* and who, in many cases, began their careers there were James Burnham (another convert from Communism), Russell Kirk, Willmoore Kendall, Frank Meyer, William Röpke, Ralph de Toledano, Richard Weaver, Bozell, Henry Hazlitt, Jeffrey Hart, George Will, Ernest van den Haag, Joseph Sobran, and Richard Brookhiser. With Buckley remaining at the editorial helm, *National Review* continues to attract the best and the brightest of conservative writers in the 1980s.

In 1952 another book, also revelatory but in a different fashion, appeared and created a stir among conservatives. *May God Forgive Us*, by Robert Welch, carried even further the charges then being leveled against the government by Senator McCarthy. Welch claimed that the Communist infiltration into the government was already so far advanced that it

Actor Charlton Heston (*left*) and publisher William Rusher greet Mrs. William F. Buckley an *National Review* dinner.

was the Communists who were shaping American foreign policy. In 1958 Welch launched the John Birch Society, attracting large numbers of upper-class white conservatives who saw a Communist inspiration behind every public policy and personality they disagreed with. Later that year, Welch went so far as to accuse President Eisenhower of being a knowing dupe of the Communists, causing most conservative groups, including the editorial board of *National Review*, to denounce Welch and the Birch Society as reactionaries rather than conservatives. The Society's membership magazine, *American Opinion*—which continues to publish, though it reaches a much smaller audience today than it did in the fifties—displayed an open disdain for democracy, which Welch claimed the Founding Fathers had never intended to be the American form of government. This rejection of democracy put the John Birch Society outside the pale of American conservatism, though in the minds of many it is still viewed as a "conservative" group. It has, in fact, much more in common with Fascism than it has with conservatism, and is rapidly withering away in the 1980s.

Eisenhower's years as President were marked by a major resurgence of the civil rights movement and a further deterioration of relations with the Soviet Union. Conservatives opposed much of the civil rights legislation that was passed in the 1950s for a variety of reasons. Some, especially those in the South, were frankly bigoted against blacks (as were large numbers of people of every other political persuasion) and wished to keep black Americans in subservient positions in society. But other, more reasonable conservatives also opposed the civil rights legislation on the basis that it gave preferential protections to one segment of society that were not being extended to all. Conservatives argued that blacks were already guaranteed full civil rights under the Constitution, and that what was needed was the enforcement of existing laws rather than the promulgation of new legislation that was subject to misinterpretation by the courts. But in the heated and emotional atmosphere engendered by the civil rights movement, such arguments were rejected by minority groups and liberals as smoke screens behind which bigotry lurked. For that and other, less sinister, reasons, conservatism has not held great appeal for American minority groups.

Shortly before the 1956 elections, Eisenhower's handling of two foreign policy crises cost him considerable support among conservatives. On October 23, demonstrations against continued Soviet occupation broke out in Budapest, Hungary, that within a week would turn into a full-scale armed insurrection. On the 29th, Israeli troops rolled into Egypt backed by British and French air cover in an attempt to force leftist Egyptian President Gamal Abdel Nasser to abandon his nationalization of the Suez Canal and return its control to a private corporation favorable to the Europeans.

Eisenhower instructed his ambassador to the United Nations (who was, ironically, Henry Cabot Lodge II, grandson of the man who had done so much to prevent America's entry into the U.N.'s forerunner, the League of Nations) to join with the Soviets in offering a Security Council resolution condemning the invasion of Egypt. The resolution was vetoed by France and Great Britain, causing a strain in relations between the United States and its two closest European allies. But Eisenhower hoped that by working with the Soviets on the Egyptian question, he could gain influence with them that would help him to resolve the Hungarian situation on terms favorable to the freedom fighters. The hope was in vain, and not a little naive. On November 23, Soviet tanks roared through Budapest and nearly demolished the city, killing at least 10,000 civilians outright (with thousands more to be executed during subsequent Soviet roundups of suspected rebels) and leaving 30,000 wounded. Six days later, the French and British agreed to abide by the Russo-American call for a cessation of hostilities in Egypt.

When it was all over, conservatives were bitter over the way Eisenhower had conducted himself. As far as they were concerned, Nasser still had his canal, anti-Communist freedom fighters lay dead by the thousands in Hungary, relations with our European allies had been strained in an effort to appease the Soviets, and perhaps worst of all, Eisenhower had placed his faith in the United Nations, which conservatives opposed as much as they had the League of Nations, and had been outmaneuvered there by the Soviet Union.

Eisenhower had easily won reelection on November 6, again beating Adlai Stevenson (whose renomination had been opposed by former President Truman, who acknowledged that Stevenson was "too much of a defeatist") by landslide proportions. But before the month was out Eisenhower knew that many people in the country were questioning his resolve in dealing with the Russians, and he was determined not to be bested by them again. In March 1957, he signed the "Eisenhower Doctrine" into law, allowing the President to provide material and, if need be, military assistance to Middle Eastern countries threatened by internal subversion or outside aggression. It was a clear warning to both the Soviets and to Nasser that the United States would not tolerate Communist or "pan-Arab" aggression against American allies in that region. He invoked the doctrine in July 1958, when a coup in Iraq threatened to spill over into Lebanon and Jordan. Eisenhower sent 5,000 Marines into Lebanon at the request of that country's government, and kept them there until the situation stabilized.

In September of that year, Eisenhower came to the assistance of the government of Formosa. After the 1949 civil war had left Mao and the Communists in charge

John Foster Dulles, Ike's
steadfast—and conservative—
Secretary of State.

of mainland China, the opposing force under the command of General Chiang Kai-shek had retreated to the island of Formosa, and there set up what they claimed was the real government of China, a claim which was then recognized by the United States and the United Nations. The Communist government on the mainland insisted upon the same claim for their government, and repeatedly launched aggressive attacks against Formosa. When Communist Chinese shelling of Formosa reached alarming proportions in 1958, and an invasion by the Communists appeared imminent, Eisenhower sent a U.S. Navy convoy to protect Formosan shipping, and to warn the Red regime that such an invasion would be met by American military resistance. The Communists continued shelling the outer island of Quemoy for some onths, but the American response had effectively blunted any plans for invasion.

After the death of conservative Secretary of State John Foster Dulles, who had been the

main proponent of Eisenhower's second term policy of confrontation with Communists, the President revived his earlier attempts to reach some sort of accommodation with the Soviets. To that end, over the hue and cry of conservatives across the country, Eisenhower entertained Soviet Premier Nikita Khrushchev on a state visit to the U.S. in September 1959. Though little of substance was accomplished, the two men agreed to meet again in Paris in May 1960. Two weeks before the summit, which included British Prime Minister Macmillan and French President de Gaulle, the Russians shot down an American spy plane over the Soviet Union. Administration officials were not at first alarmed when the plane did not return to its airbase, because it was theoretically impossible, or at least highly unlikely, that a pilot of such a plane, called a U-2, could survive a crash, which is what they assumed had happened. Four days after the incident, Khrushchev stunned the world, and no one more than Eisenhower, when he announced the downing of the plane and the capture of its live pilot, Francis Gary Powers. With Powers alive, it was impossible for the Administration to claim that the plane had simply "wandered" into the Soviet Union, and after a series of confused and conflicting statements, the Americans had to admit that Powers was spying and that there had been a program of spying on the Soviet Union from the air for some years. Although the summit opened as scheduled on the 14th of April, Khrushchev spent three days berating the Americans before walking out on the 17th, much to the delight of American conservatives, who considered continued confrontation with the Soviets to be the only course which would keep Communist expansion in check.

Eisenhower did not agree with that, despite the fact that Dulles's policy of confrontation, called "brinksmanship," had resulted in the prevention of a Communist takeover of any country from Ike's first inauguration until Dulles's death in May 1959. From that time until the end of his term, the period in which Eisenhower shaped American foreign policy by himself, conservatives would blame him for not preventing or responding to the takeover of Cuba, Laos, and the newly independent Congo by governments that were at least sympathetic to the aims of the Soviet Union, if not Communist themselves.

On balance, conservatives were disappointed by the administration of Dwight Eisenhower, though conservative spokesmen and publications such as *National Review* always kept a respectful tone toward the man himself while criticizing some of his policies. By 1960, it was apparent to conservatives that if they were to regain ascendancy in American political life, they must first take over the leadership positions of the Republican Party, which for more than a quarter of a century had been filled by liberals such as Hoover, Dewey, and former Minnesota Governor Harold Stassen. They saw the opportunity to begin doing just that in 1960, for by then Dewey had retired from active political participation (though he would continue to make his voice heard), Hoover was in his middle eighties, and Stassen had long ago begun the pattern of quixotic quadrennial quests for the Republican Presidential nomination that he continued into the 1980s and which would transform him from the party's "whiz kid" into its oldest embarrassment.

There was little doubt that the Republican nomination for President in 1960 would go to Vice President Nixon, and most conservatives were satisfied with Nixon. He had championed the anti-Communist cause since his arrival in Washington in 1946, had done much of the legwork to find the evidence which convicted Alger Hiss in 1950, had ably served as Vice President for eight years—during which time he had risked his life during a Latin American tour that turned ugly in 1958—and had forcefully defended the American way in sharp exchanges with Khrushchev during a visit to Moscow in 1959. Though he had also defended some of Eisenhower's less palatable policies, conservatives recognized his role as the Administration's point man and gave him high marks for his loyalty to Ike, even when Ike let several opportunities to show his appreciation of Nixon go by.

One man who thought Nixon too conservative was Nelson Rockefeller, since 1959 the

Opposite. Soviet leader Nikita Khrushchev and Senate Majority Leader Lyndon B. Johnson during Khrushchev's state visit to Washington in 1959.

Fidel Castro with his friend,
Soviet Premier Leonid
Brezhnev, in Havana in
1966, and in the hills of
Cuba during his revolution
to overthrow Fulgencio
Batista.

governor of New York and now the acknowledged successor to Dewey as head of the Eastern, liberal wing of the Republican Party. Though he had not entered any of the presidential primaries himself, Rockefeller was threatening Nixon with a floor fight over the party platform if at least some of the liberal planks that Rockefeller held dear were not adopted by the Nixon people beforehand. In a pre-convention meeting in New York City, Nixon and Rockefeller hammered out an agreement (known to conservatives as "The Treaty of Fifth Avenue") concerning platform modifications and the choice of a running mate, who would come from Rockefeller's wing of the party.

Conservatives were outraged. The leader of their smaller wing, Senator Barry Goldwater of Arizona, already controlled his home state's delegate vote as the favorite son. Now conservatives urged him to enter the race as a genuine candidate for the nomination, even though anyone who could add knew that Nixon could not be stopped. Despite the fact that he had denounced Nixon's truce with Rockefeller as a "domestic Munich," at the convention he told his supporters to "grow up." If they were going to compete and win in major league politics, they could not become morally outraged every time a political deal was made. After releasing his own delegates with orders to vote for Nixon, Goldwater addressed the convention, saying, "I am going to devote my time from now until November to electing Republicans from the top of the ticket to the bottom, and I call upon my fellow conservatives to do the same." But he also called upon conservatives to get to work "if we ever want to take this party back someday—and I think we can." Nixon, honoring his bargain with Rockefeller, chose Henry Cabot Lodge II as his running mate, a choice which satisfied the liberals and did not offend conservatives as much as some others would have.

The Democrats nominated Senator John Kennedy of Massachusetts for President and Senator Lyndon Johnson of Texas for Vice President, continuing that party's tradition of nominating left-of-center candidates that had begun with Bryan in 1896. Though Nixon was the early favorite to win, Kennedy campaigned more on style than on substance and his youth (he was forty-three), charm, wit, and "movie-star" good looks attracted many people to his campaign. With the race tightening up, the two Presidential candidates agreed to a series of four televised debates. This would prove to be Nixon's downfall. Nixon simply didn't look good on television, and the charismatic Kennedy was perceived to be the winner of the debates by most people who watched them. On the other hand, most people who listened to the debates on the radio thought Nixon had won. By the time they were over, Kennedy had come from behind to make the race a dead heat. It stayed that way right up until election day, when it was determined that Kennedy had won the election by two-tenths of one percent of the popular vote, or less than 120,000 out of 68 million cast. Despite widespread allegations of voter fraud in Illinois, which had gone to Kennedy by a razor-thin margin, Nixon refused to demand a recount or otherwise challenge the returns.

Kennedy's "New Frontier," as he called his domestic platform, was a reinvigoration of the New Deal, and much of the social legislation he proposed was effectively blocked by a coalition of Republicans and conservative Southern Democrats. Kennedy was perceived to be so liberal that the Republican Party as a whole moved noticeably to the right, something it had not done during all the years when Franklin Roosevelt was in office.

In January 1959, guerrilla leader Fidel Castro succeeded in toppling the regime of Cuban dictator Fulgencio Batista and set up a leftist government in its place. Despite protestations that he was not a Communist, Castro moved increasingly closer to the Soviets while relations between the U.S. and Cuba deteriorated steadily. At first Eisenhower was certain that Castro was a provisional figure who would pass from the scene, and even entertained hope that his revolution would spark a democratic uprising on the island, something that would not have been possible with Batista in power. But as Castro grew increasingly antagonistic toward the United States (and the U.S. grew increasingly tired of Castro), Eisenhower, in February 1960, gave permission for the U.S. military to begin training Cuban exiles for an invasion of the island that would topple Castro and bring about a democratic government. With the exiles not yet ready when his term ended, Eisenhower turned the project over to Kennedy, who approved continuation of the training. On April 17, 1961, the invasion of Cuba was launched with an American aircraft carrier, the *Essex*, standing offshore while six old World War II freighters, purchased by the CIA, ferried the Cuban insurgents to the shore of their island at a spot called the Bay of Pigs.

Castro had long expected an invasion, and his shore defenses knew what was coming hours before the first man hit the beach. Castro's air force cut the invasion party to pieces, while the *Essex* stood by, waiting for the President to give the orders that could launch her planes and salvage the operation. But while he was willing to back the Cuban insurgents, Kennedy was unwilling to commit American personnel to the operation, or so he told the Joint Chiefs of Staff as news of the disaster reached the White House. (This prompted one admiral to remark angrily. "Hell, Mr. President, we *are* involved!" but to no avail.) The question remains that if all along Kennedy had no plans to commit Americans to the invasion, why was the *Essex* sitting off Cuba? There is much speculation that if the invasion force was successful in establishing a beachhead, and if that then caused a general anti-Castro uprising throughout the island, the role of the *Essex* would be to serve notice on the Soviets that its presence indicated American support for the anti-Castro forces. But as it was, the beachhead was not gained, and Kennedy ordered the *Essex* to stand down. He would not let the ship salvage the operation because he did not want it known that the American government had been behind the operation from the outset.

Such an attitude was not only duplicitous, but in the minds of many American conservatives, murderous to the men who had landed at the Bay of Pigs believing they would be supported by the American military forces who had trained them. The operation caused nationwide revulsion toward the Administration, both among liberals like U.N. ambassador Adlai Stevenson, who thought we had no right even to train the rebels, and among conservatives who were frankly disgusted with Kennedy's refusal to save the men that he had sent to Cuba.

Two months after the Bay of Pigs debacle, Kennedy went to Vienna to meet Khrushchev, who was making threatening noises about the status of West Berlin. After the events of April, Khrushchev had little respect for Kennedy, and thought the young American President could be easily handled. In July he ordered the building of a wall to separate East Berlin and West Berlin to prevent anyone from the East from leaving. Kennedy rightly called the wall "the most vivid demonstration of the failures of the Communist system," but many conservatives considered it a failing of Kennedy's administration that the wall remained standing, feeling that he should have challenged the Soviets by ordering U.S. troops stationed there to remove it. But Kennedy, like Eisenhower, wanted to avoid direct confrontation with the Soviets as much as possible, hoping to reach some sort of accord with them. Like Eisenhower after the Budapest massacre, Kennedy would be disabused of the idea of Soviet-American cooperation, but because of an incident much closer to home. It was Cuba again.

To no one's great surprise, Fidel Castro announced in December 1961 that he was in fact a Communist and that his government was predicated on the ideals of Marxism-Leninism. To this end, he was aligning the interests of Cuba with those of the Soviet Union and China. From that time on, many prominent conservatives, notably New York Senator Kenneth Keating, began to make charges that the Soviets were building up a military presence in Cuba and that the possibility of their introducing nuclear missiles into Cuba was distinct. The Administration dismissed the idea, but was forced to change

The Berlin Wall, which John
Kennedy called "the most
vivid demonstration of the
failures of the Communist
system."

its position when photos sent back from reconnaissance flights over the island did indeed show the construction of bases and the installation of missiles capable of carrying nuclear warheads to the United States. For several days the President and his closest advisers agonized about how to respond to this evidence. A military air strike against the bases, the approach favored by the Joint Chiefs and others, might bring a retaliatory strike by the Soviet Union on the U.S. Kennedy's U.N. ambassador Stevenson in private angered the President by urging him practically to capitulate to this Soviet provocation by removing some of our missile bases in Europe if the Russians would take their weapons out of Cuba. (More than one senior Democrat who had known, admired, and campaigned for Stevenson in 1952 and 1956 came to the conclusion during the private sessions held by the President to discuss the crisis that it was a very good thing after all that Stevenson had not been elected.) Kennedy eventually ruled out an air strike as a first response to the crisis, deciding instead to blockade the island while communicating secretly with Khrushchev and warning him that the United States would not permit the missiles to be armed—if Khrushchev did not remove them, the U.S. Air Force would. When a Soviet ship stopped at the perimeters of the American blockade, the crisis passed and the Soviets agreed to remove the missiles in return for the removal of American missiles in Turkey—

an agreement along the lines of Stevenson's proposal. The difference was that to the world, it was the Soviets who were backing down instead of the Americans, a difference that Stevenson found difficult to see the importance of.

After Kennedy had gone on television to inform the American people of the existence of the missiles and his plan for a blockade that could lead to war with the Soviet Union, conservatives, like most Americans, rallied to support the President. In the light of history (and especially with the publication of Khrushchev's memoirs after his death) it seems certain that the Soviets would not have gone to war with the United States over Cuba, and that if Kennedy had chosen the air-strike option he could have knocked out the missiles and followed with a ground invasion of Cuba that would have toppled the Castro regime. But he could not be sure how far the Soviets would go at the time, and he earned the gratitude of the people for upholding American interests and avoiding war with Russia.

Domestically, the Kennedy Administration saw an increase in violence over the civil rights movement, a movement that Kennedy supported. His expansion of the federal government to incorporate ever more social programs was everything conservatives expected of him, and by 1962 they were gearing up to defeat his bid for reelection, still two years off.

Barry Morris Goldwater was born in Phoenix, Arizona, in 1909, and attended the University of Arizona, which he left in 1929 to work in his family's department store. He became the store's president in 1937, but gave up the post with the outbreak of World War II to accept a commission in the Army Air Force. Goldwater flew dozens of combat missions during the war and rose to the rank of lieutenant colonel. Remaining in the Reserves after the war, he would eventually attain the rank of major general. Upon his return to Arizona he was elected to the Phoenix City Council, and in 1952 won election to the U.S. Senate. His time in Washington was marked by opposition to huge budget deficits. He advocated cutting back on wasteful social programs that, as a conservative, he felt that the government had no business being involved in. He also advocated a strong defense and an aggressive foreign policy to protect American interests throughout the world. By 1960 he was the acknowledged leader of the conservative wing of the Republican Party, and he strongly supported Nixon's candidacy that year, although the two had had disagreements in the past (and would have more in the future).

After the election of 1960 had gone to Kennedy, a group of young Republicans with deeply held conservative beliefs formed themselves into an organization called the Young Americans for Freedom. Taking as their political mentors such conservative figures as William Buckley, Professor Russell Kirk, and *National Review* publisher William A. Rusher, by 1962 the group was openly campaigning for Goldwater's nomination at the next convention. After Nixon's surprising loss in the 1962 gubernatorial election in California, his political strength to stop Goldwater appeared to be New York Governor Nelson Rockefeller, the leader of the liberal wing. He had already made known his intention to seek the nomination in 1964. It was a nomination that both sides thought was well worth having, because Kennedy's penchant for lurching from crisis to crisis and his support for a civil rights movement that was daily engendering more violence made him appear vulnerable should he seek reelection in 1964.

In an effort to shore up his sagging political fortunes in the South, Kennedy decided to go on a speaking tour of Texas in November 1963. While riding in a motorcade in Dallas on the 22nd, he was shot and killed instantly. The nation was thrown into the deepest mourning it had felt since the death of McKinley, and possibly, the deepest it had ever felt.

Even people who had reason to disagree with all of John Kennedy's presidential policies were stricken with grief when he was murdered. He had brought charm, elegance, and a sense of fun to the White House that was like a breath of fresh air after the Eisenhower years. John Kennedy was such a personable man that he counted many political foes

Castro's prisoners from the Bay of Pigs invasion in 1961. President Kennedy went on television to apologize for the debacle, and was later able to ransom most of the captured insurgents.

Following pages. President and Mrs. John Kennedy brought a youthful style to the White House after the staid Eisenhower years. His appointment of his younger brother Robert (*center*) as Attorney General was denounced by conservatives as naked nepotism, but Americans of all political persuasions were grieved by his assassination in 1963.

among his closest friends, including Goldwater and fellow Catholics like Clare Booth Luce and the late Joe McCarthy. There was a great deal of anger welling up in the American people both that a man so young, with a lovely family and so much of life yet to live, would be shot down in the street, and because one man felt that he had the right to change the course of American history, picked up a gun, and did it.

Kennedy's death put Lyndon Johnson in the White House, and although in his Senate years he might have been considered more conservative than Kennedy, as President he continued his predecessor's policies and expanded on them.

Born near Stonewall, Texas in 1908, Johnson began his political career as a secretary to Congressman Richard Kleberg in 1932 and became the Texas director of the National Youth Administration, another New Deal project, in 1935. Two years later he was elected to Congress, and even as a young congressman formed a personal friendship with Franklin Roosevelt, who liked Johnson enormously. After the Japanese bombing of Pearl Harbor, Johnson became the first member of Congress to go on active duty in the armed forces, taking up his commission as a lieutenant commander in the Navy which he had earned as a member of the Reserves. He served until July 1942, when Roosevelt ordered all members of Congress who were in the military back to Washington to resume their legislative duties.

In 1949 Johnson entered the Democratic primary for nomination to the U.S. Senate along with ten other candidates. When the initial round of voting was over, Johnson had finished second behind Governor Coke Stevenson. After a runoff election widely reputed

233

Right. One of the major thrusts of the Johnson Administration was increased civil rights for blacks, but racial violence was epidemic in American cities during L.B.J.'s years in the White House.

Opposite. Lyndon Baines Johnson, thirty-sixth President of the United States, who was overwhelmed by a torrent of crises both foreign and domestic.

to have been wracked with fraud on both sides, Johnson was declared the winner—by 87 votes out of 988,000 cast.

A strong supporter of Harry Truman and the Democratic Party, Johnson was elected Senate whip by his colleagues in 1951. The following year many Texas Democrats, including Governor Allan Shivers, endorsed the Republican Eisenhower for President, but Johnson stumped the state for Stevenson. When the Democratic Senate leader, Ernest McFarland of Arizona, lost his seat to Goldwater in the Eisenhower sweep, Johnson was rewarded for his loyalty by being elected Senate Minority Leader, at forty-four the youngest Senate floor leader of either party in American history.

His years in the Senate were marked not only by his intense partisanship and, after his elevation to Majority Leader following Democratic victories in 1954, his genius for bending the Senate to his will, but by his political courage for being one of the few Southern senators to support liberal civil rights legislation, which he did consistently. Enough of a classical liberal to be liked and admired by conservative colleagues on Capitol Hill, Johnson was certainly the most powerful Democrat in the country in 1960. Though Johnson harbored some hope of being nominated by his party for President that year, he did not oppose Kennedy in any of the primaries, leaving that to Senator Hubert Humphrey of Minnesota. Many Democrats were concerned that Kennedy could not overcome the anti-Catholic feeling that had contributed to Al Smith's crushing defeat in 1928, and a "Stop Kennedy" drive led by Senator Robert Byrd of West Virginia urged Johnson to get into the race. Johnson finally declared his candidacy after Humphrey dropped out in May, but by then it was too late to pick up enough delegates to deny Kennedy the nomination. Kennedy won the on first ballot, then surprised everyone, not least his brother Robert, who was managing his campaign, by asking Johnson to be his running mate. Johnson in turn surprised everyone, not least J.F.K., by accepting.

And thus it was that within ninety minutes of the shooting in Dallas, Lyndon Johnson was being sworn in as President. For the remainder of what should have been Kennedy's term Johnson continued to push for civil rights legislation, federal social programs, and limited American involvement in Vietnam.

Vietnam had been partitioned into the Communist state of North Vietnam and the democratic state of South Vietnam after the French withdrawal from their former colony in 1954. By 1958, North Vietnam had become engaged in a guerrilla war against the South in an effort to reunify the country under Communist rule. Appealing to the United States for help, South Vietnam received assistance from the Eisenhower administration in the form of war matériel and military advisers, assistance that was continued and slightly expanded by President Kennedy. Kennedy had hoped that the South Vietnamese army would be sufficiently well-trained by 1965 to allow the withdrawal of all American military personnel, and had publicly announced '65 as the target date for bringing them home. It was Johnson's original intention to abide by that deadline for withdrawal.

In May 1963, Nelson Rockefeller divorced his wife of thirty-one years and almost immediately married Mrs. Margaretta Murphy, who was also divorced. The dissolution of one's marriage was traditionally political suicide for American politicians in the years before divorce became commonplace in this country, but with the arrogance that comes with having always gotten one's own way, Rockefeller believed he could not only conduct his personal life any way he wanted to, but could flaunt his conduct publicly less than a year before the start of the preferential primaries and still come out a winner.

He was wrong. Though he fared well in some of the early primaries, he was not winning nearly enough delegates to offset those who were daily pledging their support for Goldwater. In June, Rockefeller's last chance to stop Goldwater from getting the nomination would come in the form of the California primary, which every political analyst was saying was too close to call. But when it was over, Goldwater had won the race and the nomination.

It is impossible to predict how the election of 1964 would have turned out had John Kennedy lived to be the Democratic nominee. While he had clearly grown in confidence and competence after his abysmal kickoff with the Bay of Pigs, he was still widely perceived as being the lesser politician in his dealings with Nikita Khrushchev, and Kennedy himself was not convinced that he would be reelected.

As it was, Barry Goldwater had to face not a living, breathing President Kennedy, but the almost mythical figure he had become in death, and the personification of his suddenly sacred ideals in the form of Lyndon Johnson. This burden, combined with what can only be described as an awful campaign on his own part, led to Goldwater's massive defeat by Johnson in November 1964.

Barry Goldwater is a man of reason and sober intellect, but the stridency of his campaign, beginning with his acceptance speech at the convention, contributed to a widespread perception of him as a dangerous ultraist. At a time of increasing international tensions made frightening by the existence of nuclear weapons, Johnson won overwhelming support by projecting himself as a proven leader with a delicate touch, while the press (and too often, his own campaign staff) joined the Democrats in portraying Goldwater as a man who would gleefully slam his fist down on the nuclear button. Goldwater's attempt to offer himself as a man of decisive action was misinterpreted, or deliberately misrepresented, as *Dr. Strangelove*ism.

To shortsighted political analysts of 1964, the election was proof that conservatism as a potent political force had died with Coolidge and could not be resurrected. But such analysts missed some of the more subtle results of what appeared to be a straightforward debacle. In the first place, Goldwater finished less than four percentage points behind Adlai Stevenson's popular vote percentage in the 1956 election; with Stevenson that year

Senator Barry Goldwater of Arizona, whose nomination for President in 1964 marked the end of the liberal domination of the Rupublican Party.

perceived as an ultra-liberal and Goldwater in '64 as an ultra-conservative, it seems clear that what the American people were rejecting was extremism (Goldwater's unfortunate choice of word to summarize his political direction) rather than conservatism or liberalism. If a man as liberal as Kennedy could be elected four years after the defeat of Stevenson, it is a wonder that political analysts were refusing to admit the possibility of a conservative's election four years after Goldwater. Secondly, the Goldwater candicacy did garner twenty-seven million votes, shattering the media and intelligentsia's dearly held belief that if there were any conservatives left in the country, they were a small band of fanatical "kooks" epitomized by the John Birch Society. (At its height in the late fifties, the John Birch Society had 80,000 members.) Third, the analysts concluded that the crushing defeat of Goldwater automatically meant an abdication by conservatives of the leadership of the national Republican Party, paving the way for a 1968 nomination of an

Above. A meeting of the Young Americans for Freedom presided over by their hero, Barry Goldwater.

old guard Eastern liberal like Rockefeller, Lodge, or Governor Scranton of Pennsylvania. But the new conservative leadership had no intention of abdicating, though they knew they were in for a fight if they were going to hold on. And finally, the results of the 1964 campaign spurred two Republicans to think seriously about using the conservative base in the party that Goldwater had brought to the forefront and expanding on it to form a majority coalition of conservatives and centrists that could lead the party to victory in the 1966 congressional races and the 1968 Presidential campaign. For Richard Nixon, the crusade to forge such a majority would be his reentry into politics after his 1962 defeat in the California gubernatorial race (and his subsequent bitter and emotional press conference in which he withdrew from public life) had seemed to consign him to the past. For Hollywood actor and conservative business spokesman Ronald Reagan, it would mark his departure from the life of a movie star and his entry into the world of major-league politics. By 1965, both were ready and eager to make the attempt.

Lyndon Johnson's term as President in his own right began with as great a possibility for success—at least from the point of view of his supporters—as any in the history of the Republic. He took the oath in January 1965, having led his party to an enormous victory in the election. His social program, called the "Great Society," was legislated by Congress with record speed. (It is interesting to note that unlike his mentor, Franklin Roosevelt, and his predecessor, John Kennedy, Johnson did not label his social program "new," as in the "New Deal" and the "New Frontier." It was gratifying to conservatives to note that Johnson realized there was nothing new about a Democratic President trying to expand the welfare state.) In April, he sent a signal to the world that he would not tolerate any more Communist aggression in this hemisphere by sending the Marines to the Dominican Republic to support a military junta which had recently ousted the leftist President Donald Cabral. This move cost Johnson some support among his liberal, anti-interventionist supporters, but not nearly as much as his Vietnam policy would cost him among all Americans.

With the passing of Kennedy's target date for the withdrawal of American advisers from Vietnam, it became increasingly apparent that the South Vietnamese army was no closer to being able to fend off the invasion from the North than it had been in 1958. Lacking any tradition of democracy, the country saw the rise and fall of a series of ineffective, often corrupt leaders who could bring no cohesiveness to the war effort. By the middle of 1965 it was obvious that without a massive infusion of American military support, South Vietnam would fall to the forces of the Soviet-backed North.

In 1961, President Kennedy had gone to seek the counsel of General Douglas MacArthur, another conservative whom J.F.K. admired, and MacArthur had told him that anyone who wanted to commit American ground troops in Indochina should "have his head examined." In 1964, as the old soldier lay dying in Walter Reed Army Hospital, he repeated the advice to Lyndon Johnson. What MacArthur meant was not that Communist aggression in Asia should go unchecked, but that a repeat of Korea, with troops committed to "contain" the enemy rather than defeat it, was foolhardy. If he were President, MacArthur would deal with Vietnam in the same manner he had wanted to deal with North Korea—massive air strikes against the enemy's home bases and supply lines, undercutting his will and ability to fight. Merely holding the enemy in check while grasping for a political solution would not work in Vietnam. As MacArthur had told Congress in 1951, "In war, there can be no substitute for victory."

But like Truman, Johnson would try to substitute containment for victory. By the end of 1967 more than half a million American soldiers were in Vietnam. Demonstrations on college campuses protesting the war often turned into violent confrontations between demonstrators and police. Most of the prominent liberals in the country who had once supported Johnson now openly opposed his Vietnam policy and called on him to bring the troops home. Conservatives, meanwhile, were dismayed that American soldiers were dying by the thousands in a war that the President had made clear he had no intention of winning. Virtually every conservative spokesman in the country called on Johnson to

Above. President Grover Cleveland navigates the treacherous waters between prospective brides, and prospective office holders.

Barry Goldwater of Arizona, the father of modern American conservatism.

Below. William F. Buckley, Jr., founder and editor of *National Review*, and one of the most outspoken conservative philosophers of modern times.

Opposite. Joseph Pulitzer, newspaper baron who, along with William Randolph Hearst, helped to provoke the war in Spain in 1898.

Gerald R. Ford, moderate
Republican who succeeded
Richard Nixon after the lat-
ter's resignation from the
Presidency in August, 1974.

Among Republicans who came to prominence during the Reagan era were Elizabeth Dole, George Deukmejian, Governor of California, and political activist Phyllis Schlafly.

The fortieth President of the United States, Ronald Reagan, with Vice President George Bush.

Opposite. President Reagan and his lovely First Lady, Nancy.

George Bush and his wife Barbara on the coast of Maine.

Dr. Martin Luther King, Jr., leader of the black civil rights movement in the 1950's until his assassination in 1969. Two months after his murder, Senator Robert Kennedy, brother of the slain President and himself a candidate for the Democratic Party presidential nomination, was shot dead in Los Angeles after winning the California primary.

end the conflict quickly and save American lives by unleashing the full might of our military superiority.

In the meantime, major urban centers in American were suffering from riots that had broken out in the wake of the civil rights movement. Johnson had come into the White House more committed to civil rights than any other President in history, but his social programs had done little to alleviate the tensions that now divided black and white Americans. It was difficult for Johnson to accept that his lifelong commitment to civil rights for all Americans was not being transformed into concrete improvement in the area by the implementation of his social policies. He could not accept that passing laws does not change attitudes, that spending money does not provide opportunities. After the assassination of Martin Luther King, Jr., in April 1968, Johnson had to call out federal troops to restore order in some of the cities hardest hit by violence.

249

Above, and right. Ronald Reagan in Hollywood, with wife Nancy, and with daughter Maureen during World War II.

In 1966, the people of California rejected the reelection bid of Governor Pat Brown, the man who had defeated Richard Nixon in 1962, in favor of the Republican candidate, Ronald Reagan. Reagan began the campaign unhampered by a problem which plagues most other newcomers to elective politics, the problem of name recognition. Everyone in California knew who Ronald Reagan was long before he entered the race; he'd been a Hollywood star for twenty-five years.

Born in Tampico, Illinois on February 6, 1911, Reagan graduated from Eureka College in 1932, and shortly thereafter began his career as a sports announcer on radio. Handsome and talented, he headed for Hollywood in 1937. Two years later he rose to stardom playing the doomed George Gipp in the film *Knute Rockne—All American*. From then until he stopped making pictures, he was rarely out of work, averaging about two films a year for twenty-five years. Dubbed the "Errol Flynn of B Pictures," he also found in a niche in the early days of television as the host of *General Electric Theater* and *Death Valley Days*. By the time he gave up his acting career in the mid-sixties, Reagan was anything but a stranger to a camera.

He was originally a liberal Democrat (he voted for Franklin Roosevelt four times), and his fascination with politics led him to take an active role in the affairs of his union, the Screen Actors Guild. He was elected to five consecutive terms as president of the union from 1947 to 1952, and to a sixth term in 1959.

After Reagan began his association with General Electric as host of their television program, he also became the company's spokesman, traveling around the country giving speeches to businessmen's groups preaching the doctrine of free market capitalism. It was during this period that Reagan was converted from liberalism to conservatism, a move accelerated by his marriage to actress Nancy Davis, whose father, Loyal Davis, was an internationally renowned surgeon and an outspoken conservative. By the early '60s Reagan had become a Republican, and in October 1964, gave a televised speech in behalf of Barry Goldwater that was hailed as the highlight of an otherwise dismal campaign.

In 1965, Reagan decided to retire from acting and pursue a career in politics, convinced as he was that the conservative base of Goldwater's support needed new leadership if it was to coalesce into a winning movement. He entered the 1966 Republican gubernatorial primary and was the easy winner in June, going on to win a landslide victory over Brown in the general election that fall.

Reagan's style was combative, and he appealed to many Californians who were tired of campus disruptions, riots in the cities, and crime in the streets. His overwhelming victory made him governor of the largest state in the Union, a position which guaranteed that he could make his views known nationally and which gave him automatic standing in the leadership ranks of the Republican Party. It would, of course, be up to him to hold on to his leadership position by his actions as governor, but almost from the start, Reagan was determined to have a strong voice in shaping the affairs of the nation as well as California. Within days of his election he was being hailed in some quarters as the natural successor to Goldwater as leader of the conservative wing of the party (it was taken for granted that Goldwater himself could never again be nominated), but another Californian was equally determined to close the conservative ranks behind him and form a coalition that would win him the Republican nomination for President at the next convention. And in 1966, Dick Nixon had more experience at winning Presidential nominations than Ronald Reagan had.

Nixon had decided to run for the nomination shortly after Goldwater's defeat in 1964, and Goldwater—still titular head of the party—endorsed Nixon's candidacy in the early part of 1965. After Reagan's election as governor of California in 1966, Nixon was wary of a move on his part to gain the Presidential nomination. But he kept closer tabs on Rockefeller, letting Goldwater do much of the groundwork for him among conservatives.

Following pages.
Left. George C. Wallace, who ran a divisive third party campaign in 1968 that almost resulted in the election of Hubert Humphrey.

Right. Richard M. Nixon, thirty-seventh President of the United States.

252

This Goldwater did exceedingly well, so that by the spring of 1968 Nixon had a commanding lead among the delegates to the convention. Rockefeller dropped out of the race in March, but only because he did not want to enter the primaries, where he never did well. He still hoped to be the nominee of a brokered convention. Reagan ran unopposed in the California primary, Nixon declining to oppose him as is traditional when the governor of a state wishes to control his own delegation as the favorite son—provided he is not an active candidate. Reagan had declined to actively seek the nomination both because he felt that no one could stop Nixon and because he did not want to lose credibility with the people of California by spending a great deal of time out of state campaigning for President after less than two years as governor.

Thus, when the convention opened in Miami Beach in the early days of August 1968, the Nixon people were certain that they had the nomination sewed up. But the Rockefeller and Reagan supporters were not so sure, and word filtered around the convention hall that Nixon's support was "thin," with many people supporting him only because there was no other viable candidate in the race. On the 5th, Reagan came out into the open and announced that he was an active candidate, and the Rockefeller camp went to work with renewed vigor, hoping that a break in the conservative line would cause liberals to shake loose from Nixon as well and flock to Rocky.

It was all for naught. Most conservatives at the convention admired Reagan and thought he had a bright future, but Goldwater had done his job well and they stood fast for Nixon. Without a conservative breakaway, the liberals held on for Nixon as well, and he was nominated on the first ballot. Reagan went to the podium after the roll call was over and moved that the nomination be made unanimous, which it was.

In March 1968, President Johnson had shocked the nation when he went on television to announce that he was devoting the remainder of his term to finding a solution in Vietnam, and so would not be a candidate for reelection. The Democrats scrambled to come up with a replacement, the most prominent possibilities being Vice President Hubert Humphrey, New York Senator Robert Kennedy, brother of the late President, and Minnesota Senator Eugene McCarthy, who was the ideological twin of Bobby Kennedy and was angered by Kennedy's entry into the race. But after delivering his victory speech following his win in the California primary on June 5, Kennedy was shot by a deranged Jordanian immigrant and died the next day, adding another chapter to the book of tragedy that is the story of the Kennedy family. Kennedy's grief-stricken supporters would not join McCarthy to stop Humphrey, and the Vice President was nominated after a convention in Chicago that was marked by riots outside as the balloting proceeded inside.

The race between Humphrey and Nixon had all of the earmarks of a repeat of 1960, with the Democrat starting out behind in the polls but gradually pulling into a position to make the election a toss-up. But this time Nixon hung on, and defeated Humphrey by seven-tenths of one percent. Still, Nixon did not garner a majority of the vote because of the presence in the race of George Wallace, the pro-segregation governor of Alabama who appealed to the anti-civil rights faction and to a number of social conservatives because of his strong stand in favor of winning the war in Vietnam. Wallace captured over nine million votes, or 13.5%, and carried six states. Had he not been in the race, it is safe to assume that most of his votes would have gone to Nixon—not because Nixon was a segregationist (quite the contrary) but because Wallace's supporters were conservatives on most political issues and Nixon was far more conservative than Humphrey. If Wallace's vote is added to Nixon's, it amounts to 57% of the total—a landslide for conservatives and a nearly complete reversal of the results of 1964.

With Nixon's inauguration in January 1969, conservatives were instrumental in putting a candidate of their choosing in the White House for the first time since 1925. In that

Opposite. New York Governor Nelson Rockefeller, grandson of the oil tycoon and successor to Thomas Dewey as the leader of the liberal wing of the Republican Party. His ambition to be President was never realized, though he did serve as Vice President under Gerald Ford.

Below. Nixon on the campaign trail in 1968. He beat
Hubert Humphrey that year
by nearly as small a margin as
John Kennedy had beaten
him by in 1960.

time they had gone through periods of such languor and ineffectiveness that in 1950 social critic Lionel Trilling remarked, "In the United States at this time liberalism is not only the dominant but even the sole intellectual tradition. For it is the plain fact that there are no conservative...ideas in general circulation." Conservatives had come a long way since then, an even longer way since Coolidge left office; but though they did not know it at the time, they still had a long way to go before the conservative candidate would become a conservative President.

Above. President Nixon with his mentor, former President Dwight Eisenhower, shortly before that latter's death in 1969.

Richard Nixon enjoyed a honeymoon with orthodox conservatives for the first two years
of his administration, owing in large part to his vigorous conduct of the war in Vietnam
and the fact that he allowed his liberal critics at home to be answered by his Vice President,
the right-wing former governor of Maryland, Spiro Agnew, who struck a responsive
chord not only among conservatives but among blue-collar workers and lower-middle-
class homeowners, usually denizens of the Democratic Party but now tired of the
stridency and violence of liberals opposed to the war and opposed to Nixon in general.

But in 1971 Nixon was to lose favor among many of the more fundamentalist conservatives for his handling of issues both foreign and domestic. At home, Nixon sought to
control runaway inflation by placing a freeze on increases in salaries and prices, the most
direct government control of the economy since rationing had ended after World War II.
In foreign policy, conservatives were disturbed by his attempts to completely revamp
America's relations with both the Soviet Union and Communist China by initiating a
policy known as *détente.*

In August 1971, *National Review* magazine ran an editorial announcing that its
editorial board—made up of some the best-known and most powerful conservative
writers in the country—was "suspending" support of the President because of his foreign-
policy overtures to the Communist states, which seemed to them to be a return to the
post-Dulles policy of Eisenhower. Republican leaders, though, were not terribly concerned about the possibility of mass conservative defections away from Nixon, because
most grass-roots conservatives were pleased with his handling of the war and because by
1971 most of the contenders for the following year's Democratic nomination were
already known, and there wasn't one who even resembled a candidate that a conservative
could support. Nixon was satisfied that he had a great deal of leeway as far as conservatives
were concerned; they may not like some of his policies, but in the end, there was no place
else for them to go.

A few months after the *National Review* piece appeared, Nixon further alienated
conservatives by supporting the United Nations action to strip Taiwan (formerly Formosa) of its recognition as the true representative of the Chinese people and to give its
seat to Communist China, which in turn demanded the expulsion of Taiwan even from
the General Assembly. Many conservatives felt that Nixon's action was a betrayal of an ally
in favor of a Communist foe, but their vehemence is surprising, considering that it is the
U.N. we're discussing. For thirty years conservatives professed not to care what went on
inside the glass building on New York's First Avenue, their only position on the U.N.
being that the United States should get out of it and shake the dust from its feet as quickly
as possible. So it really should have made no difference to fundamentalist conservatives
whether the U.N. recognized the Peking government as the true Chinese government or

George McGovern, Democratic nominee for President in 1972. His far-left program was overwhelmingly rejected by the American people, and he managed to carry only Massachusetts and the District of Columbia.

the Puerto Rican legislature as the true government of the United States. But many conservatives had *never* liked Nixon despite his conservative credentials, and never would. The Taiwan flap was used as an excuse by many to vent their dislike of the President personally and their opposition to his rapprochement policy toward the Communists.

Conservatives were equally uneasy about Nixon's overtures to the Soviets, but were generally pleased that the Russians were effectively held in check in their expansionist policies throughout the course of the Nixon Administration.

When the time for Nixon's reelection had come, the Republican Party analysts proved to be right about Nixon's support among grassroots conservatives, for not only did he win reelection, carrying every state in the Union save Massachusetts, but the Congress that took office in 1973, though still controlled by the Democrats, was made up of a thin majority of ideological conservatives. Nixon took to calling conservatives "The New Majority" and vowed to shape the policies of his second term along the lines of the New Majority agenda. Even *National Review* had come out in support of Nixon's reelection (with the exception of publisher William Rusher, who loathed Nixon and, after the Taiwan-U.N. flap, wrote an *N.R.* editorial in which he vowed to "sit this one out," the alternative to Nixon being the near-hysterically liberal George McGovern).

Henry Kissinger (*center*),
Secretary of State under
Richard Nixon and Gerald
Ford. His overtures to the
Communist regimes in
China and the Soviet Union
were bitterly opposed by
conservatives, who felt he
was giving away too much
for too little.

Opposite, above. An emotion-
ally drained President Nixon
saying farewell to his staff
after his resignation following the Watergate scandal in
1974. His daughter Tricia
looks on.

Opposite, below. President
Nixon with Soviet leader
Leonid Brezhnev.

But Nixon had little attention to devote to any political agenda during his second term, when his administration was rocked by the dual scandals involving the Watergate break-in and the resignation of Vice President Agnew for having taken bribes while governor of Maryland. Conservatives were dismayed at losing Agnew, whom many hoped to see succeed Nixon as President in 1976. But Nixon's successor would come into office in 1974, for the Watergate scandal forced Nixon to become the first President ever to resign from the office.

Prior to his own resignation, Nixon had become the first President to take advantage of the Twenty-fifth Amendment to the Constitution and nominate a man to fill a vacancy in the office of Vice President, a vacancy that had come about because of Agnew's resignation. Nixon nominated the longtime House Minority Leader Gerald R. Ford of Michigan, who was swiftly confirmed by the Senate. After the release of tape recordings which clearly showed that Nixon had been involved in an obstruction of justice by trying to cover up the tracks of Attorney General John Mitchell, the man responsible for ordering the break-in at Democratic Party headquarters in the Watergate Hotel shortly before the 1972 election, the President knew he had to resign from office, and was succeeded by Ford on August 8, 1974.

Ford, who was well-liked by ideological leaders of both parties, and who himself leaned to a conservative political viewpoint, almost immediately alienated the conservatives by nominating Nelson Rockefeller to succeed him as Vice President. (Many conservatives were dismayed when their former standard-bearer, Senator Barry Goldwater, pronounced Rockefeller "acceptable" as Vice President. Those who were might have saved themselves the trouble of getting angry had they merely taken the remark at face value. *Anybody* is acceptable as Vice President; it is only upon promotion that they can be troublesome.)

Much of the rest of the nation was alienated by Ford when he issued a blanket pardon of Nixon before any charges were proffered against the former President, effectively cutting off further investigation into the Watergate scandal. (A word here about Richard Nixon: when he left office in 1974, he was reviled by many of his countrymen, and this revulsion was transferred to Ford for pardoning Nixon. But in the almost fourteen years that have transpired since Nixon's resignation, he has gained the stature of elder states-man, at least among Republicans, by his consistent championing of American interests and his acknowledged expertise in the field of foreign policy. His views on a great many issues are sought not only by political philosophers but by the President and many of the Republican candidates who hope to succeed the President. Many conservatives who disagreed vehemently with Nixon while he was in office now regard him as a premier political thinker, while others, among them Rusher, remain unreconstructed anti-Nixonians. It is the view of this writer that the restoration of Nixon to a position of respect is as it should be.)

The conservative wing sought to prevent Ford's nomination for President by the Republicans, because his selection of Rockefeller had left them uneasy and his pardon of Nixon put his chances for election in doubt. In November 1975, Ronald Reagan, having completed his second term as governor of California in January and now out of office, announced that he would seek the Republican nomination for President. Most conservatives flocked to his campaign, although some, like Senator Barry Goldwater and Senator Robert Dole of Kansas, backed Ford. Reagan did so well in the primaries that by the time the convention opened in Kansas City, no one was quite sure who would win the nomination. Reagan's own count indicated that Ford had just enough votes to win on the first ballot, so, in an attempt to shake loose some delegates from Pennsylvania who were pledged but not bound to Ford, Reagan announced that if he were nominated he would choose Richard Schweiker, the liberal Senator from Pennsylvania, to be his running mate. The move cost Reagan as many of his own delegates as he gained from the Ford camp, and

on the first roll call, Ford defeated Reagan 1,187-1,070. Ford chose as his running mate Senator Dole, who appealed to most conservatives but whose cutting manner during the campaign would cost the ticket more support than it gained.

The Democrats, meeting in New York's Madison Square Garden (which was a completely different building from the one which had housed their 1924 fiasco), nominated former Georgia Governor Jimmy Carter, who was widely if erroneously perceived to be from the conservative wing of the Democratic Party because his strong fundamentalist Christian views put him on the same side as many conservatives on "moral" issues. Carter would later back away from his former stance on such issues as abortion, which as a fundamentalist he opposed but which as the Democratic nominee he avoided discussing as much as possible.

On January 22, 1973, the Supreme Court handed down a ruling in the case of *Roe v. Wade* which completely abolished all state laws prohibiting abortion during the first trimester of a woman's pregnancy. Later rulings would effectively remove the state's right to prohibit abortion at any time during the course of a pregnancy. Almost immediately conservatives seized the issue as their own, many because their religious beliefs led them to view abortion as a perfidious moral evil, others because the ruling itself would raise vexing questions about states' rights and judicial activism. While the division was not absolute, most conservatives favored an overturn of the court's ruling to allow the individual states to decide the matter for themselves, while most liberals fought any move by Congress to "tone down" the ruling by passing laws restricting the use of federal funds

AMERICAN CONSERVATISM: AN ILLUSTRATED HISTORY

Right. Official portrait of Gerald R. Ford, thirty-eighth President of the United States.

Below. The thirty-ninth President Jimmy Carter, with Panama's President Omar Torrijos (*far right*) during the signing of the Panama Canal Treaties.

to pay for abortion, or the provision of federal funds to groups, such as Planned Parenthood, which advocated abortion as a means of birth control.

The Roman Catholic Church had always condemned abortion as a mortal sin, placing liberal Catholic politicians in an awkward position. Since abortion had become a keystone of the feminist movement's political agenda, and since the feminists had become one of the main "special-interest" groups of the Democratic Party, these politicians groped for a way to appear to be in conformity with their Church while not publicly condemning abortion or working for its restriction. After several years of trying to sidestep the issue, they hit upon the idea of "personal opposition." That is, they claimed that though they were "personally opposed" to abortion themselves, they would not attempt to "legislate their morality" or "impose their beliefs" on the rest of the country. Anti-abortionists dismissed the notion not only as duplicitous but inherently ridiculous, yet it has been the stock answer to the abortion question for such prominent liberals as Senator Ted Kennedy, New York Senator Daniel Patrick Moynihan, that state's Governor Mario Cuomo, and Representative Geraldine Ferraro, who would be the Democratic Party's nominee for Vice President in 1984. (The claim of not wishing to impose personal morality rings especially hollow in the case of Cuomo, who has vetoed death penalty legislation passed by the New York state legislature every year that he has been governor, despite the fact that opinion polls demonstrate that such legislation is widely favored by the people of New York. While as chief executive of the state Cuomo undoubtedly has the right to impose his own beliefs about the death penalty on the legislature and citizens of New York in this manner, it makes a shambles of his position on abortion.)

In 1975, James P. McFadden, then the associate publisher of *National Review*, gave up an active role with that publication to launch a new one specifically aimed at keeping public attention focused on abortion and related social issues such as the growing movement toward the legalization of euthanasia. Since its inception, the *Human Life Review* has attracted major articles condemning abortion by such leading conservatives as Ronald Reagan, Robert Dole, Jack Kemp, Clare Booth Luce, James Buckley (brother of William and a former senator from New York), and British philosopher Malcolm Muggeridge.

Among the other major issues of the 1976 campaign were inflation, women's rights, the fall of Vietnam following the American withdrawal, the covert activities of the CIA, continued unrest in the Middle East, and continued Communist aggression in Latin America, Africa, and Asia. Both Ford and Carter hewed to the center position on most issues, but the overriding theme of the campaign was integrity. Carter, an outsider to the machinations of Washington politics, was able to present an untarnished image, and constantly hammered away at Watergate and Ford's pardon of Nixon, often referring to the Republican ticket as "Nixon-Ford" rather than "Ford-Dole." Though he began the race with a wide lead in the polls, Carter's campaign lost a great deal of steam between the convention and the election, and Ford was able to pull to an almost even position. With more people defecting from Carter to Ford every day, there is a distinct possibility that had the campaign gone on for another day or two, Ford would have attracted enough voters to win the election. As it was, Carter defeated Ford on November 2 with 51% of the popular vote and 297 electoral votes to Ford's 49% and 240 electoral votes.

Because of the basically centrist positions of both of the major candidates and the near-even division of support between them, there was no clear-cut ideological victory for either conservatism or liberalism in 1976. Republican liberals found no difficulty supporting Ford, and though many G.O.P. conservatives lost their enthusiasm for the campaign that year after the defeat of Reagan at the convention, most of them cast their ballots for Ford on election day. Likewise, Carter was endorsed by the liberal wing of the Democratic Party after he secured the nomination, and his victory was attributable in

President Anwar Sadat of Egypt, President Jimmy Carter of the United States, and Prime Minister Menachem Begin of Israel during discussions at Carter's Maryland retreat that led to the Camp David Accords.

large part to his ability to woo back to the Democratic Party many social conservatives among the middle class, blue-collar workers, and farmers who had been traditionally part of the Democratic coalition but who for the last several elections had been casting their presidential votes for the Republicans.

But if Carter came into office with at least the good wishes of conservatives, who at the start considered him no worse than and little different from Gerald Ford, his performance as President would galvanize the right to such an extent that his bid for reelection would result in the election of the most ideologically conservative President at least since Coolidge, and perhaps since Grover Cleveland, and in Republican control of the Senate for the first time since 1954.

On the domestic front, Carter was severely hampered by his inability to stimulate the economy and reduce the levels of inflation, unemployment, and interest rates, after having employed what he called a "misery index" during the campaign using those three criteria. Within a short time after taking office, the "misery index" number was nearly double what it had been under the Ford administration, and Carter never mentioned it again. Carter had campaigned—and appealed to economic conservatives—on a promise to reduce the size of the federal government and make its operation more efficient. But throughout his term in office, he was hampered and effectively prevented from doing this by the congressional majority of liberal Democrats. He had been elected to office largely because he was an "outsider" to Washington, but once he was in office this translated simply into a lack of know-how that was exploited by members of his own party. (Interestingly, Carter's presidential memoirs, entitled *Keeping Faith*, begin with his inauguration and make almost no mention of the 1976 campaign, thus enabling him to avoid explanations of the "misery index," the outsider issue, and any number of campaign promises that were made but were not kept.)

With the price of oil constantly going higher because of the machinations of the Arab petroleum cartel, President Carter rightly advocated a national policy of energy conservation that would benefit Americans today and in the future. But in doing so, he made the political error of lecturing the nation as a schoolteacher would a classroom of children, calling the United States the "most wasteful nation on earth," and in general taking a tone during a nationwide address on the subject that many people found offensive. (It was during that same address that Carter referred to his energy-austerity program as the "moral equivalent of war," whose acronym many critics pointed out was MEOW.)

In foreign relations, the President alienated conservatives almost from the beginning of his term, and from then on things went from bad to worse. In 1977 he read David McCullough's *The Path Between the Seas*, a Pulitzer Prize-winning work about the building of the Panama Canal, and came away from the experience so uneasy about the U.S.'s role in building and obtaining operating rights to the canal that he felt it must be given over to Panamanian control. Conservatives immediately blasted the plan as foolhardy hand-wringing over an event that had taken place more than sixty years before and whose reversal now could have serious implications for American security should something happen to strain U.S.-Panamanian relations after the Panamanians took control. The most outspoken critic of the plan was Ronald Reagan, who had denounced a much less far-reaching proposal by President Ford to share control of the canal with the Panamanians after the dictator of that country, Omar Torrijos, had begun to make threatening noises about the continued American presence in his country. Said Reagan at the time: "When it comes to the Panama Canal, we built it, we paid for it, it's ours, and we are going to keep it!" Ford believed that Reagan won several primaries that year because of the canal issue.

But Carter went ahead with his plan, negotiated the treaty (or more accurately, treaties, as different parts of the plan were covered under separate agreements) with Torrijos, and pushed the legislation necessary for its implementation through Congress with the help of liberals in both parties anxious to strike a blow against American "imperialism." But Panama helped to rouse opposition to Carter on the right and gave new impetus to conservatives who hoped to see Ronald Reagan in the White House yet. (Conservative opposition to the Panama policy was overwhelming but not quite unanimous; among those who supported the Carter initiative were William Buckley, James Burnham, and John Wayne.)

Carter received high marks from most Americans for his attempt to bring peace to the Middle East, but his inability to effectively combat terrorist acts against American citizens in that region fueled growing feelings of frustration and anger at home. In the field of foreign policy, Carter was rapidly coming to be perceived as well-intentioned but not nearly firm enough to protect American interests. Very few people in the United States were fond of the Somoza regime in Nicaragua, for instance, but Carter did not choose to break relations with his government until he knew that doing so would result in its overthrow by the Sandinista insurgency, whose leadership was widely reported to be filled with Marxists. His vacillation over whether or not to back up the monarchy in Iran contributed directly to the fall of the Shah and the takeover of that nation by anti-American Moslem fundamentalists. His concern for human rights, while admirable, was an unsuitable basis for his foreign policy. Nicaragua and Iran may well have been guilty of human rights abuses, but so were the regimes that came to power in those countries aided by Carter's unwillingness to defend the previous governments, who were after all our allies. No government on earth, including the Nazis, has ever been more guilty of the abuse of its citizenry than the Soviet regime in Russia, but Carter willingly negotiated a

Meanwhile, back at the ranch. . . .

second arms limitation treaty with it despite incontrovertible evidence that it had repeatedly violated the first one. By 1979, Carter's insistence on human rights as the cornerstone of his foreign policy led to his no longer being taken seriously by the Soviets, a fact they demonstrated in December of that year by invading Afghanistan to prop up a failing Marxist government. Carter's response, a grain embargo which crippled the American farm economy and a boycott of the following year's Olympics, led many Americans to believe that the Soviet assessment of Carter was the correct one.

By the middle of Carter's term in office, conservatism had become the preferred political ideology of a majority of Americans, according to the national opinion polls. Americans were tired of economic "stagflation" (a combination of stagnation and inflation), tired of seeing America's allies fall to pro-Soviet or other anti-American regimes, tired of being lectured by the President about waste and about being the cause of a national "malaise," when most people who saw such a malaise, as Carter did, put the blame for it squarely at the feet of the President.

If Carter was right, if the American people were in the throes of a national malaise whatever the cause, they would be roused out of it by the events in Iran that began to unfold in November 1979. They would become so excited about it, in fact, that their volatility would lead to Carter's suffering one of the worst defeats of an incumbent President's bid for reelection in American history. And he would be replaced by the man many conservatives had been waiting for since 1968.

270

10 Triumph 1980–1988

Anti-government demonstrations by Moslem fundamentalists—long a group persecuted by the Shah—swept over Iran and turned into bloody riots in May of 1978. At first the Shah seemed not to be unduly disturbed by the uprisings, supported as he was by a strong military and an effective secret police. He kept to his regular schedule, and had no qualms about leaving the country on state visits abroad. But as months went by and the demonstrations not only continued but intensified in vehemence and violence, outside observers agreed privately that the Shah's regime was in serious trouble.

The object of the demonstrations was to force the Shah to permit the return of the Ayatollah Ruhollah Khomeini, spiritual leader of the Shiite sect, among the most orthodox Moslems in the world. Khomeini had been sent into exile after leading demonstrations against the Shah in June 1963, and had lived ever since in Iraq. But the Shah knew that the return of Khomeini could only lead to further efforts to topple his government and bring about the creation of an Islamic Republic, with the *mullahs*, the religious leaders, in charge of the civil functions of government, their laws based solely on the Koran. He had no intention of allowing Khomeini to return to Iran for as long as he sat on the Peacock Throne.

In October, 1978 the Iraqi government expelled the Ayatollah for fomenting an Iranian revolution from his base in Baghdad. He was granted asylum in Paris by French President d'Estaing, much to the surprise of many western observers and of the Iranian government as well. By November, the situation in Iran had grown so desperate that the Shah turned the government over to the military on the understanding that he would resume power as soon as they had put down the revolt.

In Washington, the Administration watched the proceedings with increasing wariness and uncertainty about what to do. Carter had proclaimed his public backing of the Shah, but had done nothing to bolster his sagging position. On December 11, and again on the 29th, millions of anti-Shah protestors marched through the streets of Teheran, demanding the return of Khomeini and the abdication of the Shah. After the second monster rally, Carter considered sending an aircraft carrier to the Persian Gulf as a show of support for the Shah, but decided against it. Privately, the President was advising the Shah to hold on to his throne, though he offered no advice on how the Shah might do that, nor did he offer to assist. On January 6, the military turned the country over to civilian rule by naming Shahpour Bakhtiar prime minister. The Shah pledged to Bakhtiar his support and his willingness to stay out of governmental affairs, saying he "needed a rest." With the Shah's power effectively gone, Carter sent him a message on January 8th advising him to get out of Iran. This the Shah had already decided to do. On the 13th Khomeini announced his intention to return to Iran after the departure of the Shah, and said he had already formed a council to fill the Shah's former position in Iran. On the 16th the Shah left Iran for Egypt, never to return. The Ayatollah left Paris and arrived in Iran on February 1. The day after the Shah's departure, Carter held a White House news conference and in reply to one question about Iran said, "We have no intention, neither ability nor desire, to interfere in the internal affairs of Iran." His use of the word "ability" left many people wondering whether it was truly the American people who were suffering a "crisis of confidence," as Carter had maintained, or their President.

The deposed Shah of Iran, pictured with former President Richard Nixon in July 1979.

Over the next several months, more massive demonstrations took place in the Iranian capital, but now they were aimed at the United States. Shortly after Khomeini's return the American embassy had been attacked and two marine guards wounded. On February 26th the State Department announced the evacuation of the families of all embassy personnel and urged any Americans remaining in Iran to leave as soon as possible. Most of them did. Anti-American rallies continued through the summer and into the fall, but Carter was unwilling to break diplomatic relations with Iran because it had still had some semblance of a civilian government that was more reasonable than the mob or the Ayatollah. On the 22nd of October the Shah, dying of cancer, entered the United States for medical treatment. Iranian students poured into the streets to protest, demanding that the United States return the Shah and his money to Iran.

The first protests seemed to be no more than what had been going on in front of our embassy since the return of Khomeini, but on the morning of November 4 a mob of around 3,000 students stormed the embassy's gate, overran the guards, and took the 57 people inside hostage. The civilian government responded to Carter's immediate protest by assuring him that they would do everything in their power to secure the release of the hostages unharmed. But the fact was that they had no power beyond that which Khomeini allowed them to exercise, and he was supporting the students. Carter himself would later write, "we and other nations had faced this kind of attack many times in the past, but never, so far as we knew, had a host government failed to attempt to protect threatened diplomats." Thus the hostage-taking in Iran with the blessings of the *de facto* government was cause for a military response by the United States. But Carter feared for the safety of the hostages, and immediately ruled out any type of military rescue attempt or reprisal against Iran. Beyond ruling out the things he did not want to do, however, he gave no indication that he knew what else to do. Two weeks after the hostages were taken, the Ayatollah announced that if the Shah was not returned the Americans would be tried as spies. A week later he ordered the release of five black and women hostages because they were among the "oppressed" people of America and as such could not be spies. That would be the last change in the situation for months.

A week after the hostages were taken Ronald Reagan announced that he would once against be a candidate for the Republican nomination for President. (Reagan had decided to run long before events to Iran reached the crisis stage and Iran was not related to the timing of his announcement.) Most public-opinion polls rated him the immediate front-runner for the nomination, though his age (he was then sixty-nine) could well be a factor in the race. His major opponents came from all three divisions of the party: Howard Baker was favored by the liberal wing, George Bush was the centrist candidate, and Robert Dole and John Connally had some support among conservatives (especially the younger, more strident members of what was called the "New Right"), although they lost much of their backing when Reagan entered the race. Baker's candidacy was rated as weak even by many of his supporters, and some of his campaign staff was ready to take part in a "Draft Ford" movement in an effort to stop Reagan should Baker fold before the convention.

In January 1980, Bush beat Reagan in the Iowa primary, briefly shifting the spotlight to his campaign. But Reagan bounced back, winning in New Hampshire in February and picking up delegates in state caucuses all across the country. After easily winning the California primary in June, Reagan had enough delegates to take the nomination on the first ballot, but Bush continued his campaign in the hope of playing a significant role at the convention. The "Draft Ford" movement fizzled, largely because the former President was reluctant to lend it any active support.

On April 17 Carter warned the government of Iran that a U.S. military response might be necessary if the hostages were not released. When there was no appreciable movement detected among the Iranians toward resolving the situation, the President went ahead with a rescue operation on April 25. Eight helicopters were dispatched to the Iranian desert to coordinate a surprise invasion of the embassy compound to free the hostages. But three of the copters developed technical malfunctions, and the operation was called off. As they were preparing to return to an aircraft carrier, one of the helicopters crashed into a transport plane, resulting in the deaths of eight servicemen. A grim-faced Carter had to go on television that morning and tell the American people what had happened. After the results of the abortive operation were learned in Teheran, most of the hostages were moved out of the embassy and scattered around the city, making a second attempt impossible. The United States could now go to war or it could do nothing, and Carter chose not to go to war.

The Republican National Convention opened on July 15 in Detroit, and on the first roll call duly nominated Ronald Wilson Reagan of California to be its candidate for President.

Following pages.
Left. Senator Robert Dole of Kansas, running mate of Gerald Ford in 1976 and candidate for the Republican nomination for President in 1980 and 1988. He is the Minority Leader in the U.S. Senate.

Right. Howard Baker, former Senate Majority Leader from Tennessee, ran for President in 1980 and served a brief stint as President Reagan's Chief of Staff late in the second term.

273

After his nomination Reagan attempted to persuade Gerald Ford to be his running mate, and the deal was nearly consummated before both backed away. Instead, Reagan chose George Bush, his main opponent in the primaries, to run with him and Bush gratefully accepted. The following month the Democrats renominated Carter, who had beaten back a primary challenge from Senator Ted Kennedy of Massachusetts. The major party candidates later agreed to meet in two debates in the fall.

If the American people were at all wary of Ronald Reagan in 1980, it was because they were concerned that a man his age might not be physically the equal of the job he was campaigning for, and because the Democrats (and in many cases, the press) had revived the tactic they had used against Barry Goldwater in 1964: they portrayed Reagan as a not terribly bright man who would rule more from emotion than intellect and thus was liable to push the final button over any perceived insult to the national honor. The face-to-face debates between Carter and Reagan laid to rest both of these notions. Reagan's doctors had often told him (and continue to tell him) that he has the metabolism of a man twenty years younger than his actual age, and his vigor and alertness came through well during the debates. On the issues, the people heard from a man with reasonable and well-reasoned opinions about which direction the country should go in over the course of the next several years. Carter also acquitted himself well during the debates, but most of the electorate had already made up its mind to vote for Reagan unless he gave them a reason not to, and Reagan was too well-prepared and comfortable in front of a camera to make the kind of blunder that Gerald Ford had made when, in the course of a debate with Carter in 1976, he denied that Poland was under Soviet domination.

Many people agreed with the assessment that Jimmy Carter was among the brightest men who had ever served as President, but he had never been able to develop the talent of transforming what he knew into what to do. His memoirs are full of instances where Carter talks about a given situation and his orders are almost invariably in the form of whom to call or whom to send to get more information. All too often, by the time he had all the facts, the moment of action had passed, and he ended up do nothing at all, wiser but not closer to his goals.

On Election Day 1980, Ronald Reagan carried forty-four states to Jimmy Carter's six, and thus was elected the fortieth President of the United States. Many liberal political analysts concluded that it was a rejection of Carter rather than acceptance of Reagan, or that it was a personal victory for Reagan rather than an embrace of conservatism. But this left them hard put to explain why the Republicans were able to capture the Senate for the first time since the election of 1952, not to mention the loss of six prominent liberal Senators that made the new Republican majority possible.

Conservative analysts, on the other hand, were immediately hailing the result as a signal that the American people had taken a permanent right turn, and they were equally wrong. The majority of American people are by nature centrists, and will vote either for the left or the right depending on whose program seems best equipped to deal with the problems currently confronting them. In many ways the Reagan victory was historic, for it did represent at long last a rejection of the New Deal programs put in by Democratic Presidents and left there by Republicans. The state of the economy was worse than it had been at any time since the start of World War II, and the American people had come to believe that the policies designed by Franklin Roosevelt to combat the Great Depression had remained in place so long that they had taken on a life of their own, and that these policies were not only not curing the economy any longer, but were making it worse. Thus the electorate was willing to give economic conservatism a chance, but they were not binding themselves to it. Reagan still had to deliver.

Carter was bitterly disappointed by the result of the election, though it is hard to imagine that he did not see it coming. The American people had lost all confidence in his

Right, and below. George Bush won the respect of conservatives for his eight years of service as Ronald Reagan's Vice President.

Water Mondale, Vice President under Jimmy Carter and Democratic President in 1984. He was crushed by Ronald Reagan in the election, with the President carrying forty-nine of the fifty states.

leadership, and had come to believe that he was, in fact, not providing any leadership at all. (Certainly, Carter must have realized that he had suffered a precipitous drop in support during his term just by reading the newspapers, for as *National Review's* Richard Brookhiser would later write, in 1980 "interest rates were kissing President Carter's popularity levels.") Carter continued working to free the hostages during his remaining time in the White House, and they were freed by the Iranians on the day that Ronald Reagan was inaugurated. It is open to speculation what effect Reagan's election had on the Iranian decision, but his Presidency started off on a high note.

And there it stayed for quite awhile. Not only had the Senate gone Republican in 1980 but the House, still under the control of the Democrats, nonetheless had a small majority of ideological conservatives, much as the one that had come into office following Nixon's reelection in 1972.

Reagan's first term in office was a virtual whirlwind of activity and accomplishment, in stark contrast to the Carter years of stagnation and malaise. Immediately upon taking office he laid out a plan for the gradual decentralization of the government, beginning with the lifting of hundreds of regulations controlling business and industry, and offering such proposals as the return of the burden of welfare to the states entirely. He pushed a 25% tax cut through Congress in his first year and more tax cuts in succeeding years, stimulating the economy and actually lowering the rate of inflation (which the experts said couldn't be done) while concurrently lowering the rate of unemployment. He demonstrated his toughness by firing air-traffic controllers who struck in defiance of the law and refused to return to work after the Secretary of Transportation gave them twenty-four hours to do so or face dismissal. Earlier, Reagan had impressed the nation with his courage after being shot by a would-be assassin in March. (He recovered quickly.) He gave a boost to the agricultural economy by lifting the grain embargo against the Soviet Union, though this was by no means an indication that he did not consider the continuing Soviet presence in Afghanistan to be a serious stumbling block in the effort to improve relations between the U.S. and the U.S.S.R.

In foreign relations, Reagan took a confrontational stance with the Soviets in the style of John Foster Dulles, having Secretary of State Alexander Haig proclaim that the U.S. could not rule out a first strike with nuclear weapons in the case of war, calling the Soviet Union an "evil empire," and reiterating his determination to block further Communist expansion anywhere in the world. To that end, he began the funding of rebel groups in Nicaragua and Angola to fight Marxist governments, pushed through massive aid bills to stabilize the faltering government of El Salvador in the face of a Communist insurgency (while at the same time warning right-wing groups there that all American aid would be cut off if they overthrew the democratically elected administration of José Napoleon Duarte), announced the inception of his Strategic Defense Initiative to develop a space-based missile shield which, if it proved feasible, could deflect a Soviet nuclear attack on the United States, and in the first deployment of U.S. combat troops since the end of the Vietnam War, sent the Marines to the island of Grenada in October 1983 to rid the island of a Cuban military contigent that had installed a Marxist government after the murder of the Prime Minister and was hastily constructing an airfield to ferry in more Cuban troops and supplies. Reagan acted to protect the lives and safety of the over 1,000 American medical students on the island and in response to an appeal from the Organization of American States.

Following pages. Three Republican Presidents in the Cabinet Room. Ronald Reagan finishes up some paper work, while Calvin Coolidge (*left*) and William Howard Taft stare down from oil paintings on the walls.

The first term had some setbacks as well. Reagan had promised to balance the budget as part of his economic program (which he called "supply side" economics, the press called "Reaganomics," and George Bush had once called "voodoo"; call it what you will, it was very much a re-packaging of the pre-New Deal economic conservatism, which held that the economy was healthiest when the most money was in the hands of the private sector rather than the government), but the national debt continued to rise to staggering proportions throughout his term. Because of the existence of pre-Reagan entitlement programs which were mandated by law and which Congress would not touch, many of the cuts that Reagan made in government expenditures were cuts in the rate of increase rather than genuine decreases.

The worst setback of Reagan's first term came in the Middle East. Reagan had sent a contingent of Marines to Lebanon as part of a peace-keeping force following the Israeli invasion of that country to drive out the Palestine Liberation Organization in June 1982. On October 25, 1983, an anti-American Moslem terrorist drove a truck filled with 2,500 pounds of explosives into the Marine compound at the Beirut airport and crashed it into the main barracks building. The explosion killed more than 250 Marines. Reagan was attacked in Congress for having the Marines in Lebanon on what his critics called an "ill-defined" mission, but Reagan at first refused to pull the troops out. But by February 1984, the political situation in Lebanon had deteriorated so badly that the President knew he was faced with a choice of pulling out or committing American forces to fight a war that could drag on for years with no guaranteed results. Reagan decided not to get bogged down in Lebanon the way Lyndon Johnson had in Vietnam, and he ordered the troops to withdraw.

The Democrats in 1984 nominated Walter Mondale for President and, in a first for one of the major parties, nominated a woman, Congresswoman Geraldine Ferraro of New York, to be his running mate. Mondale had served as Vice President under Carter, was

Edwin Meese, Reagan's embattled Attorney General who gave up the job to avoid becoming a 1988 campaign issue. Along with James Baker and Michael Deaver, Meese was one of the "troika" of advisers credited with much of the success of Ronald Reagan's first term.

closely identified with many of the failed policies of that administration, and came from the liberal wing of his party. Mondale chose as the theme of his campaign an open question to the American people: "Are you better off now than you were four years ago?" The answer was a resounding "Yes, we are!" The renominated Republican ticket of Reagan and Bush swept forty-nine of the fifty states' electoral votes, setting a new record, and tallied nearly sixty percent of the popular vote. Now that Reagan had proved that his policies worked, conservative political analysts were once again talking of a "permanent" shift to the right of the American electorate. It would not take long for them to be disabused of the idea.

In his second term, Reagan met with significantly less success than in his first, partly because his programs had shifted toward more long-range considerations and thus are not easily measured on a pass/fail system, and partly because the liberals had moved to retake the Democratic Party in the House and the Democrats were successful in recapturing the Senate in 1986. The Congresses of the second term have been admittedly and deliberately more obstructionist toward Reagan's program than those he had to work with in the first term. While there have been some notable achievements in the second term, there have also been a series of failures, made all the more notable because failures were so rare in the first term.

Mikhail Gorbachev rose to the top position in the Soviet power structure in March 1985, after the deaths of his three immediate predecessors in the space of thirty months. Gorbachev and Reagan have met at four summit meetings since then, and have held out the possibility of agreements between the United States and the Soviet Union that could significantly reduce the number of nuclear weapons in their arsenals, possibly setting the stage for an eventual ban on nuclear weapons, a policy Reagan has espoused for many years (although one he will not adopt unilaterally). But Gorbachev has always insisted that no meaningful agreement can be reached unless the Americans first scrap their Strategic Defense Initiative program, something Reagan has resolutely refused to do. The liberal opposition has attacked Reagan vehemently on this issue, asserting that SDI will never work anyway. They back up their claim by citing studies done by prominent (and prominently liberal) scientists like Carl Sagan. This leaves unanswered the question, if SDI is so obviously unworkable, why are the Soviets so anxious that we not spend any more money developing it? Surely they would enjoy seeing us waste millions of dollars on it, if they were as certain as the liberals in Congress are that it will all go for nought.

But in areas other than SDI, Reagan has taken a far less rigid and confrontational approach with the Soviets than he did in his first term. He has encouraged scientific and cultural exchanges with them (he has even offered to hand over the plans for SDI once the Americans have deployed it, and challenged future Presidents to hold to that promise if it is not deployed before he leaves office), and has been successful in winning the release of several prominent Soviet dissidents through direct appeals to Gorbachev.

For his part, Gorbachev is opening Soviet society through processes called in Russian *perestroika* and *glasnost* to a whole range of liberalizations that would have been unthinkable under any of his predecessors. Chief among these is a relaxation of strict government control of the press, so that newspapers in the Soviet Union are criticizing some of the policies of the present leadership rather than having to wait until the leaders are dead thirty years and their historical "reevaluation" comes along. Many conservatives in the U.S. are wary of Gorbachev's policies, fearing they may be nothing more than a public-relations ploy to brighten the Soviets' tarnished world image, and that there is no substance behind the new freedoms and the apparent Soviet receptiveness to some form of modified capitalism. (Such an attitude is curious, to say the least: for seventy years conservatives have been saying that Communism doesn't work; now the Communists are starting to say it and the conservatives don't believe them.)

While the second-term Reagan may be less confrontational toward the Soviets, he has become firmer in his fight against international terrorism. After a series of murders, bombings, and hijackings were traced by American intelligence officials to Libyan leader Moammar Khaddafi, Reagan first broke diplomatic relations with Libya, and when this did nothing to alleviate the problem, hit Libya with an air strike on April 15, 1986. Though one can never be sure that a man as reckless as Khaddafi has shown himself to be over the years will ever get the message, his direction of international terrorism seems at least to have been put on hold. Acts of terrorism believed to emanate from Iran continue throughout the Middle East.

Liberals have consistently criticized Reagan for not doing enough about the system of apartheid in South Africa. Apartheid enforces segregation of blacks and whites in that country, ensures continued white rule by denying blacks the right to vote, and in general keeps blacks in a subservient and poverty-stricken condition in a country where they make up the overwhelming majority of the population. Critics have urged the President to

Former Senator James Buckley (Conservative, N.Y.) debating points with *National Review* publisher William Rusher. Buckley, the brother of *National Review's* founder, was the only man ever elected to the U.S. Senate on a Conservative Party ticket without the endorsement of the two major parties.

bring pressure on the South African government to abandon the system, and have long advocated the imposition of economic sanctions as a means of doing that. But Reagan points out that long-standing American opposition to apartheid leaves him little influence with the South African government, and his lifting of the grain embargo underscores his disdain for economic sanctions generally. In South Africa's case particularly, he believes that sanctions would have a far more deleterious effect on the blacks than on the whites.

President Reagan was successful in helping to oust two long-time dictators in February 1986. After street demonstrations turned into riots in Port-au-Prince, the administration persuaded Haiti's ruler, Jean-Claude Duvalier, to leave the country to avoid further bloodshed. In the Philippines, opposition to Ferdinand Marcos jelled after the murder of Benigno Aquino, a Marcos foe who was returning to the Philippines after several years of exile in the U.S. Following an outpouring of anti-Marcos feeling all over the country, Marcos agreed to stand for election against Aquino's widow. After it became apparent that he had rigged the election, the Philippine situation almost deteriorated into civil war. Marcos then accepted Reagan's offer to come to the United States, and Mrs. Aquino succeeded him as President. Since then, Mrs. Aquino has managed to hold onto power despite several coup attempts, and may be able to establish a genuine democratic tradition in her country. But in Haiti a military junta replaced the old dictatorship; one set of elections were cancelled because of government-inspired violence against the electorate; a second set, reputed to be rife with fraud, produced a winner acceptable only to the army, and eventually, even he was deposed by the country's strong-arm general, Henri Namphy. The Reagan administration has come under fire for not taking decisive action in Haiti (even some liberals are calling for a Grenada-style invasion), but so far, the President

Sandra Day O'Connor became the first woman Justice of the Supreme Court when she was appointed by President Reagan in 1981.

has been reluctant to act. He apparently feels that no democratic government could survive the violence rampant in Haiti right now, and that an American invasion force would necessarily have to become an army of occupation, a situation he wishes devoutly to avoid.

Since the early part of his first term Reagan has advocated support for the contras, a guerrilla army fighting the forces of the Sandinista government in Nicaragua, as a means of pressuring the Sandinistas to relinquish control of the government and establish a democracy in that country. At first Reagan channeled funds to the contras through CIA contingency funds, but after Congressional objections were raised and sustained, that he was in violation of the Boland Amendment barring such aid without Congress's approval, Reagan has had to go to Congress every year and ask it to provide the necessary funds. In June of 1985 he was successful in getting $100 million for the contras, but since then, liberals in Congress who oppose the contras (and by extension, support the Sandinistas) have severely limited the funds sent to the insurgents, and have often restricted their use to

humanitarian rather than military purposes. Despite recent contra victories in the field which have been largely responsible for bringing the Sandinistas to the bargaining table and granting concessions toward democracy in Nicaragua, the Congress on February 3, 1988 voted to cut off funding for the contras by a margin of eight votes. It appears unlikely that the Congress will ever reverse itself on this issue as long as it is controlled by a liberal majority, despite a new wave of Sandinista repression of dissidents and the opposition press after a cease-fire was achieved with the contras in June 1988. The vote to deny further aid was seen as a major blow to the Administration, and may have ushered in President Reagan's "lame-duck" period nine months before the election to choose his successor.

The major reason for Reagan's lack of success with Congress in the past year has been the Iran-contra scandal. To go into all the details of the scandal here would be unwise because many of the issues that have been raised during investigations of the scandal are still unresolved, and the full story of what occurred will probably not be known until after Mr. Reagan leaves office. Briefly, some members of the Reagan administration proposed a policy of reaching out to perceived moderates in the Iranian government both in the hopes of getting them to use their influence to win release of American hostages kidnapped during random acts of terrorism throughout the Middle East, and to establish contacts in the Iranian government that could prove to be useful after the eventual death of the Ayatollah. As a show of good faith, the Iranians asked for a shipment of arms to be used in their war against Iraq. The proposal was brought to the President, who apparently authorized at least one shipment of arms (although he was in the hospital at the time, recovering from a cancer operation, and says he does not remember giving the authorization; he accepts the fact that he did). The arms were then sold to a Middle East arms dealer, who in turn sold them to the Iranians. The money that these administration officials made from the sale of the arms was then funnelled secretly to the contras in Nicaragua, apparently without the knowledge or approval of the President.

The scandal (which was originally made public by the Iranians, leading some people to believe that after the Americans made the initial contact, the rest was a set-up by the Ayatollah to embarrass Reagan) has far-reaching implications. The President had said he would never deal with terrorists to win the release of the hostages; it now appears that he did, though he says that his people believed they were dealing with moderates, not terrorists, and he was under the impression that the arms shipment was to solidify the contact, not ransom. It was certainly embarrassing for the Administration to be caught in the position of having sold arms to a country with whom we have no diplomatic relations to be used by them in a war against a country with whom we do. And the fact that some of the money ended up in the hands of the contras undoubtedly assisted liberal Congressmen in their fight against further contra aid. It is ironic that frustration over Iran contributed largely to Reagan's victory in 1980, and Iran would put such a cloud over his second term, almost as if Teddy Roosevelt had been accused of committing war crimes during the charge up San Juan Hill.

If the natural order of things prevails, Ronald Reagan will leave office on January 20, 1989. His Administration will have to be judged on much more than Iran-contra, Beirut, Grenada, or the consumer price index. It will have to be judged on how differently Americans viewed their country because of his Presidency, and how differently the world viewed America. If these are the criteria, conservatives believe that Ronald Reagan will have to be judged as eminently successful.

11 Rock of Ages: Conservatism and Religion

The presence of two ordained ministers, one Democrat and one Republican, in the 1988 Presidential primaries has renewed interest in the relationship between religion and politics. During most of the years of this country's history, it was accepted as perfectly natural that deep religious feeling spurred political action, and that there was nothing wrong with that. But with the emergence of what is generally called the "religious right" in the middle 1970s, new questions have been raised about the relationship between Church and State and whether or not religious ideas have legitimacy in public policy forums. The notion put forth by many liberals, that politicians using religion as a guide to policy-making violates the constitutional ban on the establishment of religion is not just new, but ignores the large role that religion has played in the formulation of the liberal heritage as well as the conservative.

Colonial America was in large part founded by men and women who came to this land to escape religious persecution in Europe. The people we call the "Puritans" were in their own time called "Dissenters" because they held beliefs at odds with the official teaching of the Church of England. William Penn founded Pennsylvania as a haven for his co-religionists, as did Roger Williams in Rhode Island. By the time the Constitution was written, it was an accepted fact that the nation had been founded on religious principles. The ban on the establishment of religion by the state was meant merely as a prevention against the formation of a "Church of America," with other faiths outlawed, as was then the case in England.

Deism was among the most popular religious philosophies in the late seventeenth century, claiming adherents as diverse as Thomas Jefferson and John Adams. Deism was a belief in Providence without necessarily subscribing to a particular church, and it was the influence of Deism that led to the insertion in the Constitution of the ban on the establishment of religion. But while the First Amendment to the Constitution does say that the Congress shall pass no law regarding the establishment of religion, it also says that Congress shall pass no law restricting the free exercise thereof; and nowhere does it say anything about a "separation" of Church and State that is so commonly used as an argument against the religious right in our own time. It would have been unthinkable to the Framers of the Constitution that government and religion could ever be effectively separated, nor would they want them to be. Most of them were deeply religious them-selves. They simply wanted to guarantee that the government they were incorporating would not prevent the practice of any religion, either by outlawing it or by promoting another religion.

Orestes Brownson was an early American figure whose life led him down enough paths so that he is properly hailed as part of both the conservative and liberal traditions. He was an ardent Democrat, an early exponent of Transcendentalism, an inquirer into the nature of communism (i.e., communal living), and ultimately, a Roman Catholic, after having

Bowne House, the oldest
surving house in New York
City, was a clandestine
Quaker meeting house in the
17th century. The Quakers
were looked at as both religious and political dissidents.

William Jennings Bryan,
populist politician and fundamentalist Christian who
defended the Bible against
science in the Scopes Monkey Trial in 1925.

Jonathan Edwards, firebrand
preacher of the Puritan era.

been a minister in five different Protestant sects. Through his Society for Christian Union and Progress, Brownson argued that one had a duty to take part in the affairs of society—its political affairs—as a manifestation of God's will. No one at the time would have countered that such a belief was contradictory to the American Constitution.

Abolition may rightly be seen as part of the liberal heritage, and it was unquestionably a movement founded and directed by people who felt that their participation was in answer to a call from God. William Lloyd Garrison believed that abolition was nothing less than a practical application of Christianity; Harriet Beecher Stowe, author of *Uncle Tom's Cabin*, was the daughter, sister, and wife of liberal Presbyterian ministers; John Brown was a lay preacher and son of a minister who believed that his actions had been ordained by God before the creation of the world. It is hard to imagine a liberal today decrying abolition because its leaders were trying to impose their religious beliefs on the rest of the nation and were therefore violating the First Amendment.

The movement favoring a ban on the sale of alcohol was led by people who also believed that they were doing God's work and are also a part of the liberal heritage. Much of the fight was carried on by the ladies of the Women's Christian Temperance Union. Carrie Nation thought she had a divine calling to shut down saloons; many of her followers got

William Lloyd Garrison,
newspaper publisher and
activist Christian who
directed the abolitionist
movement for twenty-five
years before the outbreak of
the Civil War.

Carrie Nation felt that her
Temperance Movement was
inspired and directed by God.

their first taste of politics pushing Prohibition, and would later join the ranks of the suffragist movment to win women the right to vote. Prohibition was also a standard plank of the Progressive Party; under the progressive leader William Jennings Bryan, it would become a standard plank of the Democratic Party as well. Bryan's fundamentalist Christianity would lead him to volunteer to assist the prosecution of the famous Scopes Monkey Trial in 1925, in which a high school teacher was tried for teaching evolution in a Tennessee classroom.

In 1911, Reverend Norman Thomas became pastor of the East Harlem Presbyterian Church. His subsequent work among the poor in that slum area of New York City led him into the Socialist Party and friendship with its leader, Eugene Debs. Thomas was also a pacifist, opposing America's entry into World War I. After Debs's death in 1926, Thomas took over the leadership of the party, and made his first run for President in 1928. Although he remained a minister until 1931, nobody accused Norman Thomas of trying to foist his religious beliefs on the rest of the country.

There was, of course, also religious movement on the right, and it is interesting to note the different treatment of religious rightists as far back as the 1930s. After Roosevelt's election to the Presidency, his socio-capitalist views were vociferously opposed by a

Right. Dr. Martin Luther
King, Jr., leader of the black
civil rights movement,
beneath a picture of
Mahatma Gandhi. Neither
was ever accused of trying to
force his religious beliefs on
his country.

Opposite. Father Charles
Coughlin, the Radio Priest
who denounced the New
Deal and was silenced by the
Vatican at the request of
F.D.R.

Detroit priest of the Catholic Church named Father Charles E. Couhglin. Father Coughlin had a radio show, and he used it to denounce the New Deal and Roosevelt personally.
He built up an enormous following among American Catholics, getting as many as
350,000 letters of support a week. Roosevelt was so concerned over Coughlin's influence
on the Catholic vote that during a visit to the United States of the Vatican Secretary
of State, Eugenio Cardinal Pacelli (later Pope Pius XII), the President asked the prelate to
do something about Coughlin, in exchange for diplomatic recognition of the Vatican.
Pacelli checked with several American bishops, and found that donations to Coughlin
were cutting into their weekly collections for the maintenance of parishes. They too
wanted something done. After returning to Rome, Pacelli quietly ordered the silencing
of Coughlin, and the priest acceded in accordance with his vow of obedience. Since his
silencing, Coughlin has often been portrayed in the press as a "demagogue" and a
right-wing kook, but the surviving records of his broadcasts do not bear out the portrait.

The civil-rights movement of the 1950s and '60s was largely led by black ministers like
the Reverend Martin Luther King, and invited participation by ministers, priests, and
rabbis from all denominations. Their religious convictions led them to take part, and no
one thought that they were violating the Constitution, except perhaps the Ku Klux Klan,
whose interpretation of that document has always been odd, to say the least. Similarly,
many protests against the war in Vietnam were led by clerics, notably Fathers Daniel and

Robert Bork, conservative jurist whose nomination to the Supreme Court was savagely scuttled by such Senators as Edward Kennedy and Joseph Biden.

Phillip Berrigan and the Reverend William Sloane Coffin. While these protests often led to the violation of several different laws, the constitutional ban on the establishment of religion was not among them.

In the middle 1970s, fundamentalist Christians began to form organizations whose mission was to bring pressure to bear on the nation's policy-makers to pass legislation that would halt what the fundamentalists viewed as the nation's slide into immorality and corruption due to the sexual revolution of the 1960s. Among the items on their agenda were laws against abortion, opposition to homosexual-rights legislation, and the return of voluntary prayer to public schools. While to the impartial observer their right to press for such legislation was equivalent to the rights of the abolitionists, the prohibitionists, the religious socialists, the civil rights workers, and the anti-war protesters, many liberals, who favored abortion, the relaxation of sexual mores, the promotion of homosexuality as an alternative lifestyle, and opposed prayer in schools began to accuse the religious right of trying to establish religion in violation of the First Amendment to the Constitution.

Most of the battles between the two opposing groups were fought not in the state legislatures or Congress, but in the courts, and the courts more often than not held with the liberals over the fundamentalists. The courts have upheld abortion, homosexual rights, and the ban on prayer in schools, with the last being ruled as in accordance with the First Amendment, no matter how voluntary the prayer program may be.

This has led to a movement among conservatives to limit "judicial activism," or the ability of courts to make rather than interpret law. The battle over judicial activism came to a head in the summer of 1987 when President Reagan nominated conservative jurist Robert Bork to fill a vacancy on the Supreme Court. It was believed by most liberals (and conservatives) that Bork's confirmation by the Senate would tip the balance of the court from liberal to conservative, endangering the existence of such court-mandated laws as abortion and school busing to achieve intergration. Despite their acknowledgement of Bork's qualifications to serve on the Supreme Court, liberal Senators such as Teddy Kennedy (still doing the Catholic fandango on abortion) and Joseph Biden (another Catholic who subscribed to the "personally opposed/publicly favored" position on abortion) spearheaded a drive to defeat Bork. Biden, chairman of the Senate Judiciary Committee, had once said publicly that if President Reagan nominated Bork, he would "have no choice" but to vote in favor of the nomination because Bork was so well-qualified. But when the nomination was proposed by the White House, Biden announced that he would lead the opposition to Bork even *before* the hearings began. When it was all over, Bork's nomination was voted down by the committee and later the full Senate, acting on the advice of the committee.

The fundamentalists and others who agreed with much of their program were angered by the liberals' handling of the Bork affair and vowed to make it an issue of the '88

The Reverend Jerry Falwell, fundamentalist Christian leader and conservative political activist.

Following pages.
Left. The Reverend Jesse Jackson, Baptist minister who ran for President in 1984 and 1988. His campaigns generated a great deal of controversy, but not because of his religious beliefs.

Right. The Reverend Pat Robertson. His religious beliefs were the object of serious press scrutiny during the 1988 campaign, when he sought the Republican nomination for President.

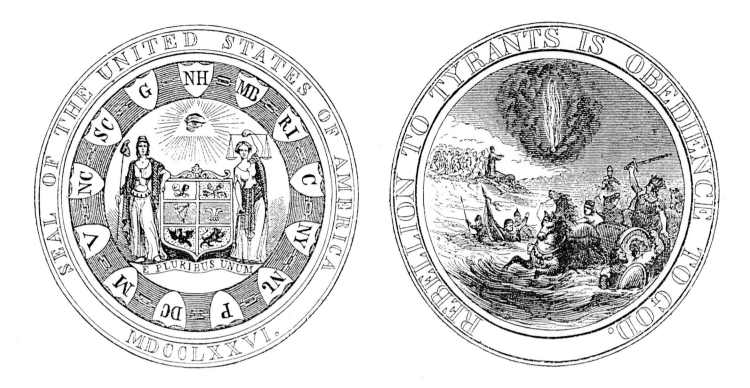

"Rebellion to Tyrants Is Obedience to God" would have been the motto of the United States had this seal designed by Thomas Jefferson not been rejected by Congress.

campaign. But at least for now, "judicial activism" appears to be a practice that will continue, as Reagan eventually had to send up the name of Judge Anthony Kennedy, perceived to be significantly more moderate than Robert Bork, to fill the vacancy on the Court.

One of the Republican hopefuls for the 1988 nomination was the Reverend Pat Robertson, a former television evangelist and a fundamentalist Christian. On the Democratic side, Baptist minister the Reverend Jesse Jackson hoped to win his party's nomination. It is again interesting to note the difference in the way the two campaigns were covered by the press. Almost all of the time and space devoted to Robertson filled with reportage of his more unorthodox religious views (he believes that he has commanded storms to turn away in God's name, etc.), while the press rarely even mentioned Jackson's religious background, almost universally omitting the title "Reverend" from his name. To dwell on Jackson as a minister, apparently, would leave him open to the same attacks as those made on Robertson, that he was trying to impose his religious beliefs on the rest of the country.

But it should be clear that the religious right and the religious left have the same right to try to have their political programs legislated by winning a majority of the votes, even if their political programs are religiously inspired. To say otherwise is to contradict nearly four hundred years of American history, beginning when the first "Dissenters" stepped on shore at Plymouth, Massachusetts, and began the tradition of religious activism in the politics of our country.

12 Future Imperfect
1988–

Concrete evidence that political analysts were premature in their proclamation of a new conservative realignment came in the form of the 1986 congressional elections, when the Republicans lost control of the Senate and ideological liberals re-established their majority in the House of Representatives. But there *was* a Reagan Revolution, and one of its most lasting effects will be that conservative candidates have as impressive a body of achievement attributable to leaders who share their political philosophy to point to as their liberal opponents have. This in no way suggests that conservatives can expect to win future elections by running on Ronald Reagan's record as President; it is simply more likely that their views will now be taken more seriously by an electorate long conditioned by the media to think of all conservatives as "right-wing kooks."

Conservatives consider that the most immediate threat to the future stability of the nation comes not from the possibility of outside military aggression, but from the consequences of this country's position as the largest debtor nation in the world. Competitive free-market economics demands that the debt be not significantly reduced but eradicated. Spending only what you have is a cherished conservative principle, and it is for this reason that President Reagan and his economic advisers pushed Congress to enact a line-item veto to enable presidents to cut the fat from spending bills. Additionally, conservatives nationwide are working toward the goal of a constitutional amendment requiring a balanced budget each and every year, and this recommendation was incorporated into the Republican Party platform in 1988. Democrats, who delight in pointing to the enormous budget deficit which accumulated during the Reagan Administration, refused to do the same in their platform.

Conservative legislators are working to formulate a practical plan for the decentralization of the federal government, with the consequent return of power to state and local governments and the individual citizen. More than merely looking for ways to cut government spending, conservatism presents to the nation a challenge to cut the government itself. As Ronald Reagan said during his first inaugural address, "Government is not the answer to our problems; government *is* our problem."

It is by no means certain that all of the states would welcome an increase in autonomy at the expense of the federal government, accustomed as many of them have become to relying on Washington for massive bailouts to meet the costs of state-mandated social welfare programs. Many of these programs would have to be streamlined or eliminated, or at least run more efficiently with greater accountability. Such proposals are often unpalatable to the politicians of larger states with a veritable menu of social service programs for its citizenry to choose from. But conservatives believe that the idea of federalism encompasses joint payment for services beneficial to all who pay (*i.e.*, defense, interstate transportation systems, etc.), not payment by all the states for programs applicable to only a few states.

The "politics of inclusion" is an idea being touted by prominent Republicans across a broad political spectrum, including conservative Rep. Jack Kemp (*far left*) and moderate New Jersey Governor Thomas Kean. Their goal is to increase the numbers of minorities and women in the GOP. Prominent Republican women who have already scored impressive political achievements include former Rep. Millicent Fenwick (*center, left*) and former U.N. Ambassador Jean Kirkpatrick.

Among the people who gained political prominence during the Reagan Era and can be expected to continue making important contributions to the process are (*left to right*) Florida's Governor Bob Martinez, activist Phyllis Schlafly, California's Governor George Deukmejian, and former Delaware Governor Pete DuPont, who waged a spirited campaign for the Republican presidential nomination in 1988.

Above. The house in Ripon, Wisconsin, where the Republican Party was born in 1854.

Opposite. Dan Quayle, conservative Senator from Indiana whose commitment to a strong defense and jobs for American workers earned him a place on the Rupublican national ticket in 1988.

Conservatives will keep their focus on national politics for the immediate future, but they realize that if they are ultimately successful in implementing conservative philosophy in national policy, then by definition the greater thrust of domestic political action will eventually be coming from the states. Thus they are beginning to lay the groundwork to make conservatism (in its practical form, the Republican Party) more localized in order to win governorships, state legislatures, mayoralties and school board elections. Conservatives in the past were often content to vote in presidential elections without even bothering to find out who was running for the school board. Liberals have had no qualms about running in such "little" races; that's why they've won so many of them and have been so much more effective on the local level. There is also a sense among conservatives that big-city mayoralties and governorships of states with large urban areas are the unassailable domain of liberal Democrats; but California is the most populous state in the Union, with huge urban areas, yet Ronald Reagan still holds the record for the largest percentage of popular vote ever won by a candidate for governor there. Underlying these qualms is the sense that urban areas are largely populated by minority groups and that conservatism does not appeal to minorities. This view ignores the existence of prominent black conservatives like Lt. Gen. Colin Powell, columnist Thomas Sowell and editorialist

Joseph Perkins, among others. It also ignores the growing Hispanic population in the United States, soon to be the largest minority group in the country and coming from a largely Catholic, family-oriented tradition similar to the background of many of today's most prominent conservative figures. A more likely explanation than that conservatism does not appeal to minorities is the probability that most conservatives, being white and middle to upper-class economically, have not taken the trouble to reach out to minorities and explain the benefits that social and economic conservatism can have for the poor who don't want to stay that way.

If they are to be successful in expanding the traditional base of conservatism to include minorities and younger voters, conservative candidates will avoid the stridency that marked and ruined the Goldwater campaign in 1964 and rely more heavily on the calm and reasoned communication of ideas that worked so well for Ronald Reagan in the 1980s. People reject candidates who try to frighten them into voting their way, but will rally behind an intelligent program for dealing with the nation's problems. Few people seriously read the publications of the John Birch Society, but Professor Allan Bloom's recent bestseller, *The Closing of the American Mind*, was remarkable in that a well-established academic would write an indictment of the liberal intelligentsia's abuse of the college curriculum to promote their political agenda, and also for the staggering number of people who read it.

In foreign relations, conservatives looking to the future are advocating plans for the exploitation of the liberalization now being undergone in both the Soviet Union and mainland China. A "carrot and stick" approach, rebuffing expansionist moves by the Communists internationally while aiding and encouraging their embryonic development of capitalism could well result in a new and safer world even by the turn of the century. George Bush espoused just such an approach in his acceptance speech at the Republican National Convention in August 1988.

Perhaps the most interesting—and telling—facet of the 1988 presidential campaign was that the nominees of both of the major parties made every effort to convince the voters that they were really more conservative than their records would indicate. Indeed, the very word "liberal" was seen as derogatory, a charge to be proferred by one side and denied by the other. Certainly, Lionel Trilling would be amazed by how things have changed in America since 1950 when he observed that liberalism was the dominant and perhaps "only" political tradition then functioning in the nation.

Before the 1980 election, George Bush was viewed as being firmly in the center of the Republican Party, and indeed was Ronald Reagan's major opponent for the nomination that year. But his eight years as Reagan's loyal Vice President won him the support of the conservatives of his party. His speech at the Republican National Convention was widely considered a triumph for a man trying to bridge the gap between the dominant conservative and still powerful moderate elements of the party.

In 1988, the conservative candidate offered the nation a clear choice for the future, embodying long-standing principles of conservative philosophy coupled with a flexibility in approach to distinctly modern problems that is becoming the hallmark of the new conservative agenda. But the "new conservatism" is the product of centuries of tried and true political values. This sense of continuity was perhaps best expressed by President Ronald Reagan in his last State of the Union address to the Congress when he quoted the ancient Chinese philosopher Lao-tzu, who said, "Govern a great nation as you would cook a small fish—do not overdo it."

Index

Acknowledgments

The author wishes to thank the following groups for the use of their photos and illustrations that appear in this book: American Enterprise Institute, (296); Americans for Robertson, (299); Ankers Photographers, (221); Bowne House Historical Society, (290[t]); Jimmy Carter Library, (266, 268); Conservative Caucus Research Analysis & Education Foundation, (226 [t], 297); Daily News Record, (220); Dorsey & Whitney, (278); The Eagle Forum, (245); Gerald R. Ford Library, (264, 265); The Goethe Institute, (114, 115); Historical Society of Pennsylvania, (37); Mr. Jim Hubbard, (246); *International News Photo*, (219); The Joint Free Public Library of Morristown and Morris Township, N.J., (124); Mr. Ray W. Jones, (290-291); Michael Kelly Collection, (194, 196, 199, 217 [b]); Ms. Eileen Leach, (293); Library of Congress, (18, 19, 26, 28, 31, 32-33, 34, 43, 47, 50, 60, 63, 64, 65, 69, 70, 71, 73, 75, 76, 77, 79, 80, 81, 82, 86, 89, 90, 91, 93, 94, 98, 99, 101, 103, 106, 108, 109, 110, 112, 113, 117, 118, 119, 121, 123, 125, 131, 132, 133, 134, 139, 140, 142, 143 [b], 145, 146, 147, 152, 153, 155, 156, 160, 163, 165, 167, 169, 170, 172-173, 177, 178, 181, 183, 185, 187 [b], 188, 190, 195, 198, 203, 204, 207, 209, 211, 212, 215 [t], 216, 223, 226 [b], 232, 235, 237, 241, 250, 252, 253, 259, 260, 266, 292, 295, 306); Los Alamos Scientific Laboratory, (204-205); Massachusetts Historical Society, (33); Metropolitan Museum of Art, (22, 23, 24 [b], 51, 93); National Archives, (38, 261, 263); National Portrait Gallery, (20, 21, 24, 42); *National Review*, (243, 284); New York Historical Society, (45-46); New York Public Library, (17, 20 [t]), 30, 48, 52, 53, 54, 55, 67, 85, 87, 94, 102, 137, 143, 148, 149, 161, 164, 166, 171, 174, 175, 177, 179, 182, 184, 187 [t], 197, 214, 215 [b], 218, 224, 229, 231, 234, 254, 256, 257, 272, 275, 294); Office of Governor Duekmejian, (245, 305); Office of Governor Kean, (302); Office of Congressman Kemp, (303); Office of the Republican Leader, U.S. Senate, (274); Office of the Vice President, (247, 248, 277, 279); Franklin D. Roosevelt Library, (201); *U.P.I. Telephoto*, (239-239); U.S. Army Signal Corps, (193, 200); U.S. Supreme Court, (285); Virginia Museum of Fine Arts, (39); The White House , (270, 280-281, 286-287).